Clinical Supervision and Teacher Development

Preservice and Inservice Applications

Clinical Supervision and Teacher Development

Preservice and Inservice Applications

Sixth Edition

M. D. Gall
Professor Emeritus, University of Oregon

Keith A. Acheson
Professor Emeritus, University of Oregon

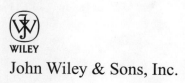

WILEY

John Wiley & Sons, Inc.

Vice President and Executive Publisher:	Jay O'Callaghan
Executive Editor:	Christopher Johnson
Acquisitions Editor:	Robert Johnston
Editorial Assistant:	Mariah Maguire-Fong
Marketing Manager:	Danielle Torio
Production Manager:	Janis Soo
Assistant Production Editor:	Annabelle Ang-Bok
Designer:	Seng Ping Ngieng

This book was set in 10/12 Times Roman by MPS Limited and printed and bound by Malloy Lithographers. The cover was printed by Malloy Lithographers.

This book is printed on acid free paper. ∞

Founded in 1807, John Wiley & Sons, Inc. has been a valued source of knowledge and understanding for more than 200 years, helping people around the world meet their needs and fulfill their aspirations. Our company is built on a foundation of principles that include responsibility to the communities we serve and where we live and work. In 2008, we launched a Corporate Citizenship Initiative, a global effort to address the environmental, social, economic, and ethical challenges we face in our business. Among the issues we are addressing are carbon impact, paper specifications and procurement, ethical conduct within our business and among our vendors, and community and charitable support. For more information, please visit our website: www.wiley.com/go/citizenship.

Evaluation copies are provided to qualified academics and professionals for review purposes only, for use in their courses during the next academic year. These copies are licensed and may not be sold or transferred to a third party. Upon completion of the review period, please return the evaluation copy to Wiley. Return instructions and a free of charge return shipping label are available at www.wiley.com/go/returnlabel. Outside of the United States, please contact your local representative.

Library of Congress Cataloging-in-Publication Data

Gall, Meredith D., 1942-
    Clinical supervision and teacher development / M. D. Gall, Keith A. Acheson. —6th ed.
      p. cm.
    Includes bibliographical references and index.
    ISBN 978-0-470-38624-8 (pbk.)
      1. Student teaching.   2. Teachers—In-service training.   3. School supervision.   4. Observation (Educational method)   5. Teachers' workshops. I. Acheson, Keith A., 1925- II. Title.
    LB2157.A3A29 2010
    370.71'1—dc22

                                             2010032266

Printed in the United States of America
10 9 8 7 6 5 4 3 2 1

Brief Contents

Detailed Contents

Preface

GOALS OF THIS BOOK

When we decided to write this book, first published in 1980, we set three goals for ourselves. One was to give the reader a comprehensive picture of what was then known about clinical supervision. To achieve this goal, we did a thorough review of the literature on clinical supervision, including both research reports and publications for education professionals. We cast a wide net, looking for all the uses of clinical supervision and all those involved in doing it, with no restrictions as to grade level, subject area, or country.

Our second goal was to write a book that clinical supervisors would find useful. For us, this meant analyzing the complex process of clinical supervision into specific techniques that supervisors could easily understand and apply. We then prepared a separate description of each technique for the book. In this most recent edition of the book, we describe 10 communication techniques, 11 conferencing techniques, and 18 classroom observation techniques.

Our third goal was to write a book that was consistent with our belief that clinical supervision is both an art and a science. We decided to present real-life cases that illustrate how clinical supervision, as an art, needs to be creatively adapted to teachers' individual situations. We also made a strong effort to identify research findings and theories that would provide a scientific foundation for designing an effective model of clinical supervision.

The fact that the book has stayed in print through five revisions over a period of more than 30 years suggests that, to some extent, we achieved these goals. It has been used by university instructors in courses on clinical supervision and teacher development, by workshop instructors preparing educators to assume the role of clinical supervisor, and by individual educators. It also has been translated into several languages (Chinese, French, and Korean), suggesting that clinical supervision, as we describe it, has universal applications. We prepared this new edition, the sixth, with the same three goals in mind as those that guided the preparation of the previous editions.

NEW TO THIS EDITION

The following are the major revisions that we made to the previous edition, each of which reflects new developments in clinical supervision and teacher development since the year 2000.

- Chapter 4 is new to this edition. It relates clinical supervision to other methods of professional development: action research, classroom walk-throughs, cognitive coaching, instructional rounds, lesson study, microteaching, peer coaching, peer consultation, and professional learning communities. These methods gradually have come into professional use independently of each other and independently of clinical supervision. We analyze similarities and differences between these methods and explain how various techniques of clinical supervision can be incorporated into these methods to strengthen them.

- Chapter 6 is also new to this edition. It examines problems of practice in clinical supervision. We wanted to highlight the fact that clinical supervision is generally beneficial, but it can break down or be problematic in certain situations. We focus on five problems of practice: teachers who have conflicting priorities; teachers who have difficulty translating insights into action; teachers who avoid contact with their supervisor; incompatibilities between student teachers and cooperating teachers; and experienced teachers who get in a rut.

- We updated each chapter to include new initiatives and methods that are relevant to clinical supervision: the No Child Left Behind (NCLB) Act; the accountability movement in education; policy initiatives to judge teachers' effectiveness based on their students' gains on standardized achievement tests; data-based teaching; tutoring as a teaching method for struggling students; school-level factors that affect teaching, learning, and supervision; the widget effect in teacher evaluation; nonverbal communication; intercultural communication; and communication accommodation theory.

- We added several new observation techniques to Unit Four: NCLB report cards; Surveys of Enacted Curriculum and other methods of determining a teacher's curriculum alignment; the Patterns of Adaptive Learning Scales to determine students' cognitive and emotional engagement in classroom activities; and teacher evaluation scales.

- We describe recent research studies whose findings are advancing educators' understanding of factors that enhance the effectiveness of clinical supervision and classroom instruction.

A NOTE TO INSTRUCTORS

Perhaps you are an instructor using this book as a course text for educators wishing to acquire or improve their clinical supervision skills. Here are several ideas for introducing them to the book and the primary concepts of clinical supervision:

- Have them recall their own experiences with clinical supervision. Ask them what their supervisor did that was helpful or not helpful. Then have them read the book's table of contents for Chapters 7–13 to see whether their supervisors used any of the techniques listed there.

- Have them read Chapter 1. Discuss the key concepts of clinical supervision that run through the book: (1) planning conferences, (2) use of observation instruments to collect data about a teacher's classroom instruction, (3) feedback conferences, and (4) the use of clinical supervision to develop teachers' capacity to help students learn.

- Ask them to make a list of effective teaching techniques and teacher characteristics. Then have them read Chapter 4 to compare their list with the techniques and characteristics described there.

A good next step is to have your students develop skills in classroom observation. If possible, have them observe student teachers or credentialed teachers at work in their classrooms. If you cannot gain access to teachers' classrooms, perhaps you can show videos of classroom teaching or have a small group of your students enact a lesson, with one of them taking the role of teacher and the others being the students. Prior to observation, have your students select a technique in Chapters 10, 11, 12, or 13, study it, and use it to collect data while observing a teacher. You can continue this activity with additional observation techniques, depending on the length of the course.

The next step is to have your students develop conferencing techniques. You can start by having them read Chapters 7, 8, and 9. If they can find a teacher who is willing to cooperate with them, they can practice these techniques with the teacher in one of more complete clinical supervision cycles—planning conference, observation, and feedback conference. Another activity you might consider is to have your students access the training manual for *Another Set of Eyes*, an ASCD publication, by going to ERIC (http://www.eric. ed.gov) and entering the accession number (ED324284). This manual includes transcripts for a planning and feedback conference for one teacher's sixth-grade math/art lesson and another teacher's high-school chemistry class. Your students can analyze the transcripts to determine which of the conferencing techniques in Chapters 7, 8, and 9 were used. They also can evaluate strengths and weaknesses of the conferences.

Finally, you can have your students read and discuss chapters about specialized topics related to clinical supervision: models of how teachers develop as professionals (Chapter 2); how clinical supervision relates to other methods of professional development (Chapter 3); the role of clinical supervision in teacher evaluation (Chapter 5); and problems that arise in real-world clinical supervision (Chapter 6).

If you give written assignments, students are likely to find it most useful to conduct one or more clinical supervision cycles with a teacher and then write a report about it. The report might contain materials from each cycle (e.g., observation data and partial transcripts of planning and feedback conferences), reflections about its strengths and weaknesses, and ideas for improving one's effectiveness as a clinical supervisor in the future.

ACKNOWLEDGMENTS

Our combined experience with clinical supervision and teacher education totals more than 90 years. (That's hard for us to believe, but it's true!) During that time, we have worked with many colleagues and students with shared interests in clinical supervision, teacher development, and effective teaching. The six editions of this book benefited enormously from their knowledge, insights, questions, and experiences. We wish to acknowledge some of these individuals here:

- At Stanford University: Dwight Allen, Horace Aubertine, Norman Boyan, Robert Bush, Jimmy Fortune, Nate Gage, Bill Johnson, Fred McDonald, Frank McGraw, Jim Olivero, Al Robertson, and Rob Spaulding.
- At the Far West Laboratory for Educational Research and Development (now Ed West), David Berliner, Walter Borg, and Ned Flanders.

- At the University of Oregon: Judy Aubrecht, Ed Beaubier, Ron Brown, Michael Carl, John Hanson, Ray Hull, Kathy Lovell, Gary Martin, Marilyn Olson, Jim Shinn, John Suttle, Peter Titze, West Tolliver, Paul Tucker, Colin Yarham, and Cal Zigler.
- At the Oregon State Department of Education: Ron Burge.
- At the Association for Supervision and Curriculum Development: Ron Brandt and Marcia D'Arcangelo.

We also wish to acknowledge the many educators worldwide who have worked with us to improve clinical supervision through their participation in our courses, workshops (especially those on Orcas Island in the state of Washington), and consultations. They have come to us, or we to them, from many states, territories (especially Guam), and countries, including Australia, Canada, Japan, Jordan, Mexico, Saudi Arabia, Singapore, and South Korea.

Finally, we wish to acknowledge the Teacher Corps, which brought the two of us together at the University of Oregon for a project on clinical supervision in the mid-1970s. That collaboration led to our long association as professors of teacher education there and coauthors of this book through its six editions.

MEREDITH "MARK" GALL
KEITH A. ACHESON

An Overview of Clinical Supervision

Chapter 1

The Nature of Clinical Supervision

Of crucial importance, is to have a supervision that is fundamentally humane, one that is emancipated from the dogma and authoritarianism and vested interests of administration and just plain trouble-making that have typified much of the supervision we have known before.

—Robert Goldhammer[1]

INTRODUCTION

Clinical supervision is a complex enterprise, but its essential elements—planning conference, classroom observation, feedback conference—are simple. The following episode from an actual case illustrates these elements. As the episode unfolds, we identify conferencing and observation techniques identified in Units 3 and 4, using the numbering system employed in them.

An Example

Arthur, a university supervisor, was assigned to supervise Jim, a student teacher at a local middle school. Arthur had an initial meeting with Jim to get acquainted, discuss his role as Jim's supervisor, and answer Jim's questions. Arthur then met with the two teachers in whose classrooms Jim would work and also with the school's principal. The teachers requested that Jim observe their classes for several weeks to become acquainted with the students and prepare several social studies units.

Once Jim had found his bearings, Arthur initiated a planning conference (see Chapter 8) with him to explain the procedures of clinical supervision and initiate a supervisory cycle. He asked Jim to describe his lesson plan for the class on Africa that Arthur would observe later in the week. Jim's plan was to organize the students into three groups and have each group read a different article about Rhodesia (a region of Africa now comprising Zambia and Zimbabwe). Then Jim wanted students in each group to state what they learned from the articles and answer questions about them.

Arthur and Jim agreed that it would be helpful to collect data on verbal interaction patterns in the lesson (Conference Technique 6). Two specific areas of focus were selected:

- the distribution of student talk during the lesson, which would be recorded on a seating chart (Observation Technique 7).
- Jim's responses to students' answers and ideas, which Arthur would record by script taping (Observation Technique 3).

Figure 1.1 shows a sample of the data collected by Arthur using each technique. When he and Jim met the following day for a feedback conference (Chapter 9), Jim was able to use the data to reach his own conclusions about how the lesson went. Arthur initiated this process by asking, "What do these data tell you about your teaching?" (Conference Technique 9). Jim realized that he had not praised or elaborated on student ideas; he had simply acknowledged them. Also, Jim saw that he was successful in getting students to talk, but the distribution of talk was unbalanced: Students sitting nearest the teacher, particularly one student, did most of the speaking.

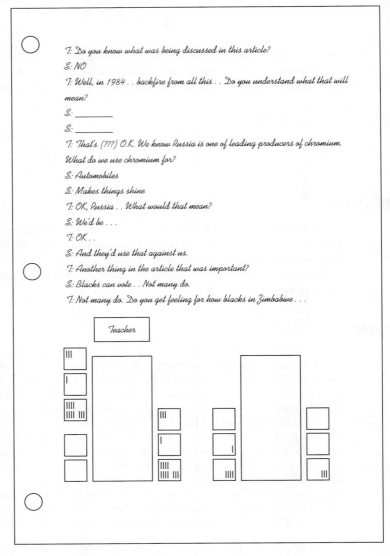

Figure 1.1 Selective verbatim and seating chart in lesson on Africa.

Arthur's next move in the feedback conference was to ask Jim why he thought these verbal patterns occurred. Jim commented that he had heard in his methods courses about the importance of responding constructively to student ideas, but he had not made the connection to his own teaching behavior until now. As for the distribution of student talk, Jim stated he was simply unaware of the imbalance. He realized, though, that he probably had called a number of times on the student who talked the most because he could depend on her to give good answers.

Arthur asked Jim what he might do based on these observations (Conference Technique 11). Jim said he would practice using praise in his next lessons and would make an effort to call on more students. Arthur suggested several ways that Jim might acknowledge student ideas and incorporate them in the lesson. He also suggested that a different arrangement of desks—perhaps a semicircle or circle—might encourage students to express more ideas and engage in discussion among themselves.

This brief example illustrates that clinical supervision consists of three primary elements: a planning conference, classroom observation, and a feedback conference. It also shows that clinical supervision includes teachers as active participants in the supervisory process and focuses on their classroom instruction. In this respect, clinical supervision differs from the typical format of teacher education courses and inservice workshops in which the instructor, rather than the student, determines the curriculum; and in which the curriculum content is not grounded in the individual teacher's classroom reality. Courses and workshops have an important role in teacher education, but they cannot substitute for the professional development that good clinical supervision promotes. Unfortunately, student teaching, the context in which preservice clinical supervision occurs, lasts only a term or less for the majority of preservice teachers, as a recent large-scale study discovered.[2] The same study found that new teachers typically viewed student teaching as "the most valuable aspect of my education program."[3]

The preceding example involved a clinical supervision episode in preservice teacher education. We use the term *preservice education* to characterize programs that prepare students (i.e., preservice teachers) for an initial position as a licensed school teacher. We use the term *inservice education* to refer to the professional development of licensed school teachers.

Traditional Teacher Supervision

Many preservice and inservice teachers react defensively to traditional supervision and do not find it helpful. In his review of research on teacher supervision, Arthur Blumberg found that teachers view supervision "as a part of the system that exists but that does not play an important role in their professional lives, almost like an organizational ritual that is no longer relevant."[4] Blumberg's review covered research up until the early 1970s, but our experience suggests that his conclusion would still hold true today.

Traditional supervision reflects the historical role of supervisors as school "inspectors." As far back as the early 18th century, lay committees in Boston were charged with inspecting schools periodically. The purpose of inspection was to evaluate teachers to ensure that instructional standards were being maintained. School inspection continued until schools grew large enough to require more than one teacher in each school. Inspection and evaluation

Figure 1.2 Nose-to-nose supervision versus side-to-side supervision.

functions then became the responsibility of one of the teachers, who was known as the "principal teacher." Eventually that title was shortened to "principal." To the extent that supervision is perceived as inspection and evaluation rather than as a source of professional development, teachers will resist it. We have more to say about teacher evaluation and the role of clinical supervision in this process in Chapter 5.

The communication pattern in traditional supervision tends not to be very helpful for the teacher. It is represented by the "nose-to-nose" characters on the left side of Figure 1.2. The supervisor offers the teacher advice or admonitions that go in one ear and out the other, or go right on by, or go off an invisible shield that "defends" the teacher.

In contrast, the "side-by-side" characters in Figure 1.2 represent a different style of communication in supervision. Both the supervisor and teacher look at objective data (such as a videotape of the teacher's lesson), analyze and interpret the data, and make decisions as colleagues rather than as adversaries. This communication style characterizes the model of clinical supervision described in this book.

A TEACHER-CENTERED MODEL OF CLINICAL SUPERVISION

The preceding portrayals of traditional teacher supervision explain, at least in part, many teachers' pervasive negative feelings about it. We propose an alternative model of supervision that is interactive rather than directive, democratic rather than authoritarian, and teacher-centered rather than supervisor-centered. This supervisory style is called clinical supervision.

We use the label *clinical supervision* because our model is based directly on the methods developed and so named by Robert Goldhammer, Morris Cogan, and other teacher educators who coordinated the Master of Arts in Teaching program at the Harvard School of Education in the 1960s.[5] The word *clinical* sometimes connotes pathology, which is inappropriate in the context of our model of clinical supervision. We certainly do not wish you to think that clinical supervision is a remedy applied by the supervisor to deficient or unhealthy behavior exhibited by the teacher. Instead, we use the term *clinical* to suggest a face-to-face relationship between the teacher and the supervisor and a focus on the teacher's actual behavior in the classroom. As Robert Goldhammer put it, "Given close observation, detailed observational data, face-to-face interaction between the supervisor and teacher, and an intensity of focus that binds the two together in an intimate professional relationship, the meaning of 'clinical' is pretty well filled out."[6]

The Three Phases of Clinical Supervision

Clinical supervision has three major phases, which together constitute a clinical supervision cycle. The supervisor:

1. meets with the teacher and plans for classroom observation;
2. observes a lesson and records information related to the objectives set during the planning conference; and
3. meets with the teacher to (a) jointly analze the data recorded by the observer, (b) interpret the meaning of this information from the teacher's perspective, and (c) reach decisions about the next steps. One of the next steps might well be to initiate another classroom observation, which becomes part of the next clinical supervision cycle. Many such cycles might occur during a supervisor's work with a teacher.

In the following sections, we describe each phase of the clinical supervision cycle in more detail.

The Planning Conference

The supervisor begins the process of supervision by holding a conference with the teacher. In the conference, the teacher has an opportunity to state personal concerns, needs, and aspirations. The supervisor's role is to help the teacher clarify these perceptions so that both have a clear picture of the teacher's current instruction, the teacher's view of ideal instruction, and possible discrepancies between the two. Next, the supervisor and teacher explore new techniques that the teacher might try in order to move the teacher's instruction closer toward the ideal.

The planning conference results in a cooperative decision by teacher and supervisor to collect observational data. For example, a teacher we know had a vaguely defined concern that he was turning off the brighter students in the class. In the planning conference, the teacher developed the hypothesis that perhaps he was spending the majority of his time with the slower students and ignoring the needs of the brighter students. Together, the teacher and supervisor decided to do a verbal flow analysis (Observation Technique 7) of the teacher's discussion behavior. This analysis involves observation of the students with whom the teacher initiates interaction and how he responds to each student's ideas. The teacher and supervisor also decided that the teacher would collect class assignments over a two-week period to determine their level of difficulty and challenge.

Recent policy initiatives, particularly the No Child Left Behind Act (NCLB), have brought new demands to hold teachers accountable for student achievement, as measured by standardized tests mandated at the state or local level. As a result, some teachers have access to test results for their classes, and they will be expected to improve on these results during the school year or from one school year to the next. If this is the case, testing data are likely to be a focus for planning conferences, particularly for clinical supervision with inservice teachers.

We discuss planning conferences in more detail in Chapter 8.

Classroom Observation

It is curious how rarely data are collected on different aspects of the teacher's classroom performance. In contrast, consider other fields. In sports, many people track statistical data that summarize observations of athletes' performance—number of home runs in baseball, percentage of completed passes in football, final and intermediate times in track events, and so forth. In medicine, business, and law, the practitioner has access to many indicators that directly reflect quality of performance—average number of lives saved following a specific medical intervention, cases settled in the client's favor, sales figures, and results of consumer satisfaction surveys. Teachers and supervisors need similar indicators of teacher performance, based on direct or indirect observation.

Collection of these indicators is the goal of classroom observation. Clinical supervisors maintain a neutral stance in the data collection process, so that the data can speak for themselves. This process is facilitated if the teacher has a hand in selecting the observation instrument (or instruments) to be used. A wide range of observation techniques is described in Chapters 10–13.

The Feedback Conference

In the final phase of the clinical supervision cycle, the teacher and supervisor meet to review the observational data, with the supervisor encouraging the teacher to make her own inferences about teaching effectiveness. For example, in viewing a videotape of their performance, teachers usually notice a number of areas in which they need to improve. They comment that they hadn't known how much they talk in class, that they tend to ignore or fail to acknowledge student comments, that they do not speak loudly enough, and the like. As the teacher reviews the observational data, the feedback conference often turns into a planning conference—with the teacher and supervisor jointly deciding in a collegial manner to collect further observational data or to plan a self-improvement program.

The Goals of Clinical Supervision

The major goal of clinical supervision is to improve teachers' classroom instruction. Teachers do other important kinds of work, such as conferring with parents, but their core work—the work that distinguishes them from professionals in other fields—is helping individuals learn within the complicated environment of classrooms and the complex organizational conditions of schools. Clinical supervision is ideally suited for helping teachers improve their core work in these demanding conditions.

The major goal of clinical supervision, which is to improve teachers' classroom instruction, can be analyzed into the following more specific goals:

- *Providing Teachers with Objective Feedback on Their Instruction.* The essence of clinical supervision is to hold up a mirror so that teachers can see what they are actually doing while teaching—which can be quite different from what teachers think they are doing. Receiving objective feedback is often sufficient stimulus for teachers to initiate a self-improvement process.

- *Diagnosing and Solving Instructional Problems.* Clinical supervisors use conference techniques and observational records to help teachers identify flaws in their instruction or better ways to accomplish an instructional goal. Teachers can occasionally do this on their own; however, the skilled intervention of a supervisor usually is necessary. A parallel situation exists in classroom instruction. Sometimes students can self-diagnose learning problems and take remedial steps on the basis of the information. At other times, students are stymied by their inability to learn a particular subject, and the teacher is needed to diagnose and remediate.

- *Helping Teachers Develop Skill in Using Instructional Strategies.* If the only purpose of clinical supervision were to help the teacher solve immediate problems and crises, its value would be severely limited. The supervisor would be needed each time the teacher had a "brush fire" to put out. The skillful supervisor uses the clinical conference and observation data to help the teacher develop enduring patterns of effective behavior—what we call instructional strategies. Our synthesis of research on effective teaching in Chapter 4 identifies instructional strategies that are evidence-based or reflect best practice.

- *Evaluating Teachers for Promotion, Tenure, or Other Decisions.* This is the most controversial function of clinical supervision. Some supervisors avoid evaluation, but most supervisors are required by their employer (typically a school district or college of education) to evaluate the teacher's competence, usually at the end of the supervisory process. The objective data collected through systematic classroom observation can and should serve as one basis for evaluating the teacher's competence.

- *Helping Teachers Develop a Positive Attitude about Continuous Professional Development.* Teachers need to view themselves as professionals who improve their skills throughout their career. Supervisors can make teachers aware of instructional strategies and programs that will improve their effectiveness and increase their enjoyment of teaching.

Is Clinical Supervision Necessary?

The model of clinical supervision that we described above incurs costs in terms of time and money for teacher education programs and school districts. Can these costs be justified?

Our starting point in answering this question is a study involving detailed observations of preschool to fifth-grade classrooms.[7] Here are some of its findings:

- Students receive fairly low levels of instructional feedback and spend the majority of their time learning basic skills rather than higher-cognitive skills.
- Interactions between teachers and students are impersonal, with few positive one-on-one interactions.
- Students spend a substantial amount of classroom time not engaged in learning activities, ranging on average from 42 percent of the time in preschool classrooms to 30 percent of the time at the fifth-grade level.

The situation was no different 25 years ago. A large national sample of classrooms was observed by John Goodlad and his colleagues.[8] In a report of their findings, one of the researchers, Kenneth Sirotnik, characterized the typical classroom thus:

> ". . . a lot of teacher talk and a lot of student listening, unless students are responding to teachers' questions or working on written assignments; almost invariably closed and factual questions; little corrective feedback and no guidance; and predominantly total class instructional configurations around traditional activities—all in a virtually affectless environment. It is but a short inferential leap to suggest that we are implicitly teaching dependence on authority, linear thinking, social apathy, passive involvement, and hands-off learning."[9]

We doubt that anyone is satisfied with this level of instructional qulity in America's classrooms. In fact, these findings probably surprise anyone who knows teachers. The vast majority of them work very hard and do their very best for their students. Why then in the quality of their classroom instruction not better?

Our answer is that teachers do not receive sufficient high-quality clinical supervision involving direct classroom observation, feedback, and guidance. No other profession or skilled trade that we know of prepares their workers so quickly and with so little supervised practice in field settings. If we look at professional sports, the disparity becomes even more obvious. Athletes require and receive expert coaching in order to reach their full potential; and coaching, if you think about it, is a form of clinical supervision.

Each chapter of this book presents knowledge and techniques that will enable clinical supervisors to provide the expert guidance found in other professions and improve the quality of classroom teaching well beyond the normative level found in the national studies described above.

Finding Time for Supervision

Finding time for supervision is a major problem. Several research studies have found that experienced teachers rarely, if ever, participate in clinical supervision designed to improve their instruction.[10] The situation is somewhat better in preservice teacher education, because a certain amount of supervision is typically mandated by state regulations. However, university supervisors often have heavy workloads, and consequently their opportunity to collect observational data and confer with student teachers is severely limited.[11] In a study of cooperating teachers who had taken a course on clinical supervision, Susan Kent found that the teachers did not engage in clinical supervision cycles more often with their student teachers because of time constraints.[12]

There is no simple explanation for the insufficient time allocated for clinical supervision in preservice and inservice education. Undoubtedly, many factors are involved. One reason might be the fact that there is a large amount of turnover in the teaching profession. Why invest in a teacher's development if there is a substantial likelihood that the teacher will not be a classroom instructor for the length of a typical career (25–30 years)? Of course, one might argue that more teachers would stay in the profession if they had access to good clinical supervision and other methods of professional development.

Let us assume for a moment that policy makers and administrators are willing to make a commitment to clinical supervision. If this happens, the allocation of time in schools and university teacher education programs will need to change. Inservice teachers might be given lighter teaching loads so that they have more time for clinical supervision and other forms of professional development. Preservice teachers might have longer programs of preparation or modify the relative amount of time allocated for university course work and field experiences. Educators have considered these and other options for reallocating time so that schools and teachers' work lives can improve.[13]

OTHER MODELS OF CLINICAL SUPERVISION

Since the seminal work of Morris Cogan and his colleagues, other educators have developed new models of clinical supervision. Edward Pajak described, analyzed, and contrasted these models.[14] His summary of the models, organized into four families, is shown in Table 1.1. None of them, including ours, is radically new; to one degree or another, all of them build on the work of the original developers.

Pajak characterizes our model of clinical supervision as technical/didactic. This label emphasizes the fact that we believe that there is a knowledge base about effective teaching techniques (see Chapter 4) that can be used to guide the supervisory process. At appropriate points in the supervisory process, the supervisor can help a teacher become aware of these evidence-based teaching techniques. We do not assume that every classroom is unique and that therefore every teacher must discover a set of teaching techniques unique to that situation.

We find much value in all the models of clinical supervision listed in Table 1.1. In our opinion, none of them is wrong or misdirected. It is a matter of emphasis. We endorse other models' emphasis on teacher reflection and self-discovery, which we incorporate in our techniques for planning and feedback conferences, but we also emphasize the knowledge base about effective teaching. We endorse other models' emphasis on education's role in social reform, but in our model we emphasize existing classroom reality and the pragmatic need to prepare teachers to succeed in that reality. We agree with other models' emphasis on the individuality of teachers and their instructional conditions, but in our model we emphasize the commonalities among teachers and their instructional conditions.

If our model of clinical supervision has any particular advantages, they involve its practical applications and comprehensiveness. After studying each technique, you should be able to apply it, if you wish, to your actual work. As for comprehensiveness, Pajak

Table 1.1 Models of Clinical Supervision

Original Clinical Models	The models proposed by Goldhammer,[15] Mosher and Purpel,[16] and Cogan[17] offer an eclectic blending of empirical, phenomenological, behavioral, and developmental perspectives. These models emphasize the importance of collegial relations between supervisors and teachers, cooperative discovery of meaning, and development of individually unique teaching styles.
Humanistic/Artistic Models	The perspectives of Blumberg[18] and Eisner[19] are based on existential and aesthetic principles. These models forsake step-by-step procedures and emphasize open interpersonal relations and personal intuition, artistry, and idiosyncrasy. Supervisors are encouraged to help teachers understand the expressive and artistic richness of teaching.
Technical/Didactic Models	The works of Acheson and Gall,[20] Hunter,[21] and Joyce and Showers[22] draw on process-product and effective teaching research from the 1970s. These models emphasize techniques of observation and feedback that reinforce certain "effective" behaviors or predetermined models of teaching to which teachers attempt to conform.
Developmental/ Reflective Models	The models of Glickman,[23] Costa and Garmston,[24] Schön,[25] Zeichner and Liston,[26] Garman,[27] Smyth,[28] Retallick,[29] and Bowers and Flinders[30] are sensitive to individual differences and the organizational, social, political, and cultural contexts of teaching. These models call for supervisors to encourage reflection and introspection among teachers in order to foster professional growth, discover context-specific principles of practice, and promote justice and equity.

Source: Pajak, E. (1993). *Supervising instruction: Differentiating for teacher success.* Norwood, MA: Christopher-Gordon. (Adapted from Table 1-1 on p. 312.) Copyright © Christopher-Gordon. Reprinted by permission of the publisher.

comments that, "Acheson and Gall provide an impressively broad array of strategies for recording behavior that generate both quantitative and qualitative data."[31]

CLINICAL SUPERVISION IN TEACHER EDUCATION PROGRAMS

Clinical supervision plays an important role in both preservice teacher education programs and inservice teacher development programs, but its characteristics differ in each context, as we explain in the next sections.

Preservice Teacher Education

In preservice teacher education, students take courses at a university and also go to neighboring schools for field experiences, where they might observe classroom teachers, assume limited classroom duties, or take full responsibility for a classroom. Unfortunately, students' coursework often is disconnected with their field experiences. University instructors might not know what their students are doing in their field experiences. Conversely, individuals responsible for their field experiences—clinical supervisors and teachers in whose classrooms the students work (we call them *cooperating teachers*)—do not know what they are learning in their courses.

This disconnect between university coursework and field experiences creates conflicts for preservice teachers. How much effort should they invest in mastering the curriculum covered in their coursework relative to acquiring instructional skills through field experiences? An answer to this question is suggested by a study by researchers at the National Bureau of Economic Research.[32] They found that new teachers produced greater student achievement if they graduated from teacher education programs that emphasized extensive, well-supervised student teaching experiences that were relevant to the schools in which they found employment. (The study involved new teachers in New York City schools.) New teachers were also more effective if they had opportunities to practice skills relevant to actual teaching.

The disconnect between coursework and field experiences can generate confusion in the clinical supervision process. For example, we know of situations where a cooperating teacher or clinical supervisor asked a preservice teacher to use a particular teaching technique, only to have the preservice teacher reply that she had learned in a course that this was not a good technique or that she should use a different technique. The obvious solution to this disconnect is for university instructors, clinical supervisors, and cooperating teachers to reach consensus about the elements of effective teaching, so that these elements are taught and reinforced both in university courses and field experiences. Consensus might not cover the totality of the teacher's role, nor need it be entirely prescriptive. It should be articulated well enough, though, that it can be conveyed clearly to the preservice teachers as a vision of what they need to learn.

Another problem that occurs with clinical supervision in the context of preservice teacher education programs involves perceptions of the students' developmental stage. Clinical supervisors typically are preoccupied with helping their student teachers acquire sufficient proficiency in classroom teaching that they can earn a teaching license and seek employment as professional teachers. In many cases, this effort involves helping the students acquire "survival skills" in the classroom.

The mindset of some university instructors is quite different. They want their students to learn evidence-based or cutting-edge teaching practices, even if they are not commonly used in schools. They might have their own unique teaching philosophy that they wish to impart to their students, or they might want their students to be change agents, advocating and incorporating school reform in their field experiences. Clinical supervisors who are struggling to help their students acquire basic classroom survival skills are likely to look askance at university instructors who have these goals. Of course, both groups have legitimate, but different aspirations for their preservice students. How can these differences be reconciled?

We believe that both clinical supervisors and university instructors need to view student teachers from a developmental perspective. That is why we wrote Chapter 2, which explains models of teacher development created by various educational theorists and professional organizations. These models posit stages of teacher proficiency, leading from novice to expert teaching. In our experience, clinical supervisors are more likely to view preservice teachers as novices, and rightly so; whereas some university instructors focus on what expert teachers can or should do.

The timeline of teacher education programs is typically designed so that preservice teachers take most of their coursework before their fieldwork. Often the culminating experience is student teaching, which typically includes most of the clinical supervision that preservice teachers receive. We suggest that it might be better to create a timeline and organizational framework that intertwines field experience and coursework more closely. As students observe and engage in classroom teaching, they are likely to observe problems and develop the desire to improve their instructional effectiveness. These problems and desires should motivate them to be receptive to the ideas that are presented in their university courses. As they interact with these ideas, they can try them out in subsequent field experiences, guided by their clinical supervisor and cooperating teacher.

This approach to preservice teacher education is easier said than done. It calls for a rigorous exploration and articulation of the roles that university coursework, field experiences, and clinical supervision play in preservice teacher education. It also is somewhat impractical in that few teacher education programs have the resources to engage in this type of exploration and then put an articulated set of university and field experiences in place. However, this ideal approach is worth stating, so that teacher educators understand the limitations under which clinical supervision currently operates—and so that they can promote the development of well-articulated teacher education programs if resources become available.

INSERVICE PROFESSIONAL DEVELOPMENT

Clinical supervision exists largely because it is mandated by state and national licensing agencies that regulate preservice teacher education programs. There is no such mandate for inservice teachers and their employer school districts. One explanation for this situation is that most school districts lack the resources to fund clinical supervision. Another is that teachers and administrators typically are overworked. Although they might value clinical supervision, it is viewed as a luxury rather than a necessity.

A major exception to this picture is the mentoring that some school districts provide for their new teachers. Mentoring might be the sole resource, or it might be one resource within an induction program that provides various kinds of support for new teachers. As we explain in Chapter 3, mentoring involves a collegial partnership in which an experienced teacher helps a novice teacher learn how to fit into the hiring school system and further develop the instructional skills that he acquired in his preservice teacher education program. The mentor teacher can use various techniques to achieve these goals, but one of the most effective is periodic clinical supervision cycles.

Another context for clinical supervision in school districts is teacher evaluation. As we explain in Chapter 5, school districts often require that administrators, typically school principals, observe teachers in their classrooms as part of their annual evaluation. With a bit more effort, this observation can be an opportunity for a complete clinical supervision cycle—planning conference, observation, feedback conference. If a teacher's performance is rated as unsatisfactory, extensive clinical supervision and other forms of professional development might be mandated by school district policies or teacher union contracts.

We believe that clinical supervision plays an important role in any effective school system. In the recent bestselling book *Outliers*, Malcolm Gladwell considers the nature of expertise and what is required to attain it.[33] From his review of research on this subject, he concludes that it takes about 10,000 hours of concerted practice for someone to become an expert in his field of interest, such as computer programming, artistic performance, or athletic competition. If this is true, one mission of an ideal school system would be to help students identify their particular talents and interests, and then facilitate the development of these students' expertise, over long periods of time, in fields of human endeavor that require these talents and interests.

If the development of expertise is a school mission, teachers will need to model it in their field of expertise, which is classroom instruction. For this to happen, school systems will need to budget for continuous professional development for teachers, with particular emphasis on clinical supervision. The experts profiled by Malcolm Gladwell, including such luminaries as Mozart and Bill Gates, did not acquire their skills simply by practicing them on their own. They had systematic coaching—involving both observation and conferencing— from individuals who themselves were experts in this type of work. Teachers will need similar coaching, in the form of clinical supervision, to become experts in classroom instruction.

SHARING RESPONSIBILITY FOR CLINICAL SUPERVISION

Supervisors of preservice and inservice teachers often have other responsibilities. University professors need to teach courses, manage programs, and engage in research and scholarship. School administrators have responsibility for public relations, curriculum development, budget, student discipline, health, safety, and nutrition, among other duties. As one of our administrator colleagues pointed out, when confronted with the fact that school administrators seem more concerned with budgets than supervision, "If you want to get fired, making a mistake in the budget is much quicker than making an omission in supervision."

If clinical supervision is to become a greater priority, educators will need to rethink and revise their roles. Ideally, educators would work together so that each preservice teacher would participate in at least 20 clinical supervision cycles (planning conference, classroom observation, feedback conference) during their program of studies, and each inservice teacher would participate in at least six clinical supervision cycles each school year. One can (and should) argue about whether these numbers are too high or too low. We present them here as our estimate of what is needed and as a starting point for discussion among our colleagues about what the ideal is.

We consider below how educators might rethink their roles in order to increase the prevalence of clinical supervision. We start by considering professional development for inservice teachers and then address preservice teacher education.

The Role of School Principals

Courts, arbitrators, and teacher oversight panels regard the principal as the person most responsible for making judgments in the evaluation of teachers. In some jurisdictions, the superintendent is responsible for teacher evaluation by law or regulation, but may delegate the responsibility to others, usually principals. Given this responsibility, the principal has the difficult task of also being a clinical supervisor in the collegial, constructive manner that we advocate.

Some principals are able to do formal evaluations *and* clinical supervision, while also maintaining a high level of trust and mutual respect with their teachers. Their competence in the techniques of clinical supervision is a major source of this respect and trust. Unfortunately, the majority of teachers do not feel that they are getting the kind of supervision they want and need.

Our response to the existing situation is twofold. First, we need more principals who are trained and experienced in systematic observation and feedback techniques. When they have become skilled, their evaluation activities can provide useful information for the improvement of instruction. These evaluation activities can be a part of instructional leadership rather than a superficial ritual. Second, the principal needs to share the instructional leadership of the school with teachers. For example, if a school district adopts peer coaching or peer consultation (see Chapter 3), principals will need to manage the logistics necessary to make collegial observation and analysis possible. If instructional rounds or walkthroughs (see Chapter 3) are adopted, principals will need to join with others in observing teachers' classroom instruction on a regular basis, reflect with them on their joint observations, and make recommendations for instructional improvement—which might include intensive clinical supervision for selected teachers.

One role we do not advocate for a principal is to be a member of the committee administering a program of assistance for a teacher if that teacher was put on notice by the principal in question. There is often a question of bias or personal conflict in such cases, and it is best to have a "neutral" administrator on the committee, as we suggest in Chapter 4.

The Role of Other Administrators

Vice principals can perform any of the supervisory functions we describe above for principals. Also, administrators in the central office of larger school districts often have skills for observing and conferencing with teachers and could benefit from spending time in the schools. This would do much to overcome their tendency to become isolated and deskbound by their customary duties.

Subject matter specialists for larger school districts are another source of instructional leadership to encourage clinical supervision. They can model effective instructional practices and train teachers in the techniques of clinical supervision. These activities would do much to facilitate the adoption of new curriculum content and new curriculum-specific teaching strategies.

Department heads in secondary schools are in a strong position to be clinical supervisors. They have the advantage of being subject matter specialists in their field. Thus they avoid the skepticism principals often receive, as reflected in comments like, "How can a former math teacher supervise and evaluate a foreign language teacher?" Department heads also are deeply familiar with the curriculum in their department. Unfortunately, though, the departments in traditional secondary schools often exist as administrative conveniences rather than as centers of instructional leadership.[34] A redefinition of the department head's role and relevant training for that role will be necessary to make department heads true instructional leaders.

The Role of Teachers

The most available source of clinical supervision expertise is teachers themselves. Most of them have the motivation to analyze their own teaching on the basis of objective data, to observe in colleagues' classrooms and record data the colleagues cannot record themselves, and to help one another analyze these data and make decisions about alternative strategies. Teachers can do these things without writing formal reports or following other procedures associated with official evaluation.

Many of the meetings teachers attend deal with procedural and bureaucratic matters. As a contrast, we invite you to envision department meetings in a secondary school or unit meetings in an elementary school where faculty members regularly view excerpts from videotapes made in their classrooms on a revolving basis. After viewing them, the teachers can analyze and discuss the content, methodology, and techniques of their teaching as a substantial part of the meeting. If this were to become a widespread practice, we should see some striking improvements in classroom instruction. Professional learning communities, which we describe in Chapter 3, are present in some school systems already and could incorporate these practices.

Assumption of the role of clinical supervisor would serve as a career ladder for teachers who do not wish to become administrators, but do want to advance in the profession. Also, teachers' involvement in clinical supervision will help them if they are called upon to serve as cooperating teachers for preservice teachers.

If successfully implemented, such a program could be cost effective. Two examples illustrate the point. In a case on which one of us consulted (K. Acheson), litigation brought by a teacher cost nearly a quarter of a million dollars in attorney fees alone. In another, a reinstated teacher became a nonproductive liability who, over the years, probably cost a half million dollars in salary, administrative time, legal fees, and the like. If these cases had been worked out cooperatively by the school districts and teacher organizations, rather than as labor-management confrontations, those same funds could have bought a lot of release time for collegial clinical supervision.

Self-Analysis

Self-analysis as a form of clinical supervision has not had the amount of use that it deserves. In the 1960s, Theodore Parsons developed guides that can be used to analyze one's own videotapes.[35] Minicourses, which we describe in Chapter 3, were designed as self-instructional units to help teachers develop new skills. They incorporated self-analysis of videotapes guided by a teacher's handbook.

The Role of Students

Students can supply useful data for the feedback process (see Chapter 13). Questionnaires can be used to tap their perceptions, and interviews with them can provide a rich source of information. Students also can operate videotape cameras for teachers who are undertaking self-analysis.

The Role of Supervisors and Cooperating Teachers in Preservice Programs

Preservice teachers generally have both supervised and unsupervised field experiences. A major advantage of unsupervised field experiences is that they are relatively inexpensive. The university program administrators only need to collaborate with participating school districts to find cooperating teachers who are willing to have a preservice intern in their classroom. Interns often function as teacher aides, and therefore are an inexpensive additional resource for school districts.

Supervised field experiences are more expensive, because university program administrators need to find clinical supervisors, train them, and pay them for their time and travel expenses. They might be retired teachers, teachers who are employed part time, or teachers who are not currently employed. In some programs, tenure-line professors will supervise student teachers. Both authors of this book have served in this capacity.

University program administrators also need to work with school districts to find cooperating teachers who will host student teachers in their classrooms. In addition, the cooperating teachers might be expected to provide clinical supervision. Even if this is not an expectation, our experience is that cooperating teachers will need to work closely with student teachers to help them gradually take over full responsibility for a class.

The principals of participating schools also play a role, albeit indirect, in the clinical supervision process. They need assurance that the preservice teachers in their school have sufficient competence to avoid creating a problem for the school. For example, we know of cases where a student teacher engaged in questionable or flagrantly illicit behavior, which could be resolved only by time-consuming interventions by the school principal in collaboration with university faculty and other educators.

For clinical supervision to work effectively in preservice teacher education, individuals in all these roles—cooperating teachers, school principals, clinical supervisors—need to be in communication with each other. Communication is facilitated if program administrators develop and distribute a brief manual that spells out everyone's roles and responsibilities in the clinical supervision process and specifies procedures for handling problems that might arise.

If university supervisors are current or former teachers, they typically have immediate credibility and rapport with cooperating teachers and school administrators. However, university professors sometimes are perceived as ivory-tower theorists who do not understand the conditions of schooling, even though many of these professors might have been former teachers themselves. To break this stereotype of university professors, it is important for them to visit the school district office and its schools occasionally. This process allows school staff to see professors as real people who are interested in student teachers and the school staff who guide their field experiences. It is also an opportunity for all of them to learn from each other.

Training for Supervisory Roles

Administrators and teachers need training and practice to develop the skills (we call them "techniques" in Chapters 7–13) required for the roles described above. We have found that 20 to 30 hours of instruction, plus an equal amount of practice (6 to 10 observations using different techniques, including 3 to 5 complete supervision cycles) should be adequate. Most likely, few administrators and teachers receive this amount of instruction. Also, several studies have found that cooperating teachers, who are key to preservice clinical supervision, receive little or no preparation for their role.[36]

The first three to five observations—each perhaps 20 to 30 minutes—should be for the purpose of practicing several different observation techniques, such as at-task, selective verbatim, interaction patterns, and classroom movement (see Unit 4). Teachers are usually willing to let a colleague practice his or her newly acquired skills in their classrooms. They are likely to be interested in seeing the data, even if a feedback conference is not part of the assignment.

When the observers feel confident, planning and feedback conferences should be added as part of the assignment. Observers who are practicing new conferencing skills are often rewarded by the response they get from teachers who find the systematic observational records to be interesting and relevant.

RESEARCH ON CLINICAL SUPERVISION

Researchers have conducted studies of the effects of clinical supervision on various outcomes. Carl Glickman and Theresa Bey reviewed this research and concluded that clinical supervision has positive effects on both teachers and students.[37] Specifically, clinical supervision has been found to improve:

- teachers' ability to reflect on their instruction and engage in higher-order thinking
- collegiality, openness, and communication among teachers and between teachers, supervisors, and principals
- retention of teachers in the profession, while also reducing teacher anxiety and burnout
- teachers' sense of autonomy, personal efficacy, and self-growth
- teachers' attitudes toward the supervisory process
- student achievement and attitudes

As one might expect, these outcomes were affected by the quality of clinical supervision that was provided for teachers. Just because an intervention is labeled "clinical supervision" does not mean that a supervisor's behavior followed the model presented in this book or the other models listed in Table 1.1. Researchers generally have found better outcomes when supervisors have been trained in techniques of clinical supervision, or when clinical supervision has been used over an extensive period of time.

Case Study Research

Jim Nolan, Brent Hawkes, and Pam Francis conducted a review of research involving six case studies of clinical supervision with inservice teachers.[38] The advantage of case studies as a research methodology is that they allow for greater depth of inquiry into complex phenomena such as clinical supervision. All the case studies revealed positive changes in teachers' ability to think productively about their instruction and improve their instruction. Among the improvements noted were the following:

- A first-year biology teacher learned how to hold her students accountable for performing intellectually.
- A third-year social sciences teacher learned how to increase the number of students who participated in class discussions.
- An elementary teacher with 10 years of experience increased his students' at-task behavior.
- A physics teacher with 15 years of experience increased his students' participation in class activities.

- An elementary teacher with 22 years of experience improved her ability to meet individual student needs, implemented process-oriented curriculum, and adopted a student-centered classroom management style.

In reviewing the case studies, Nolan and colleagues found five commonalities in supervisory behavior that facilitated these changes in teacher behavior:

1. the development of a collegial relationship in which the teacher feels safe and supported
2. teacher control over the products of supervision
3. continuity in the supervisory process over time
4. focused, descriptive records of actual teaching and learning events as the basis for reflection
5. reflection by both the teacher and supervisor as the heart of the process of postconferencing[39]

These principles of effective supervision are consistent with our model of clinical supervision.

Survey Research

Mitchell Holifield and Daniel Cline surveyed a sample of 900 teachers and 300 principals in secondary schools in 19 states about their clinical supervision practices and attitudes.[40] They wanted to learn the extent to which principals used particular techniques of clinical supervision and whether teachers and their supervisors (the school principal) believed that these techniques were worthwhile. The list of techniques, many of which are described in this book (Units 3 and 4), is shown in the first column of Table 1.2.

Each technique was rated for frequency and desirability of occurrence on a four-point scale (1 = never; 2 = seldom; 3 = usually; 4 = almost always). Inspection of Table 1.2 reveals that most clinical supervision techniques were used regularly by principals (3 = usually). Also, principals and teachers valued most of the techniques (see mean scores in the Preferred column). The researchers analyzed their data further to determine whether teachers and principals differed in their survey responses. Only slight differences were found. Principals perceived more frequent use of the clinical supervision techniques than did the teachers.

The least used (and least preferred) technique was the use of audio or video devices to collect data during the observation phase of clinical supervision. A possible explanation of this finding is that audio and video recordings are viewed as requiring too much effort for supervisors and teachers. This is unfortunate because, in our experience, video recordings provide powerful feedback to teachers on their classroom instruction.

Using the same four-point scale, the researchers asked the teachers and principals to respond to survey items about the benefits of clinical supervision. The four most common benefits, which also happen to be the most preferred benefits, were these:

- Enhances and supports teachers' desire to improve.
- Helps develop positive, professional communication and collaboration between supervisor and the teachers.

Table 1.2 Extent to Which Supervisory Practices Are Reported To Be in Use Compared with Extent to Which Respondents Preferred These Practices (Rank Ordered by Means)

		Actual		Preferred	
Item	Clinical Practices	M	Rank	Rank	M
1	Pre-observation conference prior to planned observation	3.11	9	10	3.54
2	Supervisor conducts both planned and unplanned observations	3.16	7	11	3.52
3	Collaboration occurs to identify one or more of teacher's concerns about instruction	2.96	11	8	3.60
4	Behaviors to be observed are based on teacher's concerns about instruction	2.81	15	12	3.51
5	Prior collaboration to decide focus of observation	2.93	13	9	3.58
6	Prior selection or creation of observation instrument	2.66	17	16	3.27
7	Supervisor gets clarification of what the class will be doing during upcoming observation	2.90	14	13	3.48
8	Arrange a specific time for observations	3.47	3	6	3.65
9	Stay for more than half the period	3.57	1	4	3.74
10	Supervisor focuses only on what was agreed to	2.70	16	17	3.02
11	Audio or visual recording of data during observation	1.32	19	19	2.12
12	Observation is not a distraction in class	2.95	12	18	2.96
13	Formal post-observation conference after both planned and unplanned observations	3.56	2	1	3.85
14	Objective collaboration between supervisor and teacher to review observation data	3.21	5	5	3.72
15	Collaboration to draw conclusions about teacher's performance focused on by data collection	3.21	6	3	3.74

(Continued)

Table 1.2 Cont'd

Item	Clinical Practices	Actual		Preferred	
		M	Rank	Rank	*M*
16	Supervisor & teacher collaborate to form an improvement or enhancement plan	3.04	10	7	3.64
17	Supervisor is objective, offers no value judgments	3.14	8	14	3.47
18	Supervisor is prepared for post-conference (knows the data, has logical plan for sharing them)	3.35	4	2	3.79
19	Teacher is given data prior to post-conference	2.32	18	15	3.33

Source: Table on p. 111 of Holifield, M., & Cline, D. (1997). Clinical supervision and its outcomes: Teachers and principals report. *NASSP Bulletin, 81*(590), 109–113. Copyright © 1997, National Association of Secondary School Principals. Reprinted by permission of Sage Publications.

- Helps teachers become investigators of their own teaching.
- Facilitates the building of trust between teachers and supervisors.

These survey results have limited validity, because they are based on self-report rather than direct observation. However, they strongly suggest that the model of clinical supervision presented in this book is an effective approach to promoting teachers' professional development.

In a study by James Shinn, inservice teachers responded to a survey questionnaire in which they were asked to rate the ideal frequency with which they would like school principals to use various techniques of clinical supervision, and their actual frequency of such use.[41] The questionnaire listed many of the techniques described in this book. Shinn's most significant finding was that teachers view all the techniques of clinical supervision as worthwhile; each technique was rated as meriting occasional or frequent use. This finding is strikingly similar to the findings of Holifield and Cline shown in Table 1.2, even though their study was conducted nearly 20 years later. Another noteworthy finding of Shinn's study is that, according to teachers, principals who had received training in the techniques used them more often than untrained principals did.

Gary Martin conducted a research study to determine whether training supervisors in the clinical-supervision model would affect teachers' acceptance of the model.[42] Martin surveyed a group of inservice teachers and supervisors who were trained in the observation techniques presented in Unit 4. A control group of teachers and supervisors did not receive this training. Martin found that the trained teachers believed that their annual evaluation was more helpful to them than did the untrained teachers. Also, the trained teachers were more likely to accept evaluation as a basis for promotion and tenure decisions than were the untrained teachers.

THE THEORY OF REFLECTIVE PRACTICE AS A BASIS
FOR CLINICAL SUPERVISION

Theories look behind the surface of phenomena and attempt to explain them using a system of constructs and principles relating those constructs to each other. For example, Albert Einstein invoked the constructs of energy, mass, and light to explain certain physical phenomena, and he related these constructs to each other in the famous equation, $e = mc^2$. Einstein's theory has been empirically supported and has led to many applications, including nuclear power.

Some social scientists have developed theories that can help us understand clinical supervision and perhaps lead to its improvement.[43] Among these theories, one is particularly relevant to understanding, justifying, and improving clinical supervision. Developed by Donald Schön and Chris Argyris, it is a theory about how professionals in various fields, including education, conduct their work.[44] They observed that problems of practice are often messy and not solvable by applying scientific principles or specific research findings. Skillful practitioners deal with these problems by engaging in "reflection-in-practice" (or, in shortened form, "reflection").

What does it mean for a professional to be reflective? Drawing on the theoretical work of Schön and others, Doreen Ross defines reflection as "a way of thinking about educational matters that involves the ability to make rational choices and to assume responsibility for those choices."[45] Schön and Argyris claim that this thinking is of two types: "espoused theories" and "theories-in-use." Collectively, a professional's espoused theories and theories-in-use constitute their "theory of action."

An espoused theory consists of the explanations that professionals give to others when asked to justify their actions to others and themselves. For example, a teacher might say, "I change my teaching activities frequently during a lesson, because my students have short attention spans." Activity change and attention span are the key concepts in the theory that this teacher *espouses* in order to explain and justify his teaching practice.

In contrast, a theory-in-use is the theory that actually governs a professional's practice. This is an important distinction, because, as Schön and Argyris claim:

> . . . the theory that actually governs [a professional's] actions is his theory-in-use, which may or may not be compatible with his espoused theory; furthermore the individual may or may not be aware of the incompatibility of the two theories.[46]

If Schön and Argyris are correct, one task of clinical supervisors is to elicit teachers' thinking and determine whether their espoused theory of instruction is compatible with what they actually do in the classroom. With reference to the example we stated above, it is possible that a teacher might believe in the importance of varying instructional activities, but not actually do it in the classroom. Planning and feedback conferences (see Chapters 8 and 9) provide the opportunity for a critical examination of this teacher's espoused theory and theory-in-use.

Schön and Argyris note that theories-in-use are often tacit: "Theories-in-use tend to be tacit structures whose relation to action is like the relation of grammar-in-use to speech."[47] To make theories-in-use explicit, it is necessary to infer them from careful observations of the teacher's behavior. This is one reason why observation is a key element of clinical supervision. (The four chapters of Unit 4 describe a wide range of classroom observation instruments.)

By working with a teacher to make her theory-in-use explicit, the supervisor can help her determine whether it is compatible with her espoused theory, as we stated above. Schön and Argyris explain why this type of reflection is important:

> What, then, is the advantage of explicitly stating the theories-in-use we already hold? If unstated theories-in-use appear to enable the agent to perform effectively, there may be no advantage. But if the agent is performing ineffectively and does not know why or if others are aware of his ineffectiveness and he is not, explicitly stating his theory-in-use allows conscious criticism.[48]

A major part of reflection, then, involves "conscious criticism" of one's teaching to determine whether one's theory-in-use allows one to be effective with students. The supervisor facilitates this process by collecting observational data and encouraging the teacher to interpret them and consider new, more effective ways of teaching based on a better theory-in-use.

One important source of a good theory-in-action is the knowledge base about effective teaching created by researchers (the subject of Chapter 4). Another source is reflection on practice. Ross states that the learning process of a reflective practitioner involves these elements:

- recognizing educational dilemmas.
- responding to a dilemma by recognizing both the similarities to other situations and the unique qualities of the particular situation.
- framing and reframing the dilemma.
- experimenting with the dilemma to discover the implications of various solutions.
- examining the intended and unintended consequences of an implemented solution and evaluating it by determining whether the consequences are desirable.[49]

These same elements of reflection are features of good clinical supervision. Working together, the teacher and supervisor identify "concerns and problems"—our term for "dilemmas"—in the teacher's instruction (Conference Technique 1). The supervisor then helps the teacher identify instructional techniques that may be more effective (Conference Technique 3). The teacher subsequently teaches a lesson, which the supervisor records with an appropriate observational instrument. In the feedback conference, the teacher and supervisor together examine the observational data to determine the consequences of using, or not using, particular techniques. As a result of this examination, the teacher might revise his or her espoused theory, experiment with new techniques, and determine their effects on student learning.

A study by Laurence Antil and his colleagues document a dilemma involving the teaching method called *cooperative learning*.[50] As we explain in Chapter 4, this method has been research-validated as effective in improving students' academic achievement. It involves the teacher assembling a class of students into small groups, which work collaboratively to develop each others' mastery of a lesson's content. Antil and his colleagues reviewed the literature on cooperative learning to identify the critical features of this teaching method. They then interviewed 85 elementary teachers to determine whether they used cooperative learning. Ninety-three percent of them said that they used cooperative learning; but when the researchers observed their classroom instruction, they found that very few of them were actually using this method, as defined by their criteria. The dilemma in this case is not a discrepancy between the teachers' theory-in-use (i.e., their actual use of cooperative learning) and their espoused theory (i.e., their belief that they are using cooperative learning). Rather, the dilemma is the discrepancy between the teachers' theory-in-use and the espoused theories of educational experts, which refers to particular characteristics that need to be implemented if it is to be considered cooperative learning.

Another type of dilemma was identified by Thomas Hatch, who observed a school improvement project called *ATLAS* (Authentic Teaching Learning and Assessment for All Students), which was co-led by four groups—the Coalition of Essential Schools, Education Development, Harvard Project Zero, and the School Development Program.[51] He found that differences between the espoused theories of these groups created dilemmas that made it very difficult for the project to move forward. For example, the groups differed in how much emphasis to place on winning wide support for school reform, as opposed to empowering selected individuals who had innovative ideas and wanted innovation to occur.

Hatch concluded from his research findings that it is unlikely that educators can agree on a single answer to these dilemmas. Instead, he argued for making the dilemmas explicit and reflecting on them: "Rather than trying to forge a single, common theory of action, those involved in reform efforts might be better off trying to gain a deep, respectful understanding of when and why they are likely to disagree."[52] This type of understanding is only possible if observational data are collected to identify dilemmas—and if these data become the focus of thoughtful reflection by those who are attempting to make organizational or individual professional improvements.

Hatch studied a large-scale school improvement effort, but his findings and recommendations apply equally to certain dilemmas that arise in clinical supervision. Student teachers and their cooperating teachers and university supervisors might have different espoused theories and theories-in-use. It might not be necessary to reach consensus on a single theory of action if the stakeholders can understand and accept their differences. The necessary first step is for all stakeholders to make their theories of action explicit.

There is more to the theory of reflective practice than we have presented here. However, we have described principal features of the theory, particularly those of relevance to clinical supervision.

Why is the theory of reflective practice important for teacher educators? To answer this question, we start by noting that the theory was developed and validated by observing how professionals in various fields actually perform their work. Their observations are corroborated by our own experience as teachers and teacher educators and, we trust, by your experience as well.

Assuming the theory's validity, let us consider how it matches up with conventional teacher education. The prevalent model is for preservice teachers to take a series of university courses in which they learn content-area knowledge (e.g., mathematics, history, biology), research knowledge, and generalized pedagogical knowledge. The expectation is that preservice teachers will acquire this knowledge and apply it in practicums and student teaching. University supervisors are expected to facilitate this transfer process.

This conventional model of professional education is quite different from what the theory of reflective practice suggests is needed. As we see it, the theory suggests that field experiences and clinical supervision should be at the center of teacher education. Preservice teachers should be exposed early to the "messiness" and problematic nature of classroom instruction and develop skills in problem-posing, problem-solving, experimentation, and use of observational data to refine teaching skills. Formal knowledge (typically codified in textbooks) should be brought in "just-in-time" to inform the preservice teachers' espoused theories and evolving professional skills.

Inservice education has similar problems to those of preservice education, although perhaps not to the same extent. Workshops, conference presentations, and university courses might feature more practical knowledge, but there is still the assumption that teachers will acquire the knowledge and then somehow transfer it to their classrooms. The theory of reflective practice suggests that this model of professional education is fundamentally flawed. It does not properly recognize the problematic nature of teaching and the fact that each teacher's instruction is based on his or her individual theory-in-use, which might differ substantially from the espoused theories that they learn in workshops, lectures, and courses.

In summary, we believe that the theory of reflective practice provides strong support for clinical supervision as a critical process in teacher education. Furthermore, it provides support for many of the specific conferencing and observational techniques presented in this book. Most importantly, the theory of reflective practice suggests that clinical supervision should play a different—and larger—role than it has in most teacher education programs.

ENDNOTES

1. Goldhammer, R. (1969). *Clinical supervision: Special methods for the supervision of teachers*. New York: Holt, Rinehart, & Winston. Quote appears on p. 368.

2. Levine, A. (2006). *Educating school teachers*. Available at <http://www.edschools.org/pdf/Educating_Teachers_Report.pdf>

3. *Ibid.*, p. 39.

4. Blumberg, A. (1974). *Supervisors and teachers: A private cold war*. Berkeley, CA: McCutchan. Quote appears on p. 56.

5. Their work is presented in the following books: Goldhammer, R. (1969). *Clinical supervision: Special methods for the supervision of teachers*. New York: Holt, Rinehart & Winston; Goldhammer, R., Anderson, R. H., & Krajewski, R. J. (1980). *Clinical supervision: Special methods for the supervision of teachers* (2nd ed.). New York: Holt, Rinehart, & Winston; Mosher, R. L., & Purpel, D. E. (1972). *Supervision: The reluctant profession*. Boston: Houghton Mifflin; Cogan, M. L. (1973). *Clinical supervision*. Boston: Houghton Mifflin.

6. Goldhammer, *op. cit.* Quote appears on p. 54.

7. McCaslin, M., Good, T. L., Nichols, S., Zhang, J., Wiley, C. R. H., Bozack, A. R., Burross, H. L., & Cuizon-Garcia, R. (2006). Comprehensive school reform: An observational study of teaching in grades 3 through 5. *Elementary School Journal, 106*(4), 313–331.

8. Goodlad, J. I. (1984). *A place called school: Prospects for the future*. New York: McGraw-Hill.

9. Sirotnik, K. A. (1983). What you see is what you get—consistency, persistency, and mediocrity in classrooms. *Harvard Educational Review, 53*, 16–31. Quote appears on p. 29.

10. Blankenship, G., Jr., & Irvine, J. J. (1985). Georgia teachers' perceptions of prescriptive and descriptive observations of teaching by instructional supervisors. *Georgia Educational Leadership, 1*(1), 7–10; Graybeal, N. D. (1984). Characteristics of contemporary classroom supervisory process. *Dissertation Abstracts International: Section A. Humanities and Social Sciences, 45(07)*, 2071.

11. Koehler, V. R. (1984). *The instructional supervision of student teachers*. Retrieved from ERIC database. (No. ED 271 430)

12. Kent, S. I. (2004). Supervision of student teachers: Practices of cooperating teachers prepared in a clinical supervision course. *Journal of Curriculum and Supervision, 16*(3), 228–244.

13. For other ideas about how educators might use time in the workplace differently, see Gándara, P. (Ed.) (2000).

The dimensions of time and the challenge of school reform. Albany, New York: State University of New York Press.

14. Pajak, E. (1993). *Approaches to clinical supervision: Alternatives for improving instruction.* Norwood, MA: Christopher-Gordon.

15. Goldhammer, *op. cit.*

16. Mosher & Purpel, *op. cit.*

17. Cogan, *op. cit.*

18. Blumberg, A. (1980). *Supervisors & teachers: A private cold war* (2nd ed.). Berkeley, CA: McCutchan.

19. Eisner, E. W. (1985). *The educational imagination: On the design and evaluation of educational programs* (2nd ed.). New York: Macmillan.

20. Acheson, K. A., & M. D. Gall. (2003). *Clinical supervision and teacher development: Preservice and inservice applications* (5th ed). New York: Wiley.

21. Hunter, M. (1984). Knowing, teaching, and supervising. In P. L. Hosford (Ed.), *Using what we know about teaching* (pp. 169–193). Alexandria, VA: Association for Supervision and Curriculum Development.

22. Joyce, B., & B. Showers. (1988). *Student achievement through staff development.* New York: Longman.

23. Glickman, C. D. (1985). *Supervision of instruction: A developmental approach.* Boston: Allyn and Bacon.

24. Costa, A. L., & Garmston, R. (1985). Supervision for intelligent teaching. *Educational Leadership, 42*(5), 70–80.

25. Schön, D. A. (1987). *Educating the reflective practitioner: Toward a new design for teaching and learning in the professions.* San Francisco: Jossey-Bass.

26. Zeichner, K. M., & Liston, D. P. (1987). Teaching student teachers to reflect. *Harvard Educational Review, 57,* 23–48.

27. Garman, N. B. (1986). Reflection, the heart of clinical supervision: A modern rationale for practice. *Journal of Curriculum and Supervision, 2,* 1–24.

28. Smyth, W. J. (1985). Developing a critical practice of clinical supervision. *Journal of Curriculum Studies, 17,* 1–15.

29. Retallick, J. A. (1990, April). *Clinical supervision and the structure of communication.* Paper presented at the annual meeting of the American Educational Research Association, Boston.

30. Bowers, C. A., & D. J. Flinders. (1991). *Culturally responsive teaching and supervision: A handbook for staff development.* New York: Teachers College Press.

31. Pajak *op. cit.* Quote appears on pp. 150–151.

32. Boyd., D. J., Grossman, P. L., Lankford, H., Loeb, S., & Wyckoff, J. (2009). Teacher preparation and student achievement. *Educational Evaluation and Policy Analysis, 31*(4), 416–440.

33. Gladwell, M. (2008). *Outliers: The story of success.* Boston: Little, Brown and Company.

34. Little, J. W. (1990). Conditions of professional development in secondary schools. In M. W. McLaughlin, J. E. Talbert, & N. Bascia (Eds.) *The contexts of teaching in secondary schools: Teachers' realities* (pp. 187–223). New York: Teachers College Press.

35. Parsons, T. (1968). *Guided self-analysis professional development systems. Education Series: Overview.* Berkeley: Guided Self-Analysis Professional Development Systems. Retrieved from ERIC database. (ED052151)

36. Guyton, E. (1989). Guidelines for developing educational programs for cooperating teachers. *Action in Teacher Education, 11,* 54–58; Sudzina, M., Giebelhaus, C., & Coolican, M. (1997). Mentor or tormentor: The role of the cooperating teacher in student teacher success or failure. *Action in Teacher Education, 18,* 23–35.

37. Glickman, C. D., & Bey, T. M. (1990). Supervision. In W. R. Houston, M. Haberman, & J. Sikula (Eds.), *Handbook of research on teacher education* (pp. 549–566). New York: Macmillan.

38. Nolan, J., Hawkes, B., & Francis, P. (1993). Case studies: Windows onto clinical supervision. *Educational Leadership, 51*(2), 52–56.

39. *Ibid.* p. 54. Reprinted by permission of ASCD.

40. Holifield, M., & Cline, D. (1997). Clinical supervision and its outcomes: Teachers and principals report. *NASSP Bulletin, 81*(590), 109–113.

41. Shinn, J. L. (1976). Teacher perceptions of ideal and actual supervisory procedures used by California elementary principals: The effects of supervisory training programs sponsored by the Association of California School Administrators. *Dissertation Abstracts International: Section A. Humanities and Social Sciences, 37*(06), 3567.

42. Martin, G. S. (1975). Teacher and administrator attitudes toward evaluation and systematic classroom observation. *Dissertation Abstracts International: Section A. Humanities and Social Sciences, 37*(06), 5780.

43. Anderson, J. R. (1982). Acquisition of cognitive skill. *Psychological Review, 89*(4), 369–406; Bandura, A. (1977). *Social learning theory.* New York: General Learning Press.

44. Schön, D. A. (1987). *Educating the reflective practitioner.* San Francisco: Jossey-Bass; Schön, D. A. (2000).

The reflective practitioner: How professionals think in action. New York: Basic Books; Argyris, C., & Schön, D. A. (1974). *Theory in practice: Increasing professional effectiveness*. San Francisco: Jossey-Bass.

45. Ross, D. D. (1990). Programmatic structures for the preparation of reflective teachers. In R. T. Clift, W. R. Houston, & M. C. Pugach. (Eds.), *Encouraging reflective practice in education: An analysis of issues and programs* (pp. 97–118). New York: Teachers College Press. Quote appears on p. 98.

46. Argyris & Schön, p. 7.

47. *Ibid.*, p. 30.

48. *Ibid.*, p. 14.

49. Ross, *op. cit.*, p. 98.

50. Antil, L. R., Jenkins, J. R., Wayne, S. K., & Vadasy, P. E. (1998). Cooperative Learning: Prevalence, conceptualizations, and the relation between research and practice. *American Educational Research Journal, 35*(3), 419–454.

51. Hatch, T. (1998). The differences in theory that matter in the practice of school improvement. *American Educational Research Journal, 35*, 3–31.

52. *Ibid.*, p. 25.

Unit Two

The Uses of Clinical Supervision

Chapter 2

Using Clinical Supervision to Support the Stages and Goals of Teacher Development

New teachers tend to get the neediest and lowest skill-level students or low-tracked classes. They get no extra money for supplies and resources. They have little or no collegial support.
—A mentor teacher[1]

INTRODUCTION

Graduation from a teacher education program hopefully ensures, at the least, survival skills as a classroom teacher. Once employed, teachers must continually develop in order to become master teachers. Educational theorists have developed models to identify the stages that teachers must pass through on their way to earning this status. We consider several of these models in the first part of the chapter.

Some models do not focus on stages of development, but rather on standards of professional performance that teachers should strive to achieve. In other words, these models are concerned with the goals of teacher development—in a sense, what a master teacher looks like—rather than the stages through which teachers pass on the way to achieving those goals. We describe these standards-based models later in the chapter.

HELPING TEACHERS DEVELOP AS PROFESSIONALS

Teachers wish to be seen as professionals and accorded the same status enjoyed by other professionals like doctors, lawyers, and engineers. Therefore, clinical supervisors need to focus on teachers' classroom instruction—but within the larger context of acknowledging teachers as emerging or experienced professionals.

To provide that acknowledgment, clinical supervisors need to understand what it means to be a member of a profession. Sociologists have extensively studied the characteristics of professions in the United States and elsewhere.[2] They consider a profession to be an occupation whose practitioners possess a high level of skill and perform functions that are central to society. More specifically, a profession has these characteristics:

1. A profession is an occupation which performs a crucial social function.

2. The exercise of this function requires a considerable degree of skill.

3. This skill is exercised in situations which are not wholly routine, but in which new problems have to be handled.

4. Thus, although knowledge gained through experience is important, it is not sufficient to meet professional demands and the practitioner has to draw on a body of systematic knowledge.

5. The acquisition of this body of knowledge and the development of specific skills requires a lengthy period of higher education.

6. This period of education and training also involves the process of socialization into professional values.

7. These values tend to center on the preeminence of clients' interests, and often they are made explicit in a code of ethics.

8. Because knowledge-based skills are exercised in nonroutine situations, it is essential for the professionals to have the freedom to make their own judgments with regard to appropriate practice.

9. Because professional practice is so specialized, the organizing profession should have a strong voice in the shaping of relevant social policy, a large degree of control over the exercise of professional responsibilities, and a high degree of autonomy in relation to the state.

10. Lengthy training, responsibility, and client-centeredness are necessarily rewarded by high prestige and a high level of remuneration.[3]

Clinical supervision is best suited to help teachers develop those aspects of professionalism that concern nonroutine problems and the skills, systematic knowledge, and ethical judgment needed to solve them effectively. As we explain in Chapter 1, clinical supervision is grounded in the theory of reflective practice. It provides a conceptual framework for focusing on the problematic nature of classroom practice and developing skills for handling it through experimentation, systematic observation, and reflection.

The above list of characteristics of a profession also emphasizes the "preeminence of clients' interests" and "a body of systematic knowledge." In the context of education, we interpret clients' interests to be the learning of students in teachers' classrooms. As for systematic knowledge, we demonstrate in Chapter 4 that there is a body of research-based knowledge about effective teaching methods. Although these methods cannot—and should not—be applied in a rote manner, they nonetheless can inform and enhance classroom practice. For this reason, clinical supervisors have the responsibility to draw on this body of expert knowledge (and other bodies of expert knowledge as well) in helping teachers earn recognition as true professionals.

MODELS OF TEACHER DEVELOPMENT

In times of severe teacher shortages, college graduates are recruited as classroom teachers with the barest of professional preparation. In some developing countries, a high-school diploma will suffice. While these individuals might survive in the classroom, it would be hard to argue that they are professionals by the criteria that we listed in the preceding section. Becoming a full-fledged professional teacher—what we call a master teacher—requires extensive development of one's expertise.

What are the features of this developmental process, and what role does clinical supervision play in it? To answer these questions, we review several models of teacher development in the next sections.

Leithwood's Multidimensional Model

Kenneth Leithwood reviewed various strands of theory and research about teacher development and concluded that it has three central dimensions: (1) development of professional expertise; (2) psychological development; and (3) career-cycle development.[4] Leithwood's analysis of each dimension yields a comprehensive model of how teachers develop throughout their careers. The model has significant implications for clinical supervisors, as we explain below.

Development of Professional Expertise

According to Leithwood's model of teacher development, teachers progress through six stages of professional expertise. Each stage reflects a higher level of proficiency in the classroom and other settings.

The six stages are described in Table 2.1. Teachers have different needs at each stage. Therefore, clinical supervisors need extensive knowledge about effective teaching strategies—from the most basic to the most sophisticated. In Chapter 3, we review what is known about effective teaching.

Table 2.1   The Six Stages of Teachers' Development of Professional Expertise

Stages	Characteristics of Expertise
1. Developing survival skills	• Partially developed classroom-management skills • Knowledge about and limited skill in use of several teaching models • No conscious reflection on choice of model • Student assessment is primarily summative and carried out, using limited techniques, in response to external demands (e.g., reporting to parents); may be poor link between the focus of assessment and instructional goal
2. Becoming competent in the basic skills of instruction	• Well-developed classroom-management skills • Well-developed skill in use of several teaching models • Habitual application through trial and error, of certain teaching models for particular parts of curriculum • Student assessment begins to reflect formative purposes, although techniques are not well suited to such purposes; focus of assessment is linked to instructional goals that are easiest to measure.

(*Continued*)

Table 2.1 Cont'd

Stages	Characteristics of Expertise
3. Expanding one's instructional flexibility	• Automatized classroom-management skills • Growing awareness of need for and existence of other teaching models and initial efforts to expand repertoire and experiment with application of new models • Choice of teaching model from expanded repertoire influenced most by interest in providing variety to maintain student interest • Student assessment carried out for both formative and summative purposes; repertoire of techniques is beginning to match purposes; focus of assessment covers significant range of instructional goals
4. Acquiring instructional expertise	• Classroom management integrated with program; little attention required to classroom management as an independent issue • Skill in application of a broad repertoire of teaching models
5. Contributing to the growth of colleagues' instructional expertise	• Has high levels of expertise in classroom instructional performance • Reflective about own competence and choices and the fundamental beliefs and values on which they are based • Able to assist other teachers in acquiring instructional expertise through either planned learning experiences, such as mentoring, or more formal experiences, such as inservice education and coaching programs
6. Participating in a broad array of educational decisions at all levels of the education system	• Is committed to the goal of school improvement • Accepts responsibility for fostering that goal through any legitimate opportunity • Able to exercise leadership, both formal and informal, with groups of adults inside and outside the school • Has a broad framework from which to understand the relationship among decisions at many different levels in the education system • Is well informed about policies at many different levels in the education system

Source: Leithwood, K. A. (1992). The principal's role in teacher development. In M. Fullan & A. Hargreaves (Eds.), *Teacher development and educational change* (pp. 86–103). London: Falmer Press, p. 89. Reprinted by permission of Taylor & Francis Books.

Leithwood's model of stages of professional expertise emphasizes teachers' growing capacity for reflection—from "no conscious reflection" in Stage 1 to "reflective about own competence and choices and fundamental beliefs and values on which they are based" in Stage 5. Consistent with this view, we ground clinical supervision in the theory of reflective practice (see Chapter 1). The purpose of clinical supervision is to help teachers reflect on their instruction to identify problems of practice and opportunities for improvement of their instruction.

Table 2.1 shows that when teachers reach the fifth stage of professional expertise, they are ready and eager to promote other teachers' development. One way of reaching that goal is for them to become clinical supervisors themselves—perhaps as a mentor, university supervisor, cooperating teacher, or peer consultant.

Teachers who reach the sixth and final stage of expertise in Table 2.1 contribute not only to other teachers' development, but also to their school, school system, and the entire teaching profession. In effect, they become instructional leaders. Clinical supervisors have an important role to play at this stage. Because they work directly with teachers, they are in an excellent position to identify teachers who have the expertise to be instructional leaders. They can recommend these teachers to colleagues who are responsible for teacher-based instructional leadership.

Career Development

Leithwood concluded from his review of the research literature that the careers of teachers typically pass through five stages, which are described in Table 2.2. Each stage marks a new

Table 2.2 The Five Stages of Teachers' Career Cycle

Stages	Characteristic conditions
1. Launching the career	• Easy beginnings: developing positive relationships with students and feeling a sense of instructional mastery and enthusiasm • Painful beginnings: experiencing role overload, anxiety, difficult students, close monitoring, and professional isolation
2. Stabilizing	• Making a commitment to the profession and the employer making a commitment to the teacher • Feeling confident about one's basic instructional skills • Feeling integrated into a group of peers • Possibly seeking greater responsibilities
3. Facing new challenges	• Some teachers moving into "master teacher" status or seeking promotion to positions of greater responsibility • Other teachers experiencing mediocre instructional success and considering alternative careers
4. Reaching a professional plateau	• Some teachers no longer striving for promotion and become the backbone of the school • Other teachers becoming bitter and cynical and stop seeking opportunities for professional development
5. Preparing for retirement	• Some teachers "contracting" by specializing in what they do best • Other teachers becoming disenchanted, tired, and bitter about past experiences with change

Source: Adapted from: Leithwood, K.A. (1992). The principal's role in teacher development. In M. Fullan & A. Hargreaves (Eds.), *Teacher development and educational change* (pp. 86–103). London: Falmer Press, pp. 92–93.

challenge for teachers. Many of them respond to the challenge by growing professionally. Unfortunately, some stagnate, become bitter, or decline in effectiveness.

Given how busy supervisors are, it might be easy to ignore teachers who are ready for professional growth at a particular career stage. Yet these teachers deserve the full attention of clinical supervisors and others, for they are the ones who can provide instructional leadership to schools. Indeed, they are the teachers on whom the future of the teaching profession depends.

Teachers who are in a state of stagnation or decline pose a different challenge for clinical supervisors. They require intensive clinical supervision and other forms of professional development in order to avoid having them hinder students' learning and "infect" other teachers with their negativism. In Chapter 5 we explain how these teachers become identified through a formal process of teacher evaluation and how they might be helped through plans of assistance involving clinical supervision.

Some teachers who are in a state of stagnation or decline realize their condition and need help in considering new career options. Because clinical supervision is intensive and focused on the individual teacher, the supervisor might be the first and most important colleague with whom a teacher can discuss his career frustrations. Of course, for this to happen, there must be trust and open communication between the teacher and supervisor. We discuss these aspects of communication in several chapters, but particularly in Chapter 7.

Psychological Development

Drawing on various theories of human development, Leithwood claims that teachers progress through four stages of ego, moral, and conceptual development over the course of their careers. The four stages are described in Table 2.3. As teachers move from one stage to the next, their reasoning about the moral, interpersonal, and academic aspects of classroom

Table 2.3 The Four Stages of Teachers' Psychological Development

Stages	Characteristics of teachers
Stage 1 (Simplistic)	• See choices as black and white • Believe strongly in rules and roles • View authority as the highest good • Discourage divergent thinking and rewards conformity and rote learning
Stage 2 (Conformist)	• Wish to be like their peers • Provide instruction with explicit rules that do not accommodate individual differences or special circumstances
Stage 3 (Conscientious)	• Appreciate multiple possibilities for explaining and designing instruction • Appreciate the need for exception to rules, given the circumstances • Provide rationally planned instruction that is achievement-oriented and grounded in good interpersonal communication

Stage 4 (Inner-directed)

- Appreciate the interdependent nature of relationships and therefore establish classroom control collaboratively with students
- Appreciate multiple perspectives and synthesize them
- Understand the reasoning behind rules and therefore can apply them wisely
- Can provide instruction that balances interpersonal and academic-achievement orientations
- Encourages students to engage in complex cognitive functions

Source: Adapted from: Leithwood, K.A. (1992). The principal's role in teacher development. In M. Fullan & A. Hargreaves (Eds.), *Teacher development and educational change* (pp. 86–103). London: Falmer Press, pp. 90–91.

instruction becomes more sophisticated. They also develop a more sophisticated view of themselves as members of the teaching profession.

In working with teachers as a clinical supervisor, you will find it helpful to assess their stage of psychological development. Teachers at one of the first two stages might express simplistic concerns about their instruction relative to teachers at the higher stages. Also, they might not be as able to analyze and interpret observational data, or use the data as a basis for generating more effective ways to teach. You might be tempted to do the thinking for such teachers. However, they might not be able to make sense of your ideas, or they might become overly dependent on you as an authority figure.

A more effective approach would be to ask questions that stimulate teachers at Stages 1 and 2 to think for themselves and to praise them for independent thinking. For example, a teacher might look at observational data that show many students off task for significant amounts of time, and ask you, "What should I do to correct this situation?" The temptation is to answer the question, but instead you could ask, "If you really want students to be on task, what are some things you can do?" or "When you've seen classrooms where students are on task most of the time, what kinds of things was the teacher doing?" This technique of questioning (see Chapter 9) encourages teachers to think for themselves and thus progress to Stages 3 and 4 in Leithwood's model of psychological development. A possible benefit of this approach to supervision is that these teachers will facilitate the same kind of thinking in their students.

Berliner's Model of Instructional Expertise

Researchers have become increasingly interested in the nature of expertise. They have addressed such questions as how experts and novices differ in their approach to their work and how expertise develops over time. Experts in such diverse fields as radiology and chess-playing have been studied. Experts in classroom instruction have been studied, too. David Berliner synthesized this research into a model of teacher development of instructional expertise.[5] The model is similar to Leithwood's model of professional expertise, but it has a more specific focus. Leithwood considers the full range of teachers' work—some of which occurs outside the classroom—whereas Berliner's model only involves classroom instruction.

Berliner's model specifies five stages in the development of instructional expertise.

• *Stage 1: Novice Level.* Novice teachers are learning the basic vocabulary and rules of instruction. They also are gaining classroom experience, which they are likely to view as more important than "book knowledge" about teaching. Their instructional behavior tends to be relatively inflexible. Students and many first-year teachers are at this novice stage of expertise.

• *Stage 2: Advanced Beginner Level.* Many second- and third-year teachers are at this stage of instructional expertise. They are able to link their book knowledge with their growing body of experience. When they confront new tasks and problems in their classroom, they are able to link them to previous instances in their experience and recall how they handled them. They also know the limit of instructional principles. For example, they might value the principle of waiting three seconds after asking a question in order to give students time to think, but realize that there are occasions when longer or shorter wait times might be more effective.

• *Stage 3: Competent Level.* Many third- and fourth-year teachers achieve a level of expertise characterized as competence; but according to research evidence reviewed by Berliner, some do not. Competent teachers have a sense of personal agency: They set rational instructional goals and means for achieving those goals. Also, they can size up an instructional situation and decide what is worth attending to and what can be ignored. Because they feel in control of instruction, they take more responsibility for their successes and failures than teachers at the initial stages of expertise development. They are likely to be receptive to using their students' achievement test scores as a basis for helping them learn more and achieve at a higher level on subsequent tests.

• *Stage 4: Proficient Level.* Teachers who reach this stage of expertise have achieved a certain amount of automaticity in their instruction. They are like experienced drivers who handle a car skillfully without having to consciously think about each procedure or decision. Also, they have acquired a wealth of teaching experience that allows them to see patterns in new teaching situations that less experienced teachers miss. For example, when they get a new group of students to teach or observe another teacher's class, they can "size up" the class quickly. They know which of their customary teaching strategies will work and what modifications are necessary.

• *Stage 5: Expert Level.* Expert teachers act in an effortless, fluid manner. They feel at one with their students and the curriculum, so it is not necessary to consciously plan and execute each instructional move. When things do not go as planned, expert teachers can bring their highly developed skills of analysis to improvise solutions.

By the end of the first supervisory cycle (planning conference, classroom observation, feedback conference) with a teacher, you should have a good sense of his or her level of expertise. Novice or advanced-beginner teachers will need guidance in several areas. One of them is distinguishing between significant and insignificant problems in their instruction. For example, they might feel that deficiencies in their classroom management are the central issue, whereas it might be clear to you that their inability to motivate students to learn is most important. Also, they might need guidance in seeing cause-and-effect patterns in the observational data that are reviewed in the feedback conference. This is because the ability to see patterns—rather than isolated details—requires a substantial experience base, which they lack (through no fault of their own).

Novice and advanced beginner teachers tend to feel threatened as flaws in their instruction are revealed by the supervisory process. As a clinical supervisor, you will need to build trust with novices and advanced beginners so that their anxiety and defensiveness do not block the learning process.

In working with teachers at the proficient or expert levels, you might find that your supervision is much more collegial in nature. You and the teacher will act as co-investigators of his or her classroom instruction. You will find much to admire in it, and problems of practice will be opportunities to work together to generate creative solutions. You might find it appropriate to share your own experiences and instructional strategies, because you know that the teacher will not feel threatened by them or feel compelled to adopt them in order to please you.

How long does it take for a teacher to achieve expert status? Berliner refers to a study by D. S. Turner, who studied both nonexemplary and exemplary experienced teachers.[6] The nonexemplary teachers claimed, on average, that it required 2.5 years for them to learn how to be a competent teacher. Exemplary teachers were more modest; on average, they claimed that it took them 4.5 years to achieve this status. In another study, Omar Lopez found that the students who scored highest on standardized achievement tests had teachers with seven or more years of teaching experience; but having teachers with more than seven years of teaching experience did not lead to higher test scores.[7] In other words, this study found that teachers peak out after seven years of teaching.

If we consider the case of world-class expertise in teaching, the research and case studies described by Malcolm Gladwell in his book *Outliers* suggests that 10,000 hours of study and professional practice are required.[8] That figure corresponds to approximately five years of teaching, eight hours a day, for nine months of the year. However, the individuals studied by Gladwell received expert coaching and highly stimulating environments in which to practice during their 10,000 hours. These opportunities are unavailable to most teachers.

Fuller's Model of Teacher Concerns

Frances Fuller's model of teacher development is based on changes in teachers' concerns.[9] She found that teachers progress through three major stages:

- *Covert Concerns about Self.* During student teaching and initial professional teaching, teachers tend to be concerned about where they stand in relation to their supervisors, fellow teachers, and school administrators. For example, they ask themselves questions about their responsibilities relative to the cooperating teacher during field experiences and whether they or other persons are responsible for student misbehavior in class. They have feelings of uncertainty about their authority and others' authority. These concerns are "covert" in that teachers generally feel them, but are reluctant to talk about them to others.
- *Overt Concerns about Self.* Once beginning teachers resolve their concerns about scope of responsibilities, they become concerned about their professional adequacy.

For example, they start wondering whether they are good enough to survive annual evaluations and receive contract renewals. They also worry about the adequacy of their instruction and classroom management. These concerns are more freely expressed, and therefore are labeled as "overt" by Fuller.

- *Concerns about Students.* As teachers become more experienced, the focus of concern moves from self to the students. Among other matters, they are concerned about students who fail to learn or students whom they feel they are not reaching. Teachers at this level are more likely to appreciate achievement test data about their students and reflect on their contribution to students' level of achievement as reflected by these data. In contrast, teachers whose concerns are focused on themselves, covertly or overtly, might be threatened by achievement test data about their students. They might fear the test results will reflect negatively on their competence, or they might feel powerless to raise their students' test scores to a higher level in subsequent test administrations.

Obviously, these concerns do not occur in strict progression.[10] Experienced teachers might have occasion to question their scope of responsibility, and student teachers might have mature, insightful concerns about their students. Fuller's stages of concern are broad generalizations.

You can use Fuller's model as a check on whether you are addressing teachers' felt concerns, not just the concerns that you might have about their instruction. For example, if a student teacher is concerned about the extent to which she is free to bring her own curriculum ideas into the cooperating teacher's classroom, it might be difficult for you to turn her attention to issues involving her classroom management. The teacher's felt concern needs to be addressed first. Once the concern is addressed and resolved, you will be more able to work with the teacher on concerns having to do with teaching methods and student learning.

In Chapter 8, we revisit Fuller's model in our discussion of how to address teachers' concerns as part of the planning process. In Chapter 4, we discuss Gene Hall and Shirley Hord's model of teachers' concerns about school and curriculum reforms. These educators were colleagues of Frances Fuller, and their model was influenced by hers.

TEACHER DEVELOPMENT BASED ON TEACHING STANDARDS

Several organizations and commissions currently are developing standards for teacher performance—the Interstate New Teacher Assessment and Support Consortium (INTASC—a project of the Council of Chief School Officers), the National Council for Accreditation of Teacher Education (NCATE), the Council for Exceptional Children (CEC), and the International Society for Technology in Education (ISTE).[11] Their standards constitute goals that teachers and teacher educators can use in designing professional development programs.

One of the most important and visible organizations involved in the effort to develop standards is the National Board for Professional Teaching Standards (hereafter, "National Board").[12] Just as medical specialists seek board certification to document their expertise for colleagues and patients, so teachers can document their status as a master teacher for other educators, parents, and the community by earning a National Board certificate. As we explain below, clinical supervision is helpful—perhaps essential—in facilitating the specific types of teacher development necessary to earning one.

The National Board for Professional Teaching Standards

The National Board has three purposes:

- to establish high standards that define what a master teacher should know and be able to do.
- to operate a system to assess and certify teachers who meet these standards.
- to support reforms that improve student learning.

This statement of purpose emphasizes the point that the characteristics of effective teaching need to be made explicit and public. Undoubtedly, the particular standards specified by the National Board will change as research knowledge about effective teaching improves.

Our review of research on effective teaching in Chapter 3 gives you a reference point for judging the adequacy and scope of the National Board's current list of standards. Also, one purpose of the conferencing techniques that we present in Unit 3 is to help teachers make explicit their instructional concerns and strategies. As teachers practice making them explicit, they will become more attuned to the National Board's emphasis on explicit definitions of instructional concepts and observable referents for them.

The National Board builds the standards for each certificate around five propositions:

1. Teachers are committed to students and their learning.
2. Teachers know the subjects they teach and how to teach those subjects to students.
3. Teachers are responsible for managing and monitoring student learning.
4. Teachers think systematically about their practice and learn from experience.
5. Teachers are members of learning communities.

The first three propositions address curriculum, instruction, and assessment, respectively. Unit 4 of this book presents observation instruments relating to each of these three cornerstones of classroom instruction, including their alignment with each other.

The fourth proposition involves the reflective process. The model of clinical supervision that we present in this book is built on the theory of reflective practice (see Chapter 1). As a clinical supervisor, you will help teachers develop their ability to reflect about their classroom instruction, which is consistent with this proposition.

The final proposition has to do with teachers learning together to improve their instruction. Professional learning communities, peer coaching, and other methods of professional development described in Chapter 3 support this proposition because they call for teachers to collect observational data in each other's classrooms and to hold collegial conferences to reflect on the data's implications for the improvement of instruction.

The National Board does not specify the methods by which teachers should acquire the expertise required for one of their certificates. Therefore, each teacher can take different developmental paths toward National Board certification. Some teachers' paths will take less time than others. Some might emphasize self-directed study, while others will choose to look for structured programs that will help them prepare for the National Board assessments. Whatever the path, we believe that clinical supervision can help a teacher develop the type of competence in classroom instruction required for a National Board certificate.

National Board Certificates and Assessments

The National Board has created a set of certificates, and is in the process of creating more of them. Each certificate has a subject area and developmental level associated with it, and also a set of standards. For example, teachers can earn a certificate in language arts at the adolescent and young adult level. Table 2.4 shows the 16 standards, grouped into three categories, associated with this certificate. The approach to clinical supervision that we take in this book is consistent with the view of teaching and teacher professionalism expressed in these standards.

National Board Portfolios

Candidates for a National Board certificate are required to submit a set of portfolio entries. Some of these entries ask teachers to videotape and analyze classroom instruction; others ask teachers to collect and analyze student work. For example, the following is one of the required entries for the social studies-history certificate at the early adolescence level:

> In this entry, you demonstrate your knowledge and understanding of social studies-history, and your ability to deepen student understanding of an important topic/concept/theme in social studies-history. You submit a 15-minute video recording that shows how you engage your students in a whole-class lesson that links an important social studies-history topic to the world outside the classroom and a Written Commentary that contextualizes, analyzes, and evaluates your teaching efforts to foster civic competence in your students. You will also submit instructional materials related to the lesson on the video recording.[13]

Table 2.4 National Board Standards for the English Language-Arts Certificate at Adolescence Young Adult Level (Second Edition)

The requirements for the Adolescence and Young Adulthood/English Language Arts (AYA/ELA) certificate are organized into the following sixteen standards.

Preparing the Way for Productive Student Learning

I. Knowledge of students
   Accomplished AYA/ELA teachers acquire specific knowledge about students' individual, intellectual, and social development and use that knowledge to advance students' achievement as readers, writers, speakers, listeners, and viewers in English language art.
II. Knowledge of English language arts
   Accomplished AYA/ELA teachers have a thorough command of the various domains of knowledge that compose the English language arts.
III. Instructional design and decision making
   Accomplished AYA/ELA teachers use their knowledge of students, English language arts, and pedagogy to design curricula, instruction, and assessment.
IV. Fairness, equity, and diversity
   Accomplished AYA/ELA teachers demonstrate their commitment to fairness, equity, and diversity.
V. Learning environment
   Accomplished AYA/ELA teachers establish and manage inclusive learning environments in which they engage, challenge, and support students.
VI. Instructional resources
   Accomplished AYA/ELA teachers create, select, adapt, and use a wide range of instructional resources to support their students' learning and strengthen their own teaching.

Advancing Student Learning in the Classroom

VII. Integrated instruction
Accomplished AYA/ELA teachers integrate reading, writing, listening, speaking, and viewing and producing media texts in their instruction and incorporate content from other disciplines.
VIII. Reading
Accomplished AYA/ELA teachers develop students' reading skills and their abilities to comprehend, interpret, and analyze a wide variety of texts for personal, literary, informational, and critical purposes.
IX. Writing
Accomplished AYA/ELA teachers develop and refine students' abilities to write effectively and independently different types of texts for a variety of purposes and audiences.
X. Speaking and listening
Accomplished AYA/ELA teachers advance students' abilities to speak and listen for a variety of purposes and audiences.
XI. Viewing and producing media texts
Accomplished AYA/ELA teachers enable students to critically read, evaluate, and produce messages in a variety of media.
XII. Language study
Accomplished AYA/ELA teachers develop students' abilities to use language effectively and to appreciate the different ways readers, writers, and speakers use language.
XIII. Assessment
Accomplished AYA/ELA teachers use a range of formal and informal assessment methods to plan for instruction, to monitor and evaluate student progress, to involve students in the assessment process, and to report student achievement to various audiences.

Supporting Student Learning through Long-Range Initiatives

XIV. Self-reflection
Accomplished AYA/ELA teachers continually observe, analyze, and seek to improve the quality and effectiveness of their teaching, and articulate reasons for instructional decisions.
XV. Professional community
Accomplished AYA/ELA teachers participate collaboratively in the educational community to improve instruction, advance the knowledge and practice of the field, and enhance their professional identities.
XVI. Family and community involvement
Accomplished AYA/ELA teachers work with families, caregivers, and community members to best serve the needs of students.

Clinical supervision develops teachers' ability to prepare this and other related portfolio entries for National Board certification. The conferencing techniques in Unit 3 focus on the process of analyzing and reflecting on teaching/learning processes in the teacher's classroom. Chapter 12 describes how video recordings and portfolios can be used to collect data about classroom instruction and other aspects of teachers' professional work.

National Board Assessment-Center Exercises

In addition to portfolios, candidates for a National Board certificate are required to complete a full day of assessment exercises that focus on pedagogical content knowledge. The exercises present simulations of situations to which teachers must respond or questions about pedagogical content topics and issues. For example, the following is an example of an assessment exercise for the National Board certificate for mathematics at the adolescence and young adulthood level:

> In this exercise, you will use your knowledge of algebra to explain the relationships between two important algebraic concepts. You will also create an algebraic model for a given problem and find its solution, graph the related equation(s) or inequality(ies), and interpret the graph as it relates to the solution of the problem. You will be asked to respond to two prompts. [Example of a prompt: Provide a detailed and thorough description of the relationships that exist between the degree of a polynomial equation and the number of roots of the equation.[14]

Clinical supervision does not purport to develop this type of specialized pedagogical content knowledge. However, clinical supervisors need to have a broad understanding of effective content-specific and general teaching strategies. An overview of these strategies is presented in Chapter 3.

Benefits of National Board Certification

The number of teachers holding a National Board certificate was approximately 74,000 in 2009.[15] Dolores Bohen conducted a research study of 13 National-Board-certified teachers to determine the benefits they received from the certification process.[16] The benefits she found include greater professional confidence; improved ability to analyze instruction; a stronger focus on student learning outcomes; and a greater commitment to professional growth. These benefits of National Board certification have been found in other research studies as well.[17]

For many policymakers, parents, and members of the general public, the most pressing question is whether National Board certification means that a teacher can help students make greater gains in academic achievement, as measured by standardized tests. Researchers have done studies to address this question, but their findings are inconsistent.[18] The studies employed different research methodologies and involved different grade levels and achievement tests. These differences might account for the fact that some studies found differences favoring NBCT-certified teachers, and others did not. Our view is that the instructional skills and knowledge specified in the NBPTS standards are essential elements of effective teaching, but they might not be sufficient by themselves to improve the kinds of learning measured by standardized achievement tests.

TEACHER DEVELOPMENT BASED ON STUDENTS' ACADEMIC ACHIEVEMENT

Students vary widely in their academic achievement. Some earn good grades, but many others do not. Some do well on standardized tests, and others do not. Many students complete high school, but a substantial number drop out before receiving a diploma.

These differences in academic achievement traditionally have been attributed to differences in students' IQ, motivation, ethnicity, and home environment. Increasingly, though, students' success or failure in school is attributed to their teachers' performance in the classroom. Many believe that teachers should be able to transform all their students into high achievers, not just those who have high measured IQs or who come from high-income families.

This belief underlies the No Child Left Behind (NCLB) Act of 2001, which is undoubtedly the most important, though controversial, new education policy in recent decades.[19] One key provision of this act is the requirement that schools make "adequate yearly progress," which means that student performance must improve each school year until all, or nearly all, students are considered proficient in a given school year. States must assess adequate yearly progress, using standardized tests, in each grade from kindergarten through 12th grade in reading/language arts and mathematics.

Additionally, elementary and middle schools must demonstrate adequate yearly progress in attendance rates, and high schools must demonstrate adequate yearly progress in graduation rates. Schools that do not demonstrate adequately yearly progress over a period of six years face severe consequences, such as having the school staff replaced or being reconstituted as a public or private charter school.

The NCLB Act is in the political arena and therefore is subject to revision, depending on those who lobby for and against it with legislators. For example, teacher unions have come out against some of its provisions. One of them is a recent initiative to require sophisticated data systems that would link student test results not only to individual schools, but also to individual teachers, who would be evaluated by the test results. Most likely, some groups will be reluctant to put more resources (inputs) into schools without a corresponding press on educators to use those resources to improve student learning outcomes (outputs). For example, the current national education secretary, Arne Duncan, has four billion dollars in a Race to the Top Fund. These monies will be distributed to states only if they agree to certain conditions, such as a requirement to evaluate teachers' performance on various criteria, including how well their students learn, as measured by standardized tests.

If different school districts have different curriculum standards, it is difficult to develop standardized achievement tests that reflect all of them fairly. Therefore, we are witnessing a national movement to create a common core of curriculum standards among states to simplify the development of standardized achievement tests and to facilitate comparisons of students' academic achievement within and across states. Two organizations, the Council of Chief State School Officers and the National Governors Association's Center for Best Practices, are leading this effort.

We see, then, that teachers are being asked to make two major changes in how they work with their students. One is to hold themselves accountable for their students' learning and to make adequate yearly progress in bringing all, or nearly all, of them to a high level of academic achievement. The other is to give up their traditional freedom, within limits, to develop curriculum specifically for their students, and instead adopt highly prescribed curriculum guides that are developed by agencies far removed from their classrooms.

These two changes point to a need for a model of teacher development that describes how teachers can move from their traditional practices to new practices that enable their students to make strong achievement gains on tests that measure a prescribed curriculum. In the next section, we identify several factors that need to be considered in this type of model. We also describe a relatively new approach to teacher supervision that focuses on student achievement gains.

Supervisory Techniques That Focus on Student Achievement

The models of teacher development described earlier in the chapter help us understand what might happen if teachers are required to teach a prescribed curriculum and ensure that all their students master it. Leithwood's model of teachers' development of professional expertise suggests that teachers will not be able to make these changes overnight. If they are struggling with the initial stages of expertise (developing survival skills and basic instructional skills), they will need time to master those stages. Only then can they move to the stage of expanding their instructional flexibility to individualize their instruction to accommodate the learning needs of all their students.

Fuller's model of teacher concerns points to other factors that will need to be considered. The second stage in her model has to do with concerns about professional adequacy. Indeed, many teachers are likely to question their professional adequacy when faced with accountability demands. These concerns will need to be addressed before teachers can move to the third stage of Fuller's model, which is concern about their students.

Brenda Schulz did a case study to determine the concerns of National-Board-certified elementary teachers about the impact of NCLB's accountability demands and high-stakes testing.[20] The teachers expressed concerns both about themselves and about their students. Among their self concerns was a feeling that their professionalism was being called into question by the public and a fear that they might be accused of cheating or engaging in unethical behavior while preparing students for and administering high-stakes tests. Among their student concerns were that many of their students experienced stress while preparing for and taking high-stakes tests, and that a single test did not always assess accurately whether students had mastered the skills presumably measured by the tests.[21]

The demands of NCLB, the Race to the Top Fund, and related policy initiatives will require teachers to learn new skills, some of which can be taught through workshops and courses. However, teachers also will need the type of individual clinical supervision that we describe in this book. For example, their individual concerns can be addressed in conferencing sessions. In addition, teachers and supervisors can focus on the collection of classroom tests and test results as part of the clinical supervision cycle (see Chapter 13.) Furthermore, teachers and supervisors will need to conference about these data to determine whether the teachers are following required curriculum standards and reaching all students in their classroom, not just those who are able and willing learners.

If schools are to demonstrate adequate yearly progress in student achievement, educators will need to learn how to think about school-level and classroom-level processes. NCLB requires educators to consider how all the students in a school perform on achievement tests across school years. However, students are not educated schoolwide, but rather in individual classrooms taught by individual teachers. Therefore, a school's overall results on achievement tests are dependent on each teacher's contribution to students' learning. This means that teachers who are ineffective can cancel out the contributions of effective teachers. Furthermore, an otherwise effective teacher might be impeded by a group of students who enter her classroom after a year of instruction with an ineffective teacher.

We see, then, that administrators and teachers are dependent on each teacher to contribute to the collective achievement of the school's students. An example of this interdependency is provided by the San Marcos Unified School District, which has made remarkable gains on state-mandated achievement tests at nearly every grade level and every subject for all ethnic groups.[22] The assistant superintendent for instructional services attributes these gains to the use of four strategies:

1. Teachers collectively have studied the district's curriculum standards for each grade and subject, and they have studied samples of state test questions to be sure that they are covering test-relevant curriculum content in their classrooms.

2. Teachers have agreed on "essential elements of instruction," such as approaches for motivating students and helping them remember new content. Although not stated by the assistant superintendent, this agreement on essential instructional methods likely makes classroom teaching more predictable and manageable for a school's students as they transition from one teacher and one grade level to the next.

3. Teachers administer tests frequently and analyze the results to identify which students need help and where.

4. Teachers have opportunities to share ideas with each other about effective teaching strategies.

It seems to us that this new type of learning environment, created in response to new accountability demands on teachers, calls for adaptations in the clinical supervision model that we describe in this book. Clinical supervisors will need to work with teachers both individually and collectively to make sure that the four strategies described above (plus others found to be effective elsewhere) are implemented effectively.

Performance-Based Supervision and Evaluation

James Aseltine, Judith Faryniarz, and Anthony Rigazio-DiGilio developed an approach to teacher supervision that incorporates some of the ideas described in the previous section.[23] They created their supervisory model, called *Performance-Based Supervision and Evaluation*, in response to the No Child Left Behind Act and the accountability and standards-based curriculum movements. The first step of the model is for a supervisor to help the teacher identify an area of student learning that needs to be improved. Various areas of student learning can be considered, but the one that is chosen as the target for each teacher's development must pass four tests:

- *Test #1: Essential Teaching and Learning.* Does the target represent an area of essential teaching and learning for the teacher's grade level and content area?

- *Test #2: Schoolwide and District Data.* Does an analysis of school or district performance data suggest that the target is an area needing improvement?

- *Test #3: Classroom Assessments.* Does an analysis of classroom assessment data confirm the target as an area needing improvement?

- *Test #4: The School and District Improvement Plan.* Does the target correspond to an area of emphasis in the district or school's improvement plan?[24]

The identification of a target area of student learning for improvement is the first phase in Aseltine's growth model. This phase is called *Teacher Preparation*. There are five more phases:

- Initial collaboration. The teacher and supervisor finalize the target for student academic improvement and develop a plan for the teacher to follow in improving students' performance on the target.

- Initial monitoring. The teacher learns about strategies for improving students' performance on the target, implements those strategies, and continually assesses students' learning.

- Mid-cycle review. After an appropriate period of time, the teacher and supervisor review students' achievement gains relating to the target, and modify strategies if necessary.
- Secondary monitoring. The teacher continues to implement strategies for improving students' performance on the target, while also continually assessing students' learning.
- Summative review. The teacher and supervisor review evidence about the teacher's strategies and student learning outcomes, reflect on them, and set new goals for the next supervisory cycle.

The six phases of Performance-Based Supervision and Evaluation overlap in key respects with the three phases of our clinical supervision model (preconference, observation, and postconference). In both models, supervision is initiated by a collaborative effort to identify a teacher's concerns and goals for improvement, and the cycle ends with a conference to review data, reflect on them, and set new goals for professional growth.

Performance-based Supervision and Evaluation strongly emphasizes student academic achievement as the primary focus for the teacher's professional growth. Clinical supervision, as we describe it here and as it has been traditionally practiced, places more emphasis on teachers' instructional behavior. However, we believe that clinical supervision will become more focused on student academic achievement as the movement toward teacher accountability and standards-based curriculum becomes stronger.

Educators do not yet have sufficient experience to make a good prediction about how the call for teacher accountability for student achievement will affect preservice teachers. It seems likely, though, that school administrators will be reluctant to allow student teachers to take on full responsibility for a classroom if their relative lack of instructional expertise might adversely affect the school's adequate yearly progress in academic achievement. A solution to this dilemma might be to transition student teachers to full responsibility for a classroom over a longer period of time than traditional practice and with more intensive clinical supervision, not only by a university supervisor, but also by master teachers at the school.

WORKING CONDITIONS AND TEACHER DEVELOPMENT

Ken Leithwood, who created a model of teacher development described earlier in this chapter, and his colleague Pat McAdie did a review of the literature on teachers' working conditions.[25] They wanted to know what types of work conditions affected teachers' feelings and professional knowledge, which they call "internal states." They identified eight such internal states: (1) individual sense of professional efficacy; (2) collective sense of professional efficacy; (3) organizational commitment; (4) job satisfaction; (5) stress and burnout; (6) morale; (7) engagement or disengagement from their school and profession; and (8) pedagogical content knowledge. Clinical supervisors and administrators need to be sensitive to these internal states of mind, because they affect teachers' classroom performance and responsiveness to professional development.

Leithwood and McAdie then did a literature review to identify workplace conditions that affect teachers' internal states. The workplace conditions are listed in Table 2.5. Clinical supervisors need to be aware of these conditions; this will help them assess their teachers'

Table 2.5 Working Conditions That Have a Positive Impact on Teachers' Sense of Efficacy, Organizational Commitment, Job Satisfaction, Stress, Morale, Engagement, and Professional Knowledge

Classroom-level Working Conditions

- Workload volume is perceived to be fair.
- Class sizes are reasonable.
- Out-of-classroom duties are not excessive.
- Teachers are only asked to teach subjects and grade levels for which they feel adequately prepared.
- Students are cooperative and able to learn.
- Teachers have autonomy in their classrooms.
- Instructional resources are adequate.

School-level Working Conditions

- Teachers are given goals that are clear, explicit, inspiring, and shared.
- The school atmosphere is friendly.
- Student discipline and teacher and student safety are not problematic.
- Teacher collaboration is valued.
- The school values and supports academic achievement.
- Teachers can access professional development opportunities.
- Teachers receive regular, helpful feedback if they participate in school improvement projects.
- Teachers can participate in school-level decisions, and the school's plans for improvement coincide with their priorities for improvement.
- The quality of communication throughout the school is good.
- The physical facilities enable teacher to provide good instruction.
- The school's curriculum and programs are stable and well-developed.
- Parents and the local community support and approve of the school.
- The school principal inspires teachers and advocates for continuous school improvement, but has reasonable expectations for what teachers can accomplish.
- The school principal looks out for teachers' welfare, acknowledges their good work, and exhibits personal behavior that is consistent with her expectations for teachers.
- The school principal is flexible in enforcing rules.
- The school principal follows through on decisions.
- The school principal is able to work with district administrators for the benefit of the school.

District Working Conditions

- The district provides teachers with access to meaningful professional development.
- The district's salary structure is fair and consistent with comparable districts.
- The district does not call for changes that lack teacher input, that are inconsistent with teachers' priorities, or that have unreasonable timelines.

Source: Leithwood, K., & McAdie, P. (2007). Teacher working conditions that matter. *Education Canada, 47*(2), 42-45.

willingness and ability to improve their instruction. Such conditions affect even student teachers, who only have a temporary association with a school. The working conditions of the school are likely to affect their individual sense of professional adequacy, stress, engagement with the school, and ability to obtain new pedagogical knowledge from their cooperating teacher and other teachers in the school.

One might argue that student teachers should only be placed in schools that have good working conditions, so that they, in collaboration with their clinical supervisor and cooperating teacher, can maximize their professional development. However, this might be considered unfair to struggling schools that can benefit from having energetic, idealistic student teachers. Whatever the situation, we believe that the clinical supervisor and faculty in the teacher education program should assess the working conditions of the schools in which student teachers will be placed. If the student teacher and clinical supervisor have realistic expectations about the school's working conditions, they have a better chance of maximizing the student teacher's professional development in that setting.

ENDNOTES

1. Comment by a mentor teacher cited in: Baron, W. (2006). Confronting the challenging working conditions of new teachers: What mentors and induction programs can do. In B. Achinstein & S. Z. Athanases (Eds.), *Mentors in the making: Developing new leaders for new teachers* (pp. 125–135). New York: Teachers College Press.

2. Freidson, E. (1986). *Professional powers: A study of the institutionalization of formal knowledge*. Chicago: University of Chicago Press.

3. Hoyle, E. (1995). In L. W. Anderson (Ed.), *International encyclopedia of teaching and teacher education* (2nd ed., pp. 11–15). Oxford, England: Pergamon. (Quote appears on p. 12). Copyright © Elsevier.

4. Leithwood, K. A. (1992). The principal's role in teacher development. In M. Fullan & A. Hargreaves (Eds.), *Teacher development and educational change* (pp. 86–103). London: Falmer.

5. Berliner, D. C. (2004). Describing the behavior and documenting the accomplishments of expert teachers. *Bulletin of Science Technology Society, 2004, 24*(3), 200–212.

6. Turner, D. S. (1995). *Identifying exemplary secondary school teachers: The influence of career cycles and school environments on the defined roles of teachers perceived as exemplary*. Unpublished doctoral dissertation, Macquarie University, Sydney, Australia.

7. Lopez, O. S. (1995). The effect of the relationship between classroom student diversity and teacher capacity on student performance. *Dissertation Abstracts International: Section A. Humanities and Social Sciences*, 56(06), 2064.

8. Gladwell, M. (2008). *Outliers*. Boston: Allyn & Bacon.

9. Fuller, F. F. (1969). Concerns of teachers: A developmental conceptualization. *American Educational Research Journal, 6*, 207–226.

10. The nonlinear progression of teacher concerns has been demonstrated in several studies, including: Watzke, J. L. (2007). Longitudinal research on beginning teacher development: Complexity as a challenge to concerns-based stage theory. *Teaching and Teacher Education, 23*(1), 106–122.

11. Because the work of these organizations is ongoing, we recommend that you contact their websites in order to get the most up-to-date information about their efforts to develop standards for teaching and teacher education.

12. The National Board's home page is http://www.nbpts .org/ From this home page, you can access many types of information about the National Board's philosophy and operations.

13. http://www.nbpts.org/userfiles/File/EA_SSH_Portfolio_ Instructions.pdf (Quote appears on p. 2-1.) Copyright © 2010 National Board for Professional Teaching Standards. Reprinted with permission. All rights reserved.

14. http://www.nbpts.org/userfiles/File/AYA_Math_ AssessAtaGlance.pdf Copyright © 2009 National Board for Professional Teaching Standards. Reprinted with permission. All rights reserved.

15. The most recent number of NBTS-certified teachers can be found at: http://www.nbpts.org

16. Bohen, D. B. (2001). Strengthening teaching through national certification. *Educational Leadership, 58*(8), 50–53.

17. Some of these studies are reviewed in Vandevoort, L. G., Amrein-Beardsley, A., & Berliner, D. C. (2004, September 8). National board certified teachers and their students' achievement. *Education Policy Analysis Archives, 12*(46). Retrieved from http://epaa.asu.edu/epaa/v12n46/

18. Cavalluzzo, L. C. (2004). Is National Board certification an effective signal of teacher quality? Retrieved from http://www.cna.org/documents/CavaluzzoStudy.pdf;

Goldhaber, D., & Anthony, E. (2005). *Can teacher quality be effectively assessed? National Board certification as a signal of effective teaching.* Washington, DC: Urban Institute. Retrieved from ERIC database. (ED490921); Cantrell, S., Fullerton, J., Kane, T. J., & Staiger, D. O. (2008). *National board certification and teacher effectiveness: Evidence from a random assignment experiment* (NBER Working Paper 14608). Cambridge, MA: National Bureau of Economic Research.; Rouse, W. A., Jr. (2008). National Board certified teachers are making a difference in student achievement: Myth or fact? *Leadership and Policy in Schools, 7*(1), 64–86.

19. For a recent critique of NCLB, see: Rebell, M. A., & Wolff, J. R. (2009). *NCLB at the crossroads.* NY: Teachers College Press.

20. Schulz, B. C. (2008). Teacher perspectives on how high-stakes testing influences instructional decisions and professionalism. In S. J. Zepeda & J. Glanz (Eds.), *Real-world supervision: Adapting theory to practice* (pp. 143–163). Norwood, MA: Christopher-Gordon.

21. These teacher concerns are also documented in: Nichols. S. L., & Berliner, D. C. (2007). *How high-stakes testing corrupts America's schools.* Cambridge, MA: Harvard Education Press.

22. Lieberman, B. (2009, September 13). Program boosting district's scores. *San Diego Union Tribune.* Retrieved from http://signonsandiego.com

23. Aseltine, J. M., Faryniarz, J. O., & Rigarzio-DiGilio, A. J. (2006). *Supervision for learning.* Alexandria, VA: Association for Supervision and Curriculum Development.

24. *Ibid.*, pp. 23–24.

25. Leithwood, K., & McAdie, P. (2007). Teacher working conditions that matter. *Education Canada, 47*(2), 42–45.

Chapter 3

Using Clinical Supervision to Support Other Methods of Professional Development

Today, people believe that professional development should be targeted and directly related to teachers' practice. It should be site-based and long-term. It should be ongoing—part of a teacher's workweek, not something that's tacked on. And it should be curriculum-based, to the extent possible, so that it helps teachers help their students master the curriculum at a higher level.

—James Stigler[1]

INTRODUCTION

Clinical supervision as we know it has been available to teachers since the 1960s—perhaps earlier. Other methods of teacher development have become popular more recently. In this chapter we examine 10 of these methods for two purposes. First, by examining other methods of teacher development, we bring into sharper focus the distinguishing characteristics of clinical supervision. Second, an analysis of other methods reveals how the techniques of clinical supervision can enhance their effectiveness.

Each of the methods that we describe has variations that depend on the educators who are using or writing about them. We based our descriptions on the writings of those who originally developed the methods or writings that have been widely disseminated. We group them into three categories: (1) methods in which an expert guides an individual teacher's learning; (2) methods in which pairs of teachers help each other improve their instruction; and (3) methods that focus on schoolwide improvement in addition to individual teacher development.

METHODS INVOLVING EXPERT GUIDANCE

We describe four methods of professional development in this section of the chapter: mentoring, microteaching, cognitive coaching, and action research. They are all similar in that they require a supervisor who can provide expert guidance to teachers.

Mentoring

Many professions make formal or informal use of mentoring, a method in which an experienced professional, the mentor, helps a novice professional make a successful entry into the workplace. In the teaching profession, a survey conducted in 2008 found that 22 states had a state-funded mentoring program for all new teachers, and 20 of these states had standards for selecting, training, and matching mentors with new teachers.[2] Various resources are available to help schools establish mentoring programs and determine the skills that mentors will need in working with novice teachers.[3]

Mentoring can be done either as a stand-alone activity within a school system or as part of a comprehensive induction program designed to ensure novices' effectiveness in the classroom and their retention as employees. In order for mentoring to work, mentors need to be given adequate time, resources, and training. It is also beneficial if the mentor teaches in the same certification area as the novice and is located near the novice, so that the two of them can communicate easily. If these conditions are met, the mentor can serve a variety of functions:

- helping the novice learn the norms and procedures of the school, school district, and state office of education
- socializing the novice into the norms of professional teaching and its various paths for career development
- providing emotional support
- helping the novice with curriculum, instruction, and assessment
- serving as an advocate to help the novice obtain necessary resources and desirable working conditions

This list does not include evaluation of the novice's performance. Mentors generally are experienced teachers, and they doubtless feel more comfortable serving a professional-development role than an evaluation role. A notable exception is the Program Assistance and Review (PAR) program, originally developed in Toledo, Ohio, and used in about 40 school districts nationwide.[4] Full-time mentors engage in both professional development and teacher evaluation.

Mentoring is specifically intended for new teachers. In contrast, clinical supervision can be used along the entire continuum of a teacher's career, from being a student in a preservice program to the last years of a long teaching career. Another difference is that mentors typically rely on their own teaching experience and interpersonal skills to help teachers, whereas clinical supervisors draw on specialized skills in conferencing, classroom observation, and research-based knowledge about effective teaching to help their supervisees.

We believe that mentors can increase their usefulness to novice teachers if they supplement their experience and interpersonal skills with the skills specifically associated with the clinical supervision cycle. In fact, researchers have found that new teachers valued being observed and having postobservation discussions about their teaching.[5] If school systems would include clinical supervision in their training program for mentors, it would significantly enhance the mentor's repertoire of skills for helping novice teachers succeed.

Microteaching

Microteaching was developed at Stanford University's School of Education in the 1960s.[6] It was subsequently incorporated into teacher training programs called *Minicourses*.[7] Microteaching spread rapidly around the world in the 1960s and 1970s and continues to be used in the present day in various contexts. For example, microteaching is used to develop the teaching skills of Harvard University instructors at the Derek Bok Center for Teaching and Learning.[8]

The primary features of microteaching are these:

1. The teacher is presented with a behaviorally defined teaching skill (e.g., asking higher-order questions), which he is to practice.

2. The teacher practices the skill in a short lesson (about five to 10 minutes) with four to six students; hence the label *microteaching*, which refers to "a scaled-down teaching encounter in class size and class time."[9]

3. The lesson is recorded on videotape, and subsequently the teacher views the videotape to analyze his or her use of the skill.

4. For additional practice and videotape feedback, the teacher practices the same skill again by presenting a brief videotaped lesson to another small group of pupils.[10]

In Minicourses, a group of related teaching skills are presented together in a training package. The teaching skills for one of the Minicourses, involving general questioning techniques for elementary-school teachers, is shown in Table 3.1. Teachers were asked to

Table 3.1 Questioning Techniques Taught in a Microteaching-Based Minicourse

INSTRUCTIONAL SEQUENCE 1	
Objective	To change teacher behavior (teaching techniques and practices) in order to increase pupil readiness is respond to discussion questions.
Skills Covered	Asking question, pausing three to five seconds, then calling on pupil. Dealing with incorrect answers in an accepting, nonpunitive manner. Calling on both volunteers and nonvolunteers in order to keep all pupils alert and to distribute participation.
INSTRUCTIONAL SEQUENCE 2	
Objective	To improve teacher skills so as to decrease the amount of teacher participation and increase the amount of pupil participation.
Skills Covered	Redirecting the same question to several pupils. Framing questions that call for longer pupil responses.

1. Asking for sets or groups of related facts when formulating information-level questions.
2. Avoiding Yes or No replies.

Framing questions that require the pupil to use higher cognitive processes.

INSTRUCTIONAL SEQUENCE 3

Objective	To increase teacher use of probing techniques in order to guide the pupil to more complete and thoughtful responses.
Skills Covered	Prompting. Seeking further clarification and pupil insight. Refocusing the pupil's response.

INSTRUCTIONAL SEQUENCE 4

Objective	To reduce teacher behavior that interferes with the flow of the discussion.
Skills Covered	Observing the follwing rules:

1. Teacher should not repeat his own questions.
2. Teacher should not answer his own questions.
3. Teacher should not repeat pupil answers.

Source: Borg, W. R., Kelley, M. L., Langer, P., & Gall, M. (1970). *The Minicourse: A microteaching approach to teacher education.* Beverly Hills, CA: Macmillan Educational Services. (Table 3 on p. 74.)

view videos that demonstrated each of the do's and don'ts of questioning and also to study a brief manual about them. They then practiced the skills, several at a time, in a brief videotaped lesson with five or six of their own students. Next, they viewed a video and used a checklist to evaluate their use of each of the teaching skills. This Minicourse and others were found to increase the frequency of effective teaching techniques and decrease the frequency of ineffective teaching techniques.

One of the developers of the Minicourse version of microteaching also is an author of this book (M. Gall). You can see the influence of microteaching's emphasis on behaviorally defined skills in the chapters on conferencing in Unit 3. Each of these chapters presents a set of behaviorally defined conferencing skills. Also, many of the observation techniques presented in the chapters of Unit 4 focus the observer's attention on behaviorally defined teaching skills.

Microteaching differs most from clinical supervision in the teaching behaviors that are the focus of the teacher's professional development. In microteaching, an expert instructor specifies the teaching behaviors that the teacher is to practice. In clinical supervision, however, teachers can specify teaching behaviors that they want the supervisor to observe, or a teacher and supervisor can make this decision collaboratively. Another difference is that microteaching relies on videotaping as a method of data collection, whereas clinical supervision draws on a wide range of data-collection methods, one of which happens to be videotaping. Third, microteaching involves deliberate training of skills through systematic modeling, practice, and feedback. In clinical supervision, teachers also can practice specific skills, but they do so in a more informal manner. For example, a teacher and supervisor might have a planning conference during which the teacher decides to focus on improving her classroom management. The teacher might read various writings about classroom management and decide which techniques might be effective for her. She then might incorporate these techniques into her classroom instruction for a period of weeks before asking the supervisor to collect data in her classroom. The teacher is learning, but not in a prescribed training format.

Microteaching and clinical supervision are compatible. Particularly in preservice programs, teacher educators might use both methods. Microteaching lends itself well to a university setting; there, preservice teachers can practice skills that they are studying in their courses by teaching brief lessons, with their fellow students serving in the role of students. Clinical supervision is the more appropriate method for preservice teachers who are engaged in field experience with actual classes of students.

Cognitive Coaching

Art Costa and Robert Garmston created the method of cognitive coaching to help teachers think deeply about their instructional practices.[11] They assumed that if teachers reflected on their teaching with a cognitive coach, their thinking about instruction would change, and these cognitive changes would lead to changes in their instructional behavior. This emphasis on reflection distinguishes cognitive coaching from methods like microteaching and peer coaching, which emphasize behavioral training techniques to help teachers master instructional skills.

Cognitive coaching involves a teacher and coach holding a planning conference, followed by the coach's observation of the teacher's classroom instruction, and concluding with a reflecting conference in which the coach guides the teacher in thinking about the observational data. A cognitive coach is careful not to tell the teacher how to improve her instruction, but instead asks probing questions, paraphrases what the teacher tells him, and uses silence to give the teacher time to think. These conversational techniques are intended to promote teacher self-directedness, which Costa and Garmston analyzed into three abilities: self-management, which is the ability to gather information and consider options rather than leaping immediately into action; self-monitoring, which is the ability to compare intentions with what actually is occurring; and self-modifying, which is the ability to learn from experience and put this learning into use in future experiences.

The coach's own thinking is important to this process. Therefore, cognitive coaching includes "conversation maps" that the coach can draw on while conferencing with a teacher. For example, a cognitive coach learns a Reflecting Conversation Map to use during the reflecting conference. Among other things, the map directs the coach to focus the teacher on causal patterns in the observational data instead of simply restating the data or recounting events of a lesson at a literal level. In focusing on causal patterns, the coach helps the teacher identify factors that contributed to successes and failures in the lesson. The teacher's reflections on these factors help her develop insights that lead to improvements in future lessons.

Cognitive coaching shares some similarities in process and intent with the model of clinical supervision presented in this book. The main difference is in how the two methods conceptualize the knowledge base for teaching. In cognitive coaching, the emphasis appears to be exclusively on teachers' innate capacity to develop as professionals by reflecting on their classroom experiences. In other words, teachers are expected to construct their own knowledge base. We, too, believe in this innate capacity; but we also believe that the knowledge base about teaching developed by researchers (see Chapter 4) can help teachers become more effective, if they and their supervisors access it as part of the clinical supervision process.

Action Research

Action research is a form of inquiry in which teachers or other educators collect and analyze data in order to improve their professional practice.[12] In contrast, formal research studies involve trained researchers who collect data and report findings that educators might be able to translate into practice. The claimed advantage of action research over formal research is that teachers can see the relevance of their own findings more easily and can directly apply them to improve their instruction. Teachers can do action research projects on their own or in collaboration with colleagues.

Action research projects typically involve the following steps:

1. Selecting a focus for study. Teachers might consider several problems of practice, but they will choose to study one at a time. For example, a group of three teachers decided on an action research project to reduce bullying at their school.[13]

2. Collecting data. Teachers collect data in order to understand the problem and solve it. In the bullying study, the teachers administered questionnaires to students and parents to learn about the incidence of bullying in their school. They found that the incidence was surprisingly high: half the students had been bullied at least once.

3. Taking action. The teachers in our example experimented with various interventions to reduce the incidence of bullying. For example, they asked students to create and post antibullying posters in bullying hot spots in the school.

4. Analyzing and reflecting on data. The teachers reflected on the questionnaire data and decided that the incidence of bullying was sufficiently high that lowering it should be a priority. They also collected data involving direct observation of bullying in their school before and after the interventions. They found that most types of bullying, particularly name-calling, decreased substantially in frequency.

5. Continuing or modifying practices. After reflecting on their data, teachers might decide to change their teaching practices or continue with their current practices because their new ideas did not work out as intended. In the bullying study, one teacher reached this conclusion: "[N]ow that I know the impact this intervention program has had on students, I will implement it every semester for the rest of my teaching career."[14]

6. Reporting the results. Teachers can provide support for colleagues by sharing the findings of their action research project with them. In the case of the collaborative action research project on bullying, the teachers submitted their findings to ERIC (Education Resources Information Center), an online database of bibliographic citations for educational publications and also a repository for some of these publications. The report of the bullying study can be accessed directly through ERIC.[15]

Teachers need formal training by an expert to learn how to do action research. This training often is provided in a university course. Many teachers do an action research project to fulfill a requirement for a degree or licensure program.

Unlike clinical supervision, a teacher can conduct an action research project without a supervisor, although he is likely to enlist an expert in action research as a consultant. Also, he might enlist a colleague for a project, but typically the colleague is a collaborative co-investigator who is seeking to improve his own professional practices.

Action research projects tend to be more structured and time-consuming than clinical supervision cycles, but they are similar in their emphasis on empirical data to guide the improvement of classroom teaching or schoolwide programs. The observation techniques described in Unit 4 would be useful for many action research projects.

Teachers can benefit greatly from reading the reports of action research projects conducted by other teachers in circumstances similar to theirs; they might learn about problems of practice that can be a focus for their own instructional improvement. Also, they might learn about an intervention that they wish to try with the support of their clinical supervisor. The supervisor can collect relevant observational data and reflect on them with the teacher to determine how well the intervention works in the teacher's own classroom setting.

METHODS INVOLVING TEACHER DYADS

We describe two methods of professional development in this section of the chapter—peer consultation and peer coaching. They are similar in that their process for professional development involves pairs of teachers who take turns helping each other develop their instructional skills.

Peer Consultation

One of the authors (K. Acheson) worked with colleagues in British Columbia to develop a method known as peer consultation.[16] They used peer consultation as the primary method in a professional development program known as the *Program for Quality Teaching*.

The features of peer consultation, as implemented in the *Program for Quality Teaching*, are these:

1. A group of teachers completes clinical supervision cycles—planning conference, observation, feedback conference—with each other.

2. Two-teacher teams are formed. One is the clinical supervisor, and the other is the supervisee. After several clinical supervision cycles, the roles are reversed: the clinical supervisor becomes the observed teacher, and the observed teacher becomes the clinical supervisor.

3. The teams are egalitarian. One teacher does not have more power or authority over peer consultation than the other.

4. The participants in peer consultation strive to improve their individual teaching while also helping their colleagues become better teachers. In other words, peer consultation has both individual and group goals.

5. Data about a teacher's performance that are collected during a clinical supervision cycle cannot be used for teacher evaluation.

6. Participation in peer consultation is voluntary.

7. The school principal needs to arrange for a substitute teacher for the team member who will observe the other member's classroom instruction.

8. Peer consultation typically occurs on a monthly basis, meaning that each participating teacher has a monthly opportunity to be observed in his classroom and also to serve as a clinical supervisor for another teacher.

A research study on the effectiveness of peer consultation found that teachers appreciated the breakdown in barriers that isolated them from their peers, feedback on their classroom performance, and the opportunity to learn by observing their peers.[17] Participants also developed an increased sense of respect for their colleagues as professionals.

Peer consultation is much like traditional clinical supervision, except for its reliance on voluntary participation. In preservice teacher education, for example, clinical supervision is mandated. In inservice settings, marginal teachers who are on a plan of assistance also cannot opt out of clinical supervision if that is part of their plan.

Peer Coaching

Bruce Joyce and Beverly Showers developed a method that they called *peer coaching* to overcome two problems that they perceived in other methods of professional development for teachers.[18] One problem is that the traditional approach to professional development is for teachers to attend workshops, some lasting just a few hours, about a particular teaching method and then presumably incorporate it into their classroom instruction. Research and informal observation indicate that this method does not work well, especially for complex teaching strategies that are substantially different from normative classroom instruction.

Another problem is that some professional development programs train teachers to use a teaching strategy, but the training is done in an artificial setting. For example, teachers might practice new skills by taking turns with each other in the teacher and student roles. Joyce and Showers do not believe that this training is sufficient for teachers to transfer their skills to their own classroom, where contextual factors might be very different from anything presented during training.

Joyce and Showers developed peer coaching to solve these two problems. (A more recent innovation known as *instructional coaching* is similar to peer coaching, but with less emphasis on systematic training.[19]) The first step in peer coaching is for the stakeholders—teachers, administrators, curriculum experts—to select the teaching strategy that is to be taught. Peer coaching is particularly appropriate for complex teaching strategies like those presented in the book *Models of Teaching*, coauthored by Joyce.[20] Once the teaching strategy is selected, a systematic training process occurs, involving these steps:

1. Teachers study the theoretical basis or rationale for the teaching method. This period of study might require as long as 20 to 30 hours.

2. Teachers observe demonstrations of the model by experts. Joyce and Showers recommend 15 to 20 demonstrations in several content areas and with various types of learners.

3. Teachers practice the teaching strategy under easy conditions. For example, they might teach brief lessons to their peers (as in microteaching) and to students who are relatively easy to teach. In the original peer coaching model, Joyce and Showers recommended that teachers give each other feedback on how well they implemented the model.[21] Over time, they found that this type of feedback tended to erode the spirit of collaboration necessary for peer coaching to succeed. Peer coaches tend to make evaluative comments, and teacher-learners tend to see the process as more like teacher evaluation than professional development. Therefore, Joyce and Showers revised peer coaching to include practice, but not verbal feedback.[22]

4. Teachers work in pairs or teams of four to six members to take turns coaching each other. The coach observes a colleague using the teaching strategy while teaching a lesson in her own classroom. The goal of coaching is for teachers to help each other transfer what they learned in the initial steps (study of theory, observation of experts, practice under controlled conditions) into their own classroom. An important aspect of this transfer process is developing executive control of the teaching strategy. A teacher has executive control if she understands when it is appropriate to use the teaching strategy, what learning outcomes can be expected from using it, and how to adapt it for different types of learners and curriculum content.

Peer coaching is well suited for helping teachers learn a complex teaching strategy and supporting them as they attempt to implement it with fidelity in their own classrooms. However, it requires a commitment by teams of teachers—preferably by the entire teaching staff of a school—for the process to work. In contrast, a teacher and supervisor can start a clinical supervision cycle at any time, and they can work together on any concerns or needs that the teacher has.

METHODS INVOLVING SCHOOLWIDE PARTICIPATION

We describe four methods in the sections below: instructional rounds, classroom walk-throughs, teacher learning communities, and lesson study. One similarity is that they all focus on both the professional development of individual teachers and on schoolwide improvement. Another similarity is that they involve small to large groups of educators working together to pursue shared goals. In contrast, the methods of professional development described above typically involve one teacher or a pair of teachers working together.

Instructional Rounds

Instructional rounds (hereafter *rounds*) are a relatively new method of professional development and school improvement.[23] Although intended primarily for school administrators, this method has interesting connections to clinical supervision, so we describe it here.

The rounds process is outlined in Table 3.2. The first step is for school administrators to identify a problem of practice that they wish to address. The problem of practice should be grounded in data based on classroom observation, student test results, or other empirical method. Examples of problems of practice are students not getting sufficient opportunities to practice thinking, students not applying what they have learned during instruction to solve unfamiliar math problems, and special education students doing poorly on state-administered tests.

Table 3.2 The Four Steps of Instructional Rounds

Problem of Practice	Observation of Practice	Observation Debrief	Next Level of Work
School indentifies a problem of practice that • focuses on the instructional core; • is directly observable; • is actionable (is within the school/district's control and can be improved in real time); • connects to a broader strategy of improvement (school, system). Network adopts the problem of practice as the focus for the network's learning.	Observation teams collect data that is • descriptive not evaluative; • specific; • about the instructional core; • related to the problem of practice.	Observation teams discuss the data: • *Describe* what you saw. • *Analyze* the descriptive evidence (What patterns do you see? How might you group the data?). • *Predict* what students are learning. If you were a student in this class/school and you did everything the teacher told you to do, what would you know and be able to do?	Brainstorm the next level of work: • Share district-level theory of action. • Share district context, including resources, professional development, and current initiatives. • Brainstorm the next level of work for this week/next month/by the end of the year. • Brainstorm suggestions for school level and for district level. • Tie suggestions to the district's (and school's) theory of action.

Additional Steps to Support This Element of Rounds

Problem of Practice	Observation of Practice	Observation Debrief	Next Level of Work
Provide school- or district-level context for the problem of practice. Describe optimal teaching and learning in relation to this problem of practice: • What would students be doing/saying? • What would teachers be doing/saying? • Create a working draft that captures the ongoing development of the group's learning.	May include a specific format for observation note-taking or a set of guidelines: • What are students doing/saying? • What are teachers doing/saying? • What is the task?	Use affinity protocol to group the data. Use external standards to group the data.	Ask additional questions: • What do teachers need to know to support optimal learning (described in the working draft)? • What does the school/district need to know to support optimal learning? • Build a working draft of what optimal leading and learning look like at the school and district level (What are teachers, principals, and central office administrators saying/doing?).

Source: City, E. A., Elmore, R. F., Fiarman, S. E., & Teitel, L. (2009). *Instructional rounds in education.* Cambridge, MA: Harvard Education Press. (Table appears on p. 101).

The next step is to collect observational data by having school administrators (the district superintendent, school principals, etc.) visit classrooms to collect direct observational data. The administrators become an ongoing team, traveling in small groups to a school, where they take turns rotating visits to four or five classrooms for 20 minutes each. Their data are in the form of descriptive notes, similar to the technique of anecdotal records and script taping (see Observation Technique 9). The administrators are trained to make notes that are descriptive (e.g., "Students followed directions in the text to make circuit boards") rather than judgmental (e.g., "Teacher had good rapport with students") and to emphasize fine-grained descriptions (e.g., "Teacher: 'How are volcanoes and earthquakes similar and different?'") rather than large-grained descriptions (e.g., "Teacher questions students about the passage they just read").[24] The teams also can address questions to students during class time, so long as it does not disrupt instruction.

This step gives the method its name, *instructional rounds*. It is based on the medical rounds model, which involves teams of physicians visiting patients in hospital wards to develop their skills in diagnosis and treatment. In an educational context, school administrators are the counterpart to physicians, and a class of students is the counterpart of a hospital ward's patients.

The next step is for the administrator team to meet and collectively review its descriptive data pertaining to the problem of practice. The discussion focuses on the discovery of cause-and-effect relationships involving teacher actions and student behavior and learning. Using what they have learned from this analysis, the team members proceed to the final step, which is to plan future activities that will contribute to the solution of the problem of practice. The focus is not only on solutions, however; the team also seeks to develop its understanding of teaching and learning that is relevant to the problem of practice. This understanding takes the form of a theory of action, mentioned in column 4 of Table 3.2. (We explain the theory of action in Chapter 1.)

The rounds method focuses on classroom instruction as the core of education, and it relies on observational data as the primary basis for thinking about how to improve it. Clinical supervision is based exactly on the same premise. Therefore, we believe that clinical supervision can be added to the rounds model to enhance its effectiveness. For example, clinical supervisors can be members of a team making its rounds and help it develop observation skills. Also, they contribute to the feedback conference and decision making about the next level of work. In particular, they can draw on their expertise in clinical supervision, research on effective teaching, and other methods of professional development to help the team design interventions that contribute to the solution of problems of practice.

Classroom Walk-Throughs

Management by walking around is a common practice in business. It involves managers spending a significant amount of their time visiting the business's work areas and talking with employees to learn their concerns and suggestions. In this manner, managers can provide leadership on the basis of what is actually happening in the organization, not what they think is happening. Several forms of this method have entered educational practice, including one developed by Carolyn Downey and her associates for the purpose of promoting effective leadership by administrators and professional development for educators.[25] Their version of walking about, called *walkthroughs*, has two phases: observation and reflective inquiry.

In the observation phase, a supervisor—typically a school administrator—visits the classroom of each teacher for three minutes. The supervisor observes and takes notes on five aspects of the classroom environment, in the following order:

1. Student orientation to work. The supervisor observes whether students are attending to the task at hand.

2. Curricular decision points. The supervisor identifies the lesson's curriculum objective by listening to classroom talk or examining students' worksheets or other products. Later, the supervisor analyzes the alignment of the curriculum objective with the curriculum prescribed by the school, district, or state.

3. Instructional decision points. The supervisor observes the teacher's use of (a) generic teaching methods (e.g., using examples to illustrate a principle), (b) teaching methods that have been emphasized as a focus of professional development by the school or district, and (c) research-based, subject-specific practices.

4. "Walk the Walls"—Curricular and instructional decisions. The supervisor examines the walls for materials (e.g., instructional posters, student grades, student writings) that express the teacher's curriculum and instruction. The supervisor also looks on the teacher's desk or elsewhere for materials such as student worksheets and graded essays.

5. Safety and health issues. The supervisor looks for problems such as backpacks in the aisles, lack of adequate ventilation, and broken objects that might be hazardous.

Supervisors need not provide reflective feedback to the teacher after each observation. When they do, it can take several forms: a brief written note that teachers can read at their leisure; a conversation that is directive (e.g., "Think with me about how you make decisions about wait time"); or a conversation based on reflective questions (e.g., "In planning your lessons around the district curriculum and in thinking about activities you might use, what thoughts go on in your mind about which activities to select to impact student achievement?"). The walkthrough model contains a number of guidelines for constructing reflective questions. For example, reflective questions should focus on the teacher's decision-making process and the effect of his decisions on student learning outcomes.

The walkthrough method is smaller in scale than other methods of professional development presented in this chapter. An observation and reflective conversation with a teacher might take only a total of six minutes. At the least, walkthroughs familiarize teachers and administrators with the process of classroom observation and reflection. Also, walkthroughs bring school principals directly into the school's primary work areas—namely, classrooms. This activity should make it more likely that teachers will see the principal as an instructional leader, not just a manager. Furthermore, the principal is more likely to value teachers' work and create opportunities for their professional growth, including clinical supervision for individual teachers or groups of teachers. Because both methods emphasize observation and reflective dialogue, teachers and administrators should find it easy to make the transition from walkthroughs to clinical supervision.

Professional Learning Communities

Starting around 1980, researchers began to study how school-level factors affect the work of individual teachers. In one widely cited study, Susan Rosenholtz found that teachers' efficacy was affected by how much organizational support they received for their professional development and classroom instruction.[26] Similar findings were reported about the organizational climate of businesses. Based on these findings, Peter Senge, among others, advocated that organizations support the learning of its employees, both individually and collectively, if they wished to achieve extraordinary outcomes.[27] Organizations that emphasized staff learning came to be called *learning organizations*. This concept influenced educators to introduce professional learning communities (also called *teacher learning communities*) into their organizations. These learning organizations typically are found in schools, although some exist as temporary structures that are not site-specific— for example, the National Writing Project.

The goal of teacher learning communities is to increase the ability of teachers, both individually and collectively, to improve students' learning. The communities do not work toward this goal by following a set of prescribed steps or by studying a prescribed knowledge base. Instead, each community develops its own operating procedures while following a set of shared principles. Shirley Hord identified five of these principles.[28]

1. **Supportive and shared leadership.** In a school-based learning community, teachers and building administrators learn together, and anyone can provide leadership to take action on what has been learned.

2. **Shared values and vision.** Learning communities view their mission as helping students achieve their academic potential, and they subscribe to values that support this mission.

3. Collective learning and application of learning. Participants in learning communities pursue learning that will help them achieve their goals. For example, the community might agree to a project (such as improving students' algebra skills) that requires them to engage in new learning. Some teachers might read relevant literature, while others attend workshops. Each of them has a responsibility to share what they learned with other members of the learning community, so that everyone benefits from it.

4. **Supportive conditions.** Learning communities require support and resources in order to thrive. For example, they need a time and place to meet, mutual respect and trust among all participants, administrative support, and norms of collegiality and collaboration.

5. **Shared practice.** In a learning community, each teacher needs to be willing to make her instructional practices available to colleagues. The purpose of this openness is professional development, not teacher evaluation. Hord describes it as a "'peers helping peers' process that includes teachers visiting each other's classrooms on a regular basis to observe, take notes, and discuss their observations with the teacher they have visited."[29] Also, teachers can support each other in developing new practices by engaging in peer coaching and feedback.

These five principles do not require teachers to engage in a particular type of professional development. Hord mentions peer coaching, but any of the other methods of professional development that we describe in this chapter could support the overall mission and specific projects of a teacher learning community. However, each of these methods would need to be used in such a way that whatever new knowledge a teacher acquires is shared with the entire community. For example, a pair of teachers could take turns serving as clinical supervisor and teacher in cycles of planning conferences, observation, and feedback conferences. They would take the additional step of sharing their insights with their learning community.

Lesson Study

Lesson study is widely used in Japanese schools. This method of professional education came to the attention of American educators when a cross-cultural study of mathematics instruction, called TIMSS (Third International Mathematics and Science Study), found that Japanese students were acquiring much better mathematics skills than American students.[30] Researchers who conducted this study suggested that the Japanese method of lesson study might be partly responsible for the superior learning outcomes of Japanese students. Consequently, the U.S. National Commission on Mathematics and Science Teaching for the 21st Century recommended that American teachers participate in inquiry groups modeled after lesson study as a method of professional development.[31]

Lesson study includes the following steps:

1. A group of teachers decides on a subject-matter problem that they would like to solve. For example, they might decide that students' writing skills are not developing as quickly as they would like.

2. The teachers focus their research by selecting a particular curriculum unit and objective to study. For example, they might decide to examine a unit for elementary-school students on expository writing, with the objective being that students will learn how to write a complete paragraph.

3. The teachers create a plan for a lesson (sometimes called a *research lesson*) within the unit. The lesson plan should include certain elements, including how the lesson's objectives relate to previously taught content and to content that will be taught in future lessons; learning activities and key questions; anticipated student responses to the activities; assessment procedures to check student learning; and student characteristics that were considered in the lesson design.

4. One teacher is selected to teach the research lesson to her students, while the other teachers observe and take notes on her activities and students' responses. Curriculum experts, administrators, and other educators also might observe the lesson; if so, they are asked to study the lesson plan beforehand.

5. Everyone involved in the research lesson meets to debrief it. The teacher who taught the lesson and the observers each have the opportunity to mention strengths of the lesson, its relationship to the lesson plan, and issues and concerns about the lesson.

6. The group of teachers revises the lesson plan based on what they learned from the debriefing, and another teacher is selected to teach it. Once again, the

other teachers observe the lesson, and then the teacher who taught the lesson and the observers convene to debrief it.

7. The group of teachers prepares a report that documents what they learned about the problem that they selected for study and the research lesson.

This process is primarily used at the inservice level, but some educators have experimented with its use at the preservice level.[32]

Lesson study is distinctive in that it develops teachers' skills within a sharply delineated curriculum domain. In contrast, the other methods of professional development that we describe in this chapter (and clinical supervision as well) generally focus on instructional skills that are applicable across curriculum domains. If the goal is to develop teachers' subject-matter expertise, lesson study is likely to be the most suitable method.

The major steps in a lesson study project involve a planning meeting, a classroom lesson that is observed, and a debriefing meeting. These steps closely parallel the major steps of clinical supervision—planning conference, observation, and feedback conference. Therefore, if you have learned the skills of clinical supervision, you will be well on the way to learning how to implement a lesson study project with a group of teachers. Also, preservice or inservice teachers who have had good learning experiences during clinical supervision should have the prerequisite skills and frame of mind to enter quickly into a lesson study project and benefit from it.

CONCLUDING NOTE

Most of the methods described in this chapter are based on the premise that teachers' reflection on their personal experience enables them to develop knowledge that will improve their instructional skills and improve student learning. Each teacher or group of teachers in a professional learning community needs to invent their own wheel, so to speak. A different assumption underlies microteaching, peer coaching, and clinical supervision, as we have described them here. These methods assume that there is a knowledge base of research findings upon which teachers can draw to improve their instruction. This knowledge base is described in Chapter 4. Even though this field of inquiry is relatively young, much has been learned about how to teach effectively.

Which of these two approaches is better—reflection or research-based training? We have not found comparative research studies that answer this question. A recent study, though, indirectly sheds some light on it. Researchers at the University of Michigan compared three models of school improvement to determine which was most effective in improving the learning of elementary school students.[33] Two of the models, Success for All and America's Choice, were developed by external agencies and adopted by schools involved in the experiment. In these models, the agency's staff supplied prescribed curriculum materials and trained teachers in specific instructional strategies. In the third model, the Accelerated Schools Project, the agency's staff supported teachers in developing their own instructional plans around a broadly shared philosophy of teaching and learning.

The researchers found that students whose teachers were trained in the Success for All and America's Choice models learned more than students whose teachers were given support by Accelerated Schools Project staff to improve instruction on their own. This finding suggests to us that professional development models that focus on enhancing teacher's capacity for reflection will not be sufficient to improve student learning outcomes. Models of professional development that focus on research-validated teaching strategies, applied to sound curriculum materials, are necessary.

In our view, teachers can benefit both from reflection on personal teaching experience and application of research about effective teaching. Assuming this is true, teachers need exposure to multiple methods of professional development—those that emphasize research-based teaching skills and those that emphasize reflection upon experience. Conceivably, teacher educators might be able to develop new methods of professional development that optimize both approaches.

The methods described in this chapter were designed for the professional development of inservice teachers. These methods also have the potential to enhance preservice teacher education. While formal coursework has an important place in preservice programs, student teachers need the benefit of varied forms of professional development, including clinical supervision, and extensive opportunities to apply what they have learned in real classrooms. Any of the methods of professional development described in this chapter probably would be suitable if modified for the preservice context.

ENDNOTES

1. Comment by James Stigler in: Willis, S. (2002). Creating a knowledge base. *Educational Leadership, 59*(2), 6–11. Quote appears on page 6. Reprinted by permission of ASCD.

2. Quality counts 2008: Tapping into teaching [Special issue]. (2008, January 10). *Education Week, 27,* 18. Retrieved from http://www.ed.week.org

3. Some of these resources include the following: Portner, H. (2008). *Mentoring new teachers* (3rd ed.). Thousand Oaks, CA: Corwin; Strong, M. (2009). *Effective teacher induction and mentoring: Assessing the evidence.* New York: Teachers College Press; Trubowitz, S., & Robins, M. P. (2003). *The good teacher mentor.* New York: Teachers College Press; Villani, S. (2009). *Comprehensive mentoring programs for new teachers* (2nd ed.). Thousand Oaks, CA: Corwin.

4. Information about the PAR program is available at http://www.gse.harvard.edu/~ngt/par

5. Hall, J. L., Johnson, B., & Bowman, A. C. (1995). Teacher socialization: A spiral process. *Teacher Educator, 30*(4), 25–36; Luft, J. A., & Cox, W. E. (2001). Investing in our future: A survey of support offered to beginning secondary science and mathematics teachers. *Science Educator, 10*(1), 1–9.

6. Allen, D., & Ryan, K. (1969). *Microteaching.* Reading, MA: Addison-Wesley.

7. Borg, W. R., Kelley, M. L., Langer, P., & Gall, M. D. (1970). *The minicourse: A microteaching approach to teacher education.* Beverly Hills, CA: Macmillan Educational Services.

8. http://isites.harvard.edu/fs/html/icb.topic58474/microteaching

9. Allen, D. W. (1966). *Micro-teaching: A new framework for in-service education.* Stanford, CA: Stanford University. Retrieved from ERIC database. (ED013240). Quote appears on p. 1.

10. Borg, *op cit.*, p. 33.

11. Costa, A., & Garmston, R. (2002). *Cognitive coaching: A foundation for renaissance schools.* Norwood, MA: Christopher-Gordon.

12. Dana, N. F. (2009). *The reflective educator's guide to classroom research: Learning to teach and teaching to learn through practitioner inquiry* (2nd ed.). Thousand Oaks, CA: Corwin, ; Mertler, C. A. (2009). *Action research: Teachers as researchers in the classroom* (2nd ed.). Los Angeles: Sage; Schmuck, R. A. (2009). *Practical action research: A collection of articles* (2nd ed.). Thousand Oaks, CA: Corwin.

13. Drosopoulos, J. D., Heald, A. Z., & McCue, M. J. (2008). *Minimizing bullying behavior of middle school students through behavioral intervention and instruction.* Chicago: St. Xavier University. Retrieved from ERIC database. (ED5000895)

14. *Ibid.*, p. 70.

15. Go to <http://www.eric.ed.gov> and enter <ED500895> as the search term.

16. Smith, N. S. (1989). Peer consultation as a means of professional growth: A study in British Columbia schools. *Dissertation Abstracts International: Section A. Humanities*

and Social Sciences, 51 (03), 734; Shamsher, M. (1992). Peer consultation as a means to reflective practice and classroom research: A case study of the Program for Quality Teaching in British Columbia schools. *Dissertation Abstracts International: Section A. Humanities and Social Sciences,, 54* (01), 53; Goldman, P., & Smith, N. S. (1991). *Portrait of a successful educational innovation: British Columbia's Program for Quality Teaching.* Paper presented at the annual meeting of the Canadian Association for Studies in Educational Administration, Ontario, Canada. Retrieved from ERIC database. (ED346587)

17. Goldman & Smith, *op. cit.*

18. Joyce, B., & Showers, B. (1996). The evolution of peer coaching. *Educational Leadership, 53*(6), 12–16; Joyce, B., & Showers, B. (1982). The coaching of teaching. *Educational Leadership, 40*(1), 4–8, 10.

19. Knight, J. (2007). *Instructional coaching: A partnership approach to improving instruction.* Thousand Oaks, CA: Corwin.

20. Joyce, B. R., & Weil, M. (2008). *Models of teaching* (8th ed.). Boston: Allyn & Bacon.

21. Joyce & Showers (1982), *op cit.*

22. Joyce & Showers (1996), *op cit.*

23. City, E. A., Elmore, R. F., Fiarman, S. E., & Teitel, L. (2009). *Instructional rounds in education: A network approach to improving teaching and learning.* Cambridge, MA: Harvard Education Press.

24. *Ibid.*, p. 85.

25. Downey, C. J., Steffy, B. E., English, F. W., Frase, L. E., & Poston, W. K., Jr. (2004). *The three-minute classroom walk-through: Changing school supervisory practice one teacher at a time.* Thousand Oaks, CA: Corwin; Downey, C. J., Steffy, B. E., Poston, W. K., Jr., & English, F. W. (2010). *Advancing the three-minute walk-through: Mastering reflective practice.* Thousand Oaks, CA: Corwin.

26. Rosenholtz, S. (1989). *Teachers workplace: The social organization of schools.* New York: Longman.

27. Senge, P. (1990). *The fifth discipline: The art and practice of the learning organization.* New York: Doubleday.

28. Hord, S. M. (1990). Professional learning communities: An overview. In S. M. Hord (Ed.), *Learning together, leading together: Changing schools through professional learning communities* (pp. 5–14). New York: Teachers College Press.

29. *Ibid.*, p. 11.

30. Stigler, J., & Hiebert, J. (1999). *The teaching gap: Best ideas from the world's teachers for improving education in the classroom.* New York: The Free Press.

31. National Commission on Mathematics and Science Teaching for the 21st Century. (2000). *Before it's too late.* Washington, DC: U.S. Department of Education.

32. Sims, L., & Walsh, D. (2009). Lesson study with preservice teachers: Lessons from lessons. *Teaching and Teacher Education, 25*(5), 724–733.

33. Correnti, R., & Rowan, B. (2007). Opening up the black box: Literacy instruction in schools participating in three comprehensive school reform programs. *American Educational Research Journal, 44*, 298–338.

Chapter 4

Using Clinical Supervision to Promote Effective Teaching

In various research studies I have been a part of over the past fifty years, I have found that many popular, respected practices were not supported by research. Indeed, practice often went in a direction opposite from the existing research evidence. Thus, while educational practice kept moving in the direction of the progressive, student-centered approaches, the research evidence kept growing in support of traditional, teacher-centered learning.

—Jeanne Chall[1]

INTRODUCTION

The primary goal of clinical supervision is to help teachers become more effective. But what does "effective" mean?

One way to answer this question is to examine the empirical findings of researchers who study teachers. Some educators reject this approach by arguing that effective teaching differs for every instructional situation and every teacher, and therefore no empirical generalizations are possible. We are sympathetic to this argument, but our experience and examination of the research literature suggests otherwise.

As a demonstration of this point, we suggest that you list five characteristics of an effective elementary, secondary, or college teacher. (You can elaborate on this task by also listing five characteristics of an *ineffective* teacher.) Most educators find this task relatively easy. Moreover, they usually agree with one another's lists. Rarely do we find a controversial characteristic—one that some educators think represents good teaching and other educators think represents bad teaching. Disagreement, if it occurs, usually concerns the relative importance of the characteristics.

Richard Schmuck and Patricia Schmuck interviewed more than 200 teenage students to find out, among other things, what they considered to be the characteristics of good and bad teaching.[2] Here are the most frequently occurring answers. To what extent do these characteristics agree with your list?

Characteristics of Good Teaching

- Gives students respect, is patient, and easy to get along with.
- Makes the subject interesting and fun by involving students in activities and demonstrations.
- Tells jokes and smiles a lot—good sense of humor.
- Listens to students' questions and makes changes in class to help students learn.

Characteristics of Bad Teaching

- Low respect for students, lacks patience, and treats you like you are stupid.
- Seldom smiles, very serious and stern, and issues either too harsh or too permissive discipline.
- Doesn't care about or pay attention to individuals; not helpful.
- Doesn't explain well, lazy, hands out worksheets and tests; students have to learn everything on their own.
- Has favorites; favors the smart students or one sex over the other.

Before you finalize your own list of the characteristics of effective teachers, we recommend that you read the research findings in this chapter. To understand the research, however, you need to know something about how it is done. Researchers often compare the teaching practices of more effective teachers and less effective teachers. This type of inquiry is commonly called *causal-comparative* or *correlational research*. Another research paradigm is to have a group of teachers (the experimental group) try a particular teaching practice. A different group of teachers (the control group) is asked to follow their usual practices or try a different teaching practice. If the experimental teaching practice produces superior results, it is considered effective. This type of inquiry is commonly called *experimental research*.

In correlational research, it is necessary to identify a criterion by which to define the more effective and less effective teachers whose teaching practices are to be compared. Similarly, in experimental research, it is necessary to identify a criterion to determine the relative effectiveness of the experimental and control groups.

Researchers have used various criteria in their studies. These criteria reflect different perspectives about what is important in schooling. If you do not agree with the criteria used by the researchers, you probably will disagree with their conclusions about what constitutes effective teaching. Because the criteria are so important to understanding this research, we have organized the following review of the research literature into sections that correspond to different criteria of teaching effectiveness.

EFFECTIVE TEACHING OF ACADEMIC KNOWLEDGE AND SKILLS

Much of the general public and many educators believe that the major purpose of school is to help students acquire the knowledge and skills associated with reading, mathematics, history, geography, music, art, foreign languages, and other academic disciplines studied in the K–12 curriculum. From this perspective, a teacher is more or less effective depending on how much of the academic curriculum is mastered by his or her students.

The usual research procedure for determining how much a teacher's students have learned is to give the entire class the same or a similar standardized achievement test before and after a period of instruction (usually at the start and end of a school year). Teachers whose students make substantial gains in their test scores are considered more effective, whereas teachers whose students make small gains are considered less effective.

The meaning of teacher effectiveness in this type of research obviously depends on the achievement test that is used. If a teacher's students make large gains on a reading test, the teacher can be judged to be effective in teaching reading, but that does not mean he or she is necessarily effective in teaching mathematics. It would be necessary to give the students a mathematics achievement test to make this determination. In short, the achievement test used by a researcher places limits on the generalizability of the teaching methods that are found to be effective. In the following research review, we emphasize teaching methods that were found to be effective across several school subjects.

Nine Teacher Characteristics Associated with Gains in Student Academic Achievement

Barak Rosenshine and Norma Furst synthesized the research that had been done on teacher effectiveness up until approximately 1970.[3] They identified nine characteristics of teachers whose students make greater gains in academic achievement than students of other teachers:

1. clarity.
2. variety in use of materials and methods.
3. enthusiasm.
4. task-oriented, businesslike approach to instruction.
5. avoidance of harsh criticism.
6. indirect teaching style.[4]
7. emphasis on teaching content covered on the criterion achievement test.
8. use of structuring statements that provide an overview for what is about to happen or has happened.
9. use of questions at multiple cognitive levels.

Research studies reported after 1970 have continued to demonstrate the effectiveness of these teacher characteristics in promoting student learning. In one recent study, researchers did not relate teacher characteristics to student learning gains, but rather asked college and graduate students in 68 different degree programs to describe three to six characteristics that they believed effective college instructors should possess.[5] Analyzing the responses, they identified nine teacher characteristics that were repeatedly mentioned:

1. Sensitive to students' needs.
2. Well informed on course content.
3. Organized in preparing course.
4. Animated in delivery of course material.
5. Clearly conveys course material.

6. Available to students.

7. Expert in his or her field.

8. Impartial.

9. Lets students know how well he or she has done or can improve.

These characteristics parallel those on Rosenshine and Furst's list to a large degree. Both lists portray the same kind of effective teacher, even though the first list was based on research with elementary and secondary students, and the second list involved university students.

Direct and Indirect Teaching

Ned Flanders initiated an important line of research on effective teaching in the 1960s.[6] He identified two contrasting styles of teaching: direct and indirect. Direct teaching is characterized by teacher reliance on the following:

1. lecture.

2. criticism.

3. justification of authority.

4. giving directions.

Indirect teaching is characterized by teacher reliance on:

1. asking questions.

2. accepting students' feelings.

3. acknowledging students' ideas.

4. giving praise and encouragement.

Many research studies have found that students of "indirect" teachers learn more and have better attitudes toward learning than students of "direct" teachers.[7] However, Flanders believes that both direct and indirect behaviors are necessary in good teaching. For example, teachers can effectively use a direct teaching strategy, such as lecture and demonstration, to clarify a difficult curriculum topic. Even in this situation, however, the teacher can make the lecture and demonstration more indirect by asking questions occasionally to determine whether students are following the presentation. Effective teaching behavior, then, involves appropriate use of indirect teaching techniques, not total reliance on them.

The Explicit Teaching Model

Researchers have made a concerted effort to identify teacher behaviors that facilitate student learning in specific curriculum areas. Much of this research has focused on reading and mathematics instruction at the primary and elementary school levels, because mastery of these subjects is critical to subsequent academic achievement.

Barak Rosenshine synthesized the findings of this body of research into an organized model of teaching, which he calls "explicit teaching."[8] The teaching is "explicit" because the teaching goals and steps are predictable and can be clearly analyzed and

Table 4.1 The Six Elements of the Explicit Teaching Model

1. *Review*. Each day, start the lesson by correcting the previous night's homework and reviewing what students have recently been taught.
2. *Presentation*. Tell students the goals of today's lesson. Then present new information a little at a time, modeling procedures, giving clear examples, and checking often to make sure students understand.
3. *Guided practice*. Allow students to practice using the new information under the teacher's direction; ask many questions that give students abundant opportunities to correctly repeat or explain the procedure or concept that has just been taught. Student participation should be active until all students are able to respond correctly.
4. *Correction and feedback*. During guided practice, give students a great deal of feedback. When students answer incorrectly, reteach the lesson if necessary. When students answer correctly, explain why the answer was right. It is important that feedback be immediate and thorough.
5. *Independent practice*. Next, allow students to practice using the new information on their own. The teacher should be available to give short answers to student's questions, and students should be permitted to help each other.
6. *Weekly and monthly reviews*. At the beginning of each week, the teacher should review the previous week's lessons. At the end of the month, the teacher should review what students have learned during the last four weeks. It is important that students not be allowed to forget past lessons once they have moved on to new material.

Source: Adapted from: Rosenshine, B.V. (1986). Synthesis of research on explicit teaching. *Educational Leadership, 43*(7), 60–68. Reprinted by permission of ASCD.

described. The six parts of the explicit teaching model are described in Table 4.1. You will note that the first five parts of the model correspond approximately to a daily lesson plan. The sixth part—review—is incorporated into the lesson plan at periodic intervals.

There is a striking correspondence between Rosenshine's explicit teaching model and Madeline Hunter's model of effective teaching.[9] Her model, sometimes called *Instructional Theory into Practice* (ITIP), has had a major influence on American education. The seven components of the model and their counterpart in the explicit teaching model (in parentheses) are as follows:

1. anticipatory set (review).
2. stating of objectives (presentation).
3. information input (presentation).
4. modeling (presentation).
5. checking for understanding (presentation; correction and feedback).
6. guided and independent practice (guided practice; independent practice).
7. closure (weekly and monthly review).

Hunter based her model on a different, older base of research knowledge than did Rosenshine, yet they drew similar conclusions about the elements of effective teaching.

Rosenshine claims that the explicit teaching model is applicable to any "well-structured" school subject, such as "mathematical procedures and computations, reading decoding, explicit reading procedures such as distinguishing fact from opinion, science facts and concepts, social studies facts and concepts, map skills, grammatical concepts and rules, and foreign language vocabulary and grammar."[10] These examples represent what is generally known as lower-cognitive objectives. Effective teaching of higher-cognitive objectives requires different methods, which are discussed in the next section. Rosenshine further delimited the situations for which the explicit teaching model is effective:

> It would be a mistake to say that this small-step approach applies to all students or all situations. It is most important for young learners, slow learners, and for all learners when the material is new, difficult, or hierarchical. In these situations, relatively short presentations are followed by student practice. However, when teaching older, brighter students, or when teaching in the middle of a unit, the steps are larger, that is, the presentations are longer, less time is spent in checking for understanding or in guided practice, and more independent practice can be done as homework because the students do not need as much help and supervision.[11]

These qualifications about the use of the explicit teaching model have an important implication for the supervision of teachers. Specifically, they imply that a supervisor should not use the explicit teaching model, or any other teaching model, as an absolute set of criteria for evaluating a teacher or for setting improvement goals. Rather, the supervisor needs first to determine the teacher's instructional objectives through a planning conference (see Chapter 8). Then the supervisor and teacher can discuss appropriate teaching methods for addressing these objectives.

Effective Teaching of Thinking Skills

Bloom's taxonomy classifies six cognitive levels of thinking.[12] The knowledge, comprehension, and application levels generally are considered to represent lower-cognitive thinking, whereas the analysis, synthesis, and evaluation levels represent higher-cognitive thinking. Nancy Cole observed that lower-cognitive and higher-cognitive curriculum objectives reflect different theories about learning.[13] With respect to lower-cognitive learning, Cole observed:

> By the 1960s, behavioral psychology dominated conceptions of learning in psychology and in education. The learning theory with which a generation of educators grew up came directly from this field. It was heavily based on studies of animal learning and was closely connected with the learning of specific, discrete skills described as precise, well-delimited behaviors. . . .
>
> The theories that supported behavioral psychology were well suited to the political times of increasing public concern that children were not learning to read, write, or perform basic arithmetic operations. There was also public concern that students were not learning basic factual information. The result of this merging of theoretical and political orientation was a decade (the seventies) in which the strongly dominant conception of educational achievement in public discussion was in terms of specific, separate, basic skills and facts.[14]

Much of the research that led to the development of the explicit teaching model described above involved this conception of learning.

Cole observed that another conception of learning was starting to become prominent:

> Alongside the conception of achievement as mastery of basic skills and facts, and often competing with it, stands a dramatically different conception of educational achievement. This conception focuses on a more complex level of achievement—the achievement of higher order skills (using such terms as critical thinking or problem solving) and of advanced knowledge of subjects (using words such as understanding or expertise).[15]

If you and the teacher value the teaching of thinking skills, you will need to decide which teaching practices and assessment techniques are effective for this purpose. Research on this problem is still fragmentary, but it does provide general guidance.

The Discussion Method

The discussion method is, at this time, the best validated approach for promoting higher-cognitive learning.[16] Most of this research has involved college students and other adult learners. There is no reason why younger students would not benefit from discussion teaching, but it might be more difficult to create the necessary classroom conditions. For example, M. D. Gall and Joyce Gall found that the essential elements of a discussion are small group size (six to eight students) and students talking to each other rather than to the teacher.[17] The teacher can set the problem for discussion, but then serves primarily as moderator and facilitator of student-to-student interaction. We (and others) have found it possible to train even young students in discussion skills and to organize them into small groups.

Higher-Cognitive Questions

Another teaching practice to promote the development of thinking skills is asking higher-cognitive questions. These questions can be asked in a variety of instructional contexts: in discussions, in inquiry teaching, in review sessions before tests, or interspersed throughout an explanation of new curriculum content.

Researchers have not yet determined for certain the effectiveness of higher-cognitive questions. Philip Winne reviewed the research and concluded that it made no difference to student learning whether the teacher emphasized higher-cognitive or lower-cognitive questions.[18] Doris Redfield and Elaine Rousseau reviewed essentially the same research, but concluded that teacher emphasis on higher-cognitive questions led to more learning.[19] Complicating the picture is Barak Rosenshine's review of three major classroom studies, from which he concluded that lower-cognitive questions were more effective.[20] Also problematic is the fact that most of the studies included in the reviews did not differentiate the effects of higher-cognitive questions on thinking skills and on lower-cognitive learning outcomes.

Our view of the situation is that asking higher-cognitive questions is probably necessary, but not in itself sufficient, for the development of students' ability to think. Higher-cognitive questions cue students that thinking is expected and important. However, these questions might be ineffective if the student is unable to respond appropriately. For example, the three studies reviewed by Rosenshine were done in primary-grade classrooms in low-achieving urban schools. Higher-cognitive questions, in the absence of any other intervention, might not promote learning in this context. In contrast, Christiaan Hamaker found in his review of research that higher-cognitive questions inserted in reading passages had a consistently positive effect on students' thinking skills.[21] Most of this research involved college students, a population that would be able to handle the response demands of questions at the higher-cognitive levels.

For younger students, we think teachers should ask higher-cognitive questions routinely, but also provide appropriate instruction and conditions for answering them. This means, for example, modeling the appropriate thinking processes, which can be done by "thinking aloud" for students. Also in contrast to explicit teaching, the teacher needs to give students opportunities for self-expression (rather than carefully defined tasks), substantial projects and tasks (rather than drill-type worksheets), and elaborated, open-ended feedback (rather than correct–incorrect feedback).

Constructivist Teaching

Some educators conceptualize the teaching of thinking skills as a process of helping the learner construct deep understandings of a particular academic discipline. This type of teaching is sometimes called constructivist teaching, as Jacqueline and Martin Brooks explain:

> Traditionally, learning has been thought to be a "mimetic" activity, a process that involves students repeating, or miming, newly presented information . . . in reports or on quizzes and tests. Constructivist teaching practices, on the other hand, help learners to internalize and reshape, or transform new information. Transformation occurs through the creation of new understandings . . . that result from the emergence of new cognitive structures. . . . For example . . . many high school students read Hamlet, but not all of them transform their prior notions of power, relationships, or greed. Deep understanding occurs when the presence of new information prompts the emergence or enhancement of cognitive structures that enable us to rethink our prior ideas.[22]

Robert Marzano, Debra Pickering, and Jane Pollock identified several instructional strategies that are consistent with constructivist principles and that also have been demonstrated by researchers to promote students' academic achievement.[23] Four of them are listed below:

1. Identifying similarities and differences. The teacher asks students to identify similarities and differences between several subjects. The teacher also might ask students to create categories for grouping subjects that have a particular similarity.
2. Summarizing. The teacher asks students to prepare a highly condensed synthesis that expresses the content of a body of information, such as a passage of text or entire book.
3. Making nonlinguistic representations. The teacher asks students to elaborate on newly acquired verbal knowledge by making graphic organizers, physical models, or mental pictures or by engaging in kinesthetic activities.
4. Generating and testing hypotheses. The teacher states a generalization and then asks students to state a hypothesis based on the generalization and test it. (We can think of a hypothesis as a type of prediction.) Alternatively, the teacher has students discover a generalization and then asks them to state a hypothesis based on their generalization and test it. In either situation, the teacher continually asks students to state the reasoning underlying the hypothesis and method of testing it.

Each of these strategies is explained and illustrated by Marzano and his colleagues.[24] A checklist for observing constructivist teaching methods is presented in Chapter 13 (see Observation Technique 16).

Although constructivist teaching methods appear to have merit, some educators are concerned that they might be difficult to implement in conventional classroom settings.[25] For example, Lee Shulman and Kathleen Quinlan reviewed research indicating that the quality of teaching for understanding is dependent on the teacher's own understanding of the subject matter and ability to transform that understanding into accurate representations (e.g., examples, models, and explanations of concepts such as ecology in biology, the preterite tense in Spanish, and acceleration in mathematics).[26] Teachers who lack this understanding and skill will have difficulty implementing constructivist instruction. In fact, a substantial percentage of teachers are "misassigned," meaning that they teach subjects for which they hold no teaching license or endorsement during some or all of a school day.[27]

Effective Use of Time in Teaching

Classroom instructional time is a limited resource. Researchers have found that teachers' use of this resource affects how well students master the curriculum.

One aspect of time is *allocated time*, which is the amount of time that the teacher provides for instruction on each subject or topic. David Berliner and his colleagues found that some elementary teachers spend as little as 16 minutes per average day on mathematics instruction, whereas other teachers spend as much as 50 minutes per average day.[28] The range of allocated time was even greater in reading instruction: from a low of 45 minutes per average day to a high of more than two hours per average day. Walter Borg concluded from his review of research on allocated time that the more time a teacher allocates to instruction in a particular content area, the more students learn about that content area.[29]

If allocated time is the focus of supervision, the supervisor and teacher can review how the teacher plans the amount of time to be spent on each subject during a typical school day. In secondary school instruction, this type of planning is not relevant if the length of class periods and course subjects are fixed. However, most secondary teachers have discretion about allocation of time for particular topics—for example, in a U.S. history class, how much time to spend on the Civil War versus the Reconstruction period following the war. Similarly, the teacher might have discretion about how much time to allocate to historical facts versus historical concepts. The teacher and supervisor can discuss alternative time allocation patterns and their respective merits, especially in relationship to curriculum alignment, which we explain later in this chapter and in Chapter 13.

Students are seldom attentive during the total time allocated for each subject. The percentage of allocated time that students are attentive is called *engaged time* or *at-task time*. Walter Borg concluded from the review of research mentioned above that classes with a high percentage of at-task time have better academic achievement than classes with a low percentage of at-task time. For this reason, at-task time is a frequent focus of clinical supervision. Chapter 11 describes procedures for collecting observational data about it.

If the percentage of students' at-task time is found to be low, the supervisor and teacher should consider methods for improving it. One option for the teacher is to increase substantive interaction with students—for example, explaining content to them, asking questions, giving feedback, and providing assistance during seat work. Charles Fisher and colleagues found that teachers who had more of these substantive interactions with their students had a higher percentage of student at-task time.[30] Their research involved elementary teaching, but it seems reasonable that a similar relationship would be found in secondary school teaching.

Homework extends the amount of allocated time for students to be engaged in learning. Harris Cooper concluded from his review of research on homework that it has relatively little effect on elementary school students' achievement, but a substantial effect on the achievement of older students.[31] The supervisor and teacher can review the teacher's homework policy to determine whether homework is desirable for her students and, if so, the amount and type of homework that should be assigned and how it should be reviewed in class and graded.

Tutoring

In the 1980s, Benjamin Bloom reviewed the research literature on effective teaching and concluded that tutoring is the most effective method.[32] He challenged educators to search for methods of classroom instruction that equaled its effectiveness. To our knowledge, no such method has been found, undoubtedly because tutoring enables a teacher to work individually and intensively with a student, adjusting his or her instruction as much and as often as necessary to meet the student's needs. Tutoring simply is not possible in school classrooms, which might have anywhere from 12 to 50 students or more.

Some schools are able to provide tutoring if supplemental resources are available. In particular, some elementary schools are able to hire tutors for children who are struggling to learn basic reading and mathematics skills. Also, schools might have resources for after-school or summer programs in which tutoring can be used to help students who do not make sufficient learning gains through regular classroom instruction. For example, Valley High School in Las Vegas, Nevada, helps struggling students by providing tutoring sessions after school, on Saturdays, and during vacations.[33] Because of this tutoring program and other efforts, Valley High School has made dramatic gains in the percentage of students passing the state's achievement tests: from 44 percent of students passing the math test in 2004 to 80 percent passing it in 2009; and from 54 percent of students passing the language arts test in 2004 to 92 percent passing it in 2009. This case example is supported by research studies, which have found that tutoring is effective for struggling students.[34]

The fact that a tutor has been assigned to help an individual student does not ensure that tutoring will be effective. As with any other form of instruction, clinical supervision can provide useful feedback to the tutor and the opportunity to consider how tutoring can be made more effective for the student.

We believe that teacher educators should consider introducing their preservice students to the subtleties of teaching and learning by having them serve as tutors in local schools. One advantage is that preservice teachers would be practicing the most effective teaching method currently available. They can use their experiences with this method as a kind of gold standard for comparing the methods that they will observe and use in total-group instruction in school classrooms.

Generic Guidelines for Good Teaching

Jere Brophy synthesized the literature on teaching to derive a set of principles that teachers can use to design and deliver effective instruction.[35] These principles are summarized in Table 4.2. They are derived from the research that we review in this chapter and from theory and research on curriculum-instruction-assessment alignment, social-constructivist instruction, and standards-based curriculum. The principles do not define a single model of teaching (e.g., explicit teaching), but are at a level of generality that can accommodate

Table 4.2 Generic Guidelines of Good Teaching

1. *Supportive classroom climate.* Students learn best within cohesive and caring learning environments.
2. *Opportunity to learn.* Students learn more when most of the available time is allocated to curriculum-related activities and the classroom management system emphasizes maintaining students' engagement in those activities.
3. *Curricullar alignment.* All components of the curriculum are aligned to create a cohesive program for accomplishing instructional purposes and goals.
4. *Establishing learning orientations.* Teachers can prepare students for learning by providing an initial structure to clarify intended outcome and cue desired learning strategies.
5. *Coherent content.* To facilitate meaningful learning and retention, content is explained clearly and developed with emphasis on its structure and connections.
6. *Thoughtful discourse.* Questions are planned to engage students in sustained discourse structured around powerful ideas.
7. *Practice and application activities.* Students need sufficient opportunities to practice and apply what they are learning, and to receive improvement-oriented feedback.
8. *Scaffolding students' task engagement.* The teacher provides whatever assistance students need to enable them to engage in learning activities productively.
9. *Strategy teaching.* The teacher models and instructs students in learning and self-regulation strategies.
10. *Cooperative learning.* Students often benefit from working in pairs or small groups to construct understandings or help one another master skills.
11. *Goal-oriented assessment.* The teacher uses a variety of formal and informal assessment methods to monitor progress toward learning goals.
12. *Achievement expectations.* The teacher establishes and follows through on appropriate expectations for learning outcomes.

Source: Brophy, J, (2001). Introduction. In J. Brophy (Ed.), *Advances in research on teaching* (Vol. 8, pp. 1–23). Oxford: JAI Elsevier.

various teaching methods, school subjects, and grade levels. Therefore, they have wide applicability in clinical supervision.

Elaine McEwan developed a list of 10 traits of highly effective teachers, based on her own experience as a teacher and teacher educator and on her review of the research literature.[36] The 10 traits, as labeled by McEwan, and a brief description of each one are shown in Table 4.3. The list reflects general personality characteristics that are likely to give rise to effective classroom instruction. These personality characteristics are illustrated well in a set of classroom stories collected by Adrienne Mack-Kirschner.[37] The stories, all written by teachers who have attained certification by the National Board for Professional Teaching Standards, illustrate in particular the traits of being passionate, positive, real, and street smart. These teachers treat each student as important and deserving of individual attention so that their learning needs are met.

The 10 traits listed in Table 4.3 are well-aligned with the research-validated instructional methods and styles described in this section of the book: Rosenshine and Furst's list of effective teacher characteristics; Flanders' indirect teaching style; Hunter's and

Table 4.3 Ten Traits of Highly Effective Teachers

Traits That Reflect Personal Character

Trait 1: Mission-driven and Passionate
The teacher feels a call to teach and has a desire to help students learn to their full potential.

Trait 2: Positive and Real
The teacher is sincere, empathic, and respectful in relating to students and others.

Trait 3: Teacher-Leader
The teacher takes the lead in working with others to develop meaningful goals and ways to accomplish them.

Traits That Get Results

Trait 4: With-It-Ness
The teacher is constantly attentive to everything happening in the classroom, including the organization of the classroom, student engagement with learning activities, and use of time.

Trait 5: Style
The teacher displays her unique personality in a way that makes her an interesting, engaging human being for her students and others.

Trait 6: Motivational Expertise
The teacher motivates students to learn by setting high behavioral and academic expectations for their students and by their own personal sense of teaching efficacy.

Trait 7: Instructional Effectiveness
The teacher can communicate effectively and can draw on a broad repertoire of instructional strategies to help students learn.

Trait 8: Book Learning
The teacher has a sound understanding of the academic disciplines that he is teaching and also of the school's curriculum standards.

Trait 9: Street Smarts
The teacher knows students' personal lives and what is happening in the school and community, and can use that knowledge to solve students' learning problems.

Trait 10: A Mental Life
The teacher is constantly reflecting about her instructional effectiveness and how to improve it, while also being attuned to changing conditions in her classroom, school, and the larger community.

Adapted from: McEwan, E. K. (2002). *10 traits of highly effective teachers*. Thousand Oaks, CA: Corwin.

Rosenshine's explicit teaching model; the use of discussion, higher-cognitive questions, and constructivist instruction; an emphasis on at-task time; tutoring; and Brophy's generic guidelines for good teaching. Teacher educators might use McEwan's list as one basis for generating criteria for selecting students into a teacher education program. Clinical supervisors might use the list as a basis for conferencing with teachers about their concerns and aspirations.

Effective Teaching in the Context of the No Child Left Behind Act

The No Child Left Behind Act (NCLB) is having a major impact on educational practice. Among its provisions are two requirements: that all schools test students in reading and mathematics; and that they demonstrate year-to-year gains in test scores until all students in a school achieve proficiency as measured by the tests. In response to these requirements, educators are continually searching for ways to improve students' performance on these tests. Fortunately, stories from the field suggest potentially effective methods.

One such story comes from the school district in Mamaroneck, New York.[38] One of the elementary schools in the district has a particularly diverse student population and low achievement test scores. An administrator was appointed to oversee students' academic achievement. She meets monthly for two hours with all staff associated with students at a particular grade level, and they review achievement test profiles for individual students and students as a whole. The sharing of these data in a public forum is similar to a clinical supervisor and teacher conferencing about classroom data collected during the teacher's actual instruction.

In sharing test data, the teachers were surprised to find that some students were not making expected progress in reading skills. This realization led teachers to use a classroom observation technique that we describe in this book (Observation Technique 10): "[It] involved videotaping students reading as a way to jointly examine both teacher practice and student behaviors during instruction."[39]

When the videotapes were shown at the monthly meetings, the team was able to develop hypotheses about why some students were not making expected progress, generate ideas for instructional changes based on these hypotheses, and try them out during classroom instruction. This approach, similar to clinical supervision cycles, led to improvement in test results. For example, the percentage of fourth-grade students who scored at or above state standards increased from 52 percent to 68 percent over a two-year period.

Another example of data-based teaching comes from the Pueblo del Sol Middle School, which was one of 490 Arizona schools that did not make NCLB-mandated adequate yearly progress in 2009.[40] One of the principal's primary strategies for solving this problem was to hire two academic coaches to observe classes and give feedback to teachers. In performing these functions, the coaches are very similar to clinical supervisors, differing in name only.

The principal also created a Student Data Analysis Center, which has whiteboards listing individual students and their state test scores in relation to state standards. The students have individual magnets to represent them, and the magnet is moved on the whiteboard to reflect each student's progress on benchmark tests administered quarterly. This system provides objective data, which teachers individually and, in school-based professional learning communities, can use to consider instructional improvements tailored to the needs of individual students.

These two cases demonstrate that, by working together, teachers and administrators can create a school-level system that enables all of them to be more effective in meeting NCLB requirements than if they worked alone—administrators in their offices and teachers in their individual classrooms. Several features of an effective school-level system are illustrated by these two cases. Researchers have discovered additional school-level practices that lead to improved student achievement. Robert Marzano reviewed several syntheses of this research and used them to create his own synthesis.[41] He identified five school-level factors that research has demonstrated to improve students' academic achievement. We describe each factor below and show how it can be translated into school-level and teacher-level practices.

1. *A guaranteed and viable curriculum.* A curriculum, that is, the academic content that is to be taught to students, exists at several levels. The public version of the curriculum typically is stated as a set of written standards that specify the content to be taught at each grade level for major subjects, such as language arts, mathematics, science, and social studies.

   This intended curriculum might differ from the curriculum actually implemented by individual teachers. Discrepancies can occur if teachers do not follow the intended curriculum or if they use textbooks or other materials whose content differs from the intended curriculum or does not cover it in sufficient depth. It is easy to imagine what can happen if the intended curriculum is used to create high-stakes tests for a teacher's students, but the teacher's implemented curriculum omits some of the content of the intended curriculum. Students' academic achievement will suffer. A similar problem will occur if teachers' implemented curriculum differs from their own teacher-made tests.

   If a teacher's students perform poorly on tests mandated by the district or state, the clinical supervisor and the teacher should consider whether the problem involves a lack of alignment between the intended curriculum and the teacher's implemented curriculum. In the case of poor student performance on teacher-made tests, the clinical supervisor and the teacher will need to determine whether there is a lack of alignment between the academic content taught during classroom instruction and the content covered by the test. These various types of alignment collectively are called *curriculum alignment* (see Chapter 13).

   Full-scale curriculum alignment is well beyond the scope of clinical supervision. It requires expertise and leadership at the school, district, and state levels. However, the clinical supervisor and teacher can examine some aspects of curriculum alignment in their conferences and classroom observations. For example, a clinical supervisor and teacher can jointly examine students' performance on tests and reflect on whether their performance might be affected, either positively or negatively, by the teacher's curriculum-alignment practices (see Observation Technique 14).

2. *Challenging goals and effective feedback.* Research studies have found that students achieve at a higher level when school leaders set challenging goals for them. NCLB states challenging goals in terms of year-to-year gains in student achievement on standardized tests and school attendance. Lowering the dropout rate is another challenging goal. In addition to these schoolwide goals, school leaders also need to consider setting goals for individual students. This type of goal is important, because while students on average can make an improvement, individual students might continue to do poorly and be lost in group statistics.

   Challenging goals can be stated at the school level, but they must be translated by each teacher into actions that they take in their individual classrooms. Clinical supervisors and teachers can conference about effective ways to communicate goals to students, followed by the collection of observational data about how teachers actually communicate goals during classroom instruction. Clinical supervisors and teachers also can conference about how best to set goals for students who might need special help.

Goal-setting depends on continual assessment at both the school and classroom level for it to be effective. The two cases described above illustrate how continual assessment can be provided as feedback to teachers, who use it to improve their classroom instruction.

3. *Parent and community involvement.* Research studies have found that parent and community involvement, if it is positive in its intent, benefits students' academic achievement. Criticism of parents or the community has the opposite effect. Marzano's synthesis of research findings revealed that three types of involvement are effective: (1) communication between school educators, parents, and the community; (2) providing ways for parents to participate in school activities, such as by serving as teacher aides or guest presenters in classrooms; and (3) giving parents and community members a voice in school-level decision making—for example, by forming parent advisory councils.

4. *Safe and orderly environment.* Marzano cites research studies indicating that violence in schools is a significant problem. Too often teachers are assaulted, and students experience physical harm and bullying from other students. When violence is present, teachers' energy for teaching and students' motivation to learn suffers. The converse of violence—a safe and orderly environment—is conducive to students' academic achievement. This type of environment is fostered by the establishment of schoolwide rules for handling misbehavior, enforcement of consequences for breaking the rules, and programs that teach students self-discipline and responsibility.

   We know of instances where preservice teachers experience student misbehavior in their classroom and other areas of the school, but are at a loss about how to deal with it. This problem is most likely to occur if a preservice teacher has not been given an orientation to school policies about misbehavior or if there are no such policies. In this situation, the clinical supervisor needs to learn what the school policies are and help the preservice teacher follow them. If there are no policies, the clinical supervisor will need to talk to school administrators about how preservice teachers should respond to various kinds of student misbehavior.

   Preservice teachers might feel uncomfortable about occurrences of student misbehavior and try to ignore them, hoping that they are isolated instances and will not recur. Also, they might be in a state of denial about occurrences of student misbehavior, because they feel that the occurrences are a result of their inability to manage students effectively. Clinical supervisors can handle this denial by presenting the preservice teacher with nonjudgmental observational data about incidents of student misbehavior. They then can work together to determine possible causes of the misbehavior, how best to deal with it, and what can be done to forestall future occurrences. Otherwise, student misbehavior is likely to accelerate and put the student teacher's progress in jeopardy.

5. *Collegiality and professionalism.* Marzano found in his review of research studies that students' academic achievement is better in schools where teachers act collegially toward each other. Collegiality involves such teacher practices as openly acknowledging and analyzing each other's successes and failures, and displaying

respect toward each other. Professionalism also plays a role in improving students' academic achievement. It involves various factors: feeling a sense of efficacy in one's work; having appropriate licenses and certificates; and having good subject-matter knowledge and pedagogical knowledge in one's areas of instructional responsibility.

Clinical supervisors can support collegiality and professionalism by modeling them in their own work. They can make collegiality a prominent feature of the work they do with teachers whom they are supervising and, at the preservice level, with the teachers in whose classrooms a preservice teacher is gaining experience. They can model professionalism by being knowledgeable about clinical supervision, school curriculum, and assessment.

A recent research study of middle schools supports the findings of Marzano's synthesis.[42] The researchers administered surveys to school administrators and teachers in 303 California middle schools and also collected students' scores on standardized achievement tests (the California Standards tests) of language arts

Table 4.4 Differences in School-level Practices between Middle Schools with Higher and Lower Levels of Student Academic Achievement

Middle-school students are more likely to have a higher level of achievement in language arts and mathematics if:

- they study a curriculum designed to prepare them for high school.
- their curriculum is coherent and well-aligned with the state's academic standards and state-adopted curriculum programs.
- administrators emphasize improving student achievement across all grades, closing subgroup achievement gaps, and getting as many students to proficient as possible.
- their teachers have uninterrupted instructional time.
- their teachers and the school principal frequently communicate with parents about the school's academic standards and students' progress, provide ways for parents to support their students' academic achievement, and have requirements or contracts for parent participation.
- their teachers and administrators make extensive use of data to improve instruction and student learning.
- their teachers and administrators provide early, proactive academic interventions for students with special needs, such as English learner students and students at risk of failure in the current school year.
- their teachers are provided with useful professional development, meaningful teacher evaluations, and time to collaborate to evaluate lessons and discuss student work.
- their teachers report that the middle grades are their current first choice of teaching assignment.
- the school principal ensures a clean, safe, and disciplined school environment.
- the superintendent evaluates school principals on their effectiveness in improving student achievement.

Source: Williams, T., Kirst, M. W., Haertel, E., et al. (2010). *Gaining ground in the middle grades: Why some schools do better.* Mountain View, CA: EdSource.

and mathematics. They analyzed the data to determine whether certain school-level practices differentiated between middle schools whose students had higher and lower scores on these tests (controlling for differences between the schools in such factors as socioeconomic status and parent education). Table 4.4 summarizes the main findings of the study. You can see that these findings are quite consistent with those of Marzano's synthesis, described above.

EFFECTIVE DEVELOPMENT OF STUDENT ATTITUDES AND MOTIVATION TO LEARN

Attitudes and learning motivation involve the affective domain of education. They are not easy terms to define, but their manifestations are easy to recognize. We can tell through observation whether students are eagerly involved in a learning task or bored by it. Most students, if asked, will tell you which school subjects they like and dislike.

Researchers distinguish three components of attitudes: beliefs, feelings, and actions. For example, a student who has a positive attitude toward mathematics might believe that math plays an important role in the world of work, experience positive feelings when working on a challenging math problem, and act by choosing to learn something new about mathematics rather than engaging in some other activity. Of the three components of attitudes, the most observable—and probably the most important—is action. By observing how students act in situations that allow choice, we can tell fairly well whether they have a positive or negative attitude toward an "object" (a person, event, book, place, etc.). A positive attitude is manifested by choosing to approach the object, whereas a negative attitude is manifested by choosing to avoid the object.

School attitudes can be internalized at different levels of personality. At a superficial level of internalization, the student is motivated to learn, but only with proper stimulation by the teacher. At the deepest level of internalization, the attitude has become an integral part of the student's personality. We can say that the attitude has become a value when it motivates much of the student's life without external prompting. David Krathwohl and colleagues developed a taxonomy that differentiated the various levels at which attitudes can be internalized.[43]

The development of positive academic attitudes is an important educational outcome, as John Dewey noted:

> Perhaps the greatest of all pedagogical fallacies is the notion that a person learns only the particular thing he is studying at the time. Collateral learning in the way of formation of enduring attitudes of likes and dislikes may be and often is much more important than the spelling lesson or lesson in geography or history that is learned. For these attitudes are fundamentally what count in the future.[44]

In the public school curriculum, academic knowledge and skills are given more emphasis than attitudes, yet some instructional outcomes involving attitudes can be found. Teachers of social studies typically want students to develop informed beliefs about important social issues and to act as responsible citizens. Teachers of foreign languages want students to appreciate the cultures that speak the language they are teaching. And teachers of scientific disciplines want students to value scientific inquiry and to develop an appreciation of the natural world.

Researchers have investigated the effects of teacher enthusiasm on student attitudes. A. Guy Larkins and colleagues reviewed this research and concluded that teaching with enthusiasm generally promotes positive student attitudes.[45] Indicators of teacher enthusiasm are described in Chapter 8 (see Conference Technique 2).

Another teaching technique whose effect on student attitudes has been investigated is use of praise. N. L. Gage reviewed this research and concluded that teacher praise has a positive effect on student attitudes.[46] More recent research suggests that the effectiveness of teacher praise depends on its content and context.[47] Guidelines for effective use of praise are presented in Chapter 10 (see Observation Technique 3).

Wilbert McKeachie and James Kulik reviewed research at the college level, comparing the effectiveness of the lecture method and the discussion method in changing attitudes.[48] They concluded that discussion is the more effective method. In a review of research involving younger students, Joyce Gall and M. D. Gall similarly concluded that the discussion method has positive effects on the attitudes of elementary- and high-school students.[49] However, discussions have the potential to be misused. For example, a discussion can reinforce existing negative attitudes, such as racial prejudice, if all the students in the group feel the same way about the topic being discussed.[50] This problem usually can be avoided by forming heterogeneous discussion groups.

Cooperative learning has become a popular teaching method in recent years. It is similar to the discussion method in that students contribute to each other's learning by working together in small groups. It differs from the discussion method, however, because it usually requires the completion of a specific academic task—such as a list of ideas, a visual display, or the solution to a problem—that can be evaluated and graded. By contrast, discussion does not usually have a tangible goal that can be evaluated, and students are not required to cooperate with each other, except by listening carefully to each other and avoiding personal attacks.

Research on cooperative learning has found that it is effective both for improving students' academic achievement and for developing important social attitudes. Robert Slavin, who reviewed this body of research, stated that these attitudinal outcomes include: increased liking and respect among students of different racial or ethnic backgrounds; improved social acceptance of mainstreamed students by their classmates; more friendships among students; gains in self-esteem; and increased liking of school and of the subject being discussed.[51]

Student motivation to learn is not quite the same thing as an attitude, but it is similar. We can think of motivation to learn as how the student feels about becoming engaged in instruction, whereas an attitude is how the student feels about a specific aspect of instruction, such as the topics being taught. For example, a student might not like learning calculus, but might be motivated to learn it, perhaps because it will increase his chances of college admission.

Jere Brophy identified two basic principles of motivating students to learn:

> In order to motivate their students to learn, teachers need both to help their students appreciate the value of academic activities and to make sure that the students can succeed in these activities if they apply reasonable effort.[52]

For example, if students believe that they are likely to fail their general science course even if they apply effort, they will lack motivation and develop a negative attitude toward the course and toward science generally. Also, if students do not see the relevance of science to their lives or do not value the consequences of doing well in the course (e.g., a good grade, teacher and parent approval), they will not be motivated to learn. Teaching methods that allow students to be successful or that show them the importance of the topic being studied are likely to be effective in improving students' motivation to learn.

Up to this point we have considered instructional methods for creating positive student attitudes and motivation. Unfortunately, some teachers act in ways that have the opposite effect. Carolyn Orange documented many of these inappropriate behaviors.[53] She collected her data by asking preservice teachers to write about their worst experience with a teacher. Here are two vignettes and Orange's analysis of them.

> **Vignette 1.** My high school junior English teacher was constantly on my case about talking (maybe because I'm a guy), but she would let the class valedictorian and salutatorian (both girls) talk away right next to me. I really disliked that teacher. That was the first time I ever got a C in any class.[54]

Orange suggests that the key to avoiding this type of inappropriate behavior is for teachers to avoid showing favoritism toward individual students or types of students (e.g. males and females, fast learners and slow learners).

> **Vignette 2.** The worst experience ever with a teacher was in kindergarten when a substitute teacher asked me to color a worksheet that had a witch on it. I decided to color my witch orange. After I had finished coloring my picture, I proudly went to show it to my substitute and she proceeded to tell me how ugly it was and that witches were supposed to be black, so she made me color it over in black.[55]

Orange suggests that teachers can avoid this negative effect on students' motivation by encouraging their creativity and originality rather than making premature artistic or value-laden judgments.

These and other teaching methods can improve students' attitudes and motivation to learn.[56] The implications for clinical supervision are clear. If a teacher is concerned about her students' attitude toward instruction, the supervisor and teacher can plan to collect observation data on the teacher's use of the practices described above—enthusiastic teaching style, praise, discussion, cooperative learning, the opportunity for students to experience academic success, and helping students see the relevance and value of learning.

TEACHER EFFECTIVENESS IN RESPONDING TO STUDENT DIVERSITY

In research on teacher effectiveness, the typical criterion is how much the teacher's class as a *whole* learns over a particular period of time. By this criterion, a teacher is effective if the mean score of the class on an achievement test increases from its first administration to the second. The mean score masks the possibility that the gain resulted from a small number of students benefiting substantially from a particular teaching method, with other students learning relatively little.

Some researchers do not look at classroom learning as a whole, but at whether teachers behave differently toward different groups of students. Other research concerns whether different teaching practices are effective for different groups of students. For example, teaching method A might be effective for male students, whereas teaching method B is effective for female students.

In this section, we review major findings on effective teaching for different types of students.

Effective Teaching of Students Who Differ in Achievement Level

Thomas Good reviewed the research literature on differential teacher treatment of high-achieving and low-achieving students.[57] He identified 17 teaching practices that are used with different frequencies with these two groups of students. The teaching practices are

Table 4.5 Differences in Teacher Behavior toward High-Achieving and Low-Achieving Students

1. Wait less time for "lows" to answer questions.
2. Give "lows" the answer or call on someone else rather than try to improve their responses by giving clues or using other teaching techniques.
3. Reward inappropriate behavior or incorrect answers by "lows."
4. Criticize "lows" more often for failure.
5. Praise "lows" less frequently then "highs" for success.
6. Fail to give feedback to the public responses of "lows."
7. Pay less attention to "lows" or interact with them less frequently.
8. Call on "lows" less often to respond to questions, or ask them only easier, nonanalytical questions.
9. Seat "lows" farther away from the teacher.
10. Demand less from "lows."
11. Interact with "lows" more privately than publicly and monitor and structure their activities more closely.
12. Grade tests or assignments in a differential manner, so that "highs" but not "lows" are given the benefit of the doubt in borderline cases.
13. Have less friendly interaction with "lows," including less smiling and less warm or more anxious voice tones.
14. Provide briefer and less informative feedback to the questions of "lows."
15. Provide less eye contact and other nonverbal communication of attention and responsiveness in interacting with "lows."
16. Make less use of effective but time-consuming instructional methods with "lows" when time is limited.
17. Evidence less acceptance and use of ideas given by "lows."

Source: Good, T. L. (1987). Two decades of research on teacher expectations: Findings and future directions. *Journal of Teacher Education, 38*(4), 32–47. Copyright © 1987 by the American Association of Colleges for Teacher Education. Reprinted by permission of SAGE Publications.

listed in Table 4.5. They define a pattern of diminished expectations for low-achieving students' ability to learn.

Academic achievement is highly correlated with social class, meaning that low-achieving students are more likely to come from disadvantaged home backgrounds, whereas high-achieving students are likely to come from advantaged home backgrounds. Therefore, the differential teaching practices listed in Table 4.5 suggest a pattern of discrimination based on students' social class as well as their achievement level.

If observational data reveal that a teacher treats high-achieving and low-achieving students differently, the clinical supervisor can help the teacher recognize this pattern of behavior and adopt more equitable and effective patterns. For example, suppose a teacher discovers that he waits less time for low-achieving students to respond than he waits for high-achieving students. The teacher might set the goal of giving low-achieving students at least as much time to respond, and perhaps more time if they need it.

Effective Teaching of Ethnically Diverse Students

There is research evidence that some teachers act differently toward students depending on their ethnic background. Gregg Jackson and Cecilia Cosca studied whether elementary and secondary teachers in the Southwest distribute their verbal behavior differentially among Anglo and Chicano students.[58] Using a modified form of the Flanders Interaction Analysis System (see Observation Technique 17), observers classified each verbal interaction and whether it was directed to, or initiated by, an Anglo student or a Chicano student.

Jackson and Cosca found that teachers directed significantly more of their verbal behaviors toward Anglo students than toward Chicano students. The teachers "praised or encouraged Anglos 35% more than they did Chicanos, accepted or used Anglos' ideas 40% more than they did those of Chicanos, and directed 21% more questions to Anglos than to Chicanos."[59] The researchers also found that Anglo students initiated more verbal behaviors than did Chicano students. In a review of related research, M. D. Gall and Joyce Gall found that black students tend to participate less in discussions than white students.[60]

These are older studies, so they might not accurately represent current teacher practice. However, because of the importance of student ethnicity and race, clinical supervisors should be sensitive to whether teachers provide equal opportunities for students of all ethnic backgrounds to learn.

Educators differ in what they consider effective teaching practices to accommodate for ethnic differences between students. The differences reflect different philosophies of multicultural education. James Banks distinguished between three such philosophies.[61] They are as follows:

1. *Cultural pluralism:* the goal of the curriculum is to help students function more effectively in their own ethnic culture and to help liberate them from ethnic oppression.

2. *Assimilationism:* the goal is to help students develop a commitment to the common culture and its values.

3. *Multiethnicism:* the goal is to help students learn how to function effectively within the common culture, their own ethnic culture, and other ethnic cultures.

Table 4.6 Effective Practices in Culturally Responsive Teaching

1. Acknowledging the legitimacy of the cultural heritages of different ethnic groups, both as legacies that affect students' dispositions, attitudes, and approaches to learning and as worthy content to be taught in the formal curriculum.
2. Building bridges of meaningfulness between home and school experiences as well as between academic abstractions and lived sociocultural realities.
3. Using a wide variety of instructional strategies that are connected to different learning styles.
4. Teaching students to know and praise their own and each others' cultural heritages.
5. Incorporating multicultural information, resources, and material in all the subjects and skills routinely taught in schools.

Source: Gay, G. (2000). *Culturally responsive teaching: Theory, research, & practice*. (p. 29). New York: Teachers College Press.

Clinical supervisors can help teachers clarify for themselves which of these philosophies, or other philosophy, guides their instruction. Otherwise, they run the risk of ignoring multicultural aspects of teaching, or, worse, succumbing to personal prejudices and thereby depriving some students of equal opportunity for learning.

Geneva Gay reviewed the literature on effective multicultural teaching practices and teacher characteristics to create a model of instruction that she labels *culturally responsive teaching*.[62] The key characteristics of culturally responsive teaching are listed in Table 4.6. (The characteristics are consistent with other syntheses of the literature on effective multicultural pedagogy.[63]) These probably are effective teaching practices and qualities, irrespective of the teacher's philosophy of multicultural education. The picture that emerges from the list is of a teacher who respects all students, takes responsibility for knowing about their cultural backgrounds, and uses this knowledge in his or her teaching.

Effective Teaching of Male and Female Students

Researchers have found that some teachers treat boys and girls differently during classroom instruction. For example, Jere Brophy found that teachers interact more frequently with boys, give them more feedback and help, and criticize and praise them more frequently.[64] These differences perhaps are more pronounced in traditionally male-stereotyped subjects, such as mathematics. For example, in research on fourth-grade mathematics classes, Elizabeth Fennema and Penelope Peterson found that teachers did the following:

1. initiated more interactions with boys for the purpose of socializing and classroom management.
2. received and accepted more "callout" responses from boys.
3. more frequently called on boys for both the answers and the explanations of how the answers were obtained when working on word problems.[65]

These findings indicate that teachers tend to treat boys more favorably than girls. If a teacher is observed to do this, the clinical supervisor can help the teacher reallocate interaction patterns so that girls are treated equitably. In the case of traditionally male-stereotyped subjects, more radical changes might be necessary. Fennema and Peterson found that competitive games tended to help boys learn basic math skills, but tended to interfere with girls' learning of these skills. A different pattern was found for cooperative learning activities: They tended to help girls, but not boys, learn math problem-solving skills. These findings suggest that teachers need to learn how to maintain an appropriate balance of competitive and cooperative activities, so that both boys and girls have equal opportunity to use learning styles that are effective for them. Fennema and Peterson also recommend, "Perhaps the most important thing that a teacher can do is to expect girls to work independently. Teachers should encourage girls to engage in independent learning behavior and praise them for participating in and performing well on high-level cognitive mathematics tasks."[66]

Although Fennema and Peterson's recommendations focus on mathematics instruction, they seem appropriate to other male-stereotyped subjects, such as the physical sciences and technology.

Effective Teaching in Response to Individual Students' Interests and Needs

The preceding discussion focused on effective methods for teaching particular groups of students, such as males and females or students who share a certain ethnicity. However, each student is also a unique individual. Teachers must attempt to understand and accommodate this uniqueness if they are to be truly effective.

Research knowledge about how teachers can effectively respond to individual diversity among students is scant. There has been some theoretical work, in particular, the theory of multiple intelligences developed by Howard Gardner.[67] However, there is little empirical research testing the theory's validity and its educational implications. At the present time, then, we must look to "best practices," that is, the practices recommended and used by expert teachers and other educators.[68] In general, best practices for accommodating student diversity involve:

- using the theory of multiple intelligences to identify and develop each student's strengths and weaknesses.
- acknowledging students' different interests by giving them choices with respect to curriculum, class assignments, and homework.
- representing facts, concepts, and skills in different forms (e.g., examples, analogies, videos, demonstrations) to accommodate individual differences in students' preferences for cognitive processing.
- providing extra time to complete assignments and tests for students who need it.
- providing extra instruction (e.g., by peer tutoring and cooperative learning) for students who need it.

Carol Ann Tomlinson compiled a list of these and other best practices for accommodating student diversity.[69] It is presented in Chapter 13 (see Observation Technique 16).

EFFECTIVE CLASSROOM MANAGEMENT

Daniel Duke defines classroom management as "the provisions and procedures necessary to establish and maintain an environment in which instruction and learning can occur."[70] This definition implies that classroom management is not the same thing as teaching, but is a necessary precondition for teaching. As one would expect, researchers have found that students' academic achievement is higher in well-managed classrooms.[71] This is probably because students are more on task in such classrooms, and their learning processes are better organized.

Many teachers, both preservice and inservice, have difficulty managing their classroom. This difficulty typically is manifested in two ways: (1) the progression of classroom events is disorganized and frequently interrupted, and (2) many of the students are off task. The occurrence of these problems is usually distressing for the teacher as well as for the clinical supervisor. Therefore, supervisors should know effective classroom management practices that can help the teacher bring the class under control.

Carolyn Evertson reviewed the research that she and others have done to identify practices used by teachers who are effective classroom managers.[72] The practices are listed in Table 4.7, and they demonstrate that carefully formulated rules and procedures are at the heart of a good classroom management system. Walter Doyle's comprehensive analysis of classroom management suggests that rules and procedures are needed for all the tasks and situations shown in Table 4.8.[73] The list of tasks and situations demonstrates that managing a classroom is a complex process. It also suggests how a class can easily get out of control if students do not have clear rules and procedures to follow.

Another important aspect of classroom management is the teacher's procedures for handling student misbehavior. Common types of misbehavior are: tardiness, cutting class,

Table 4.7 Practices of Teachers Who Are Effective Classroom Managers

Rules and Procedures

1. *Analysis.* The teacher carefully analyzes the rules and procedures that need to be in place so that students can learn effectively in the classroom setting.
2. *Description.* The teacher states the rules and procedures in simple, clear language so that students can understand them easily.
3. *Teaching.* The teacher systematically teaches the rules and procedures at the start of the school year, or when beginning a new course with new students.
4. *Monitoring.* The teacher continuously monitors students' compliance with the rules and procedures, while also maintaining careful records of their academic performance.

Physical Arrangement of Classroom and Supplies

1. *Visibility.* Students should be able to see the instructional displays. The teacher should have a clear view of instruction areas, students' work areas, and learning centers to facilitate monitoring of students.
2. *Accessibility.* High-traffic areas (areas for group work, pencil sharpener, door to the hall) should be kept clear and separated from each other.
3. *Distractibility.* Arrangements that can compete with the teacher for students attention (seating students facing the windows to the playground, door to the hall, face to face with each other but away from the teacher) should be minimized.
4. *Supplies.* The teacher takes care to secure an adequate supply to textbooks and materials for all the students in the classroom.

Source: Evertson, C. M. (1987). Managing classrooms: A framework for teachers. In Berliner, D. C., & Rosenshine, B.V. (Eds.). *Talks to teachers* (pp. 54–74). New York: Random House.

Table 4.8 Classroom Tasks and Situations for Which a Teacher Needs Rules and Procedures

1. Seat assignment in the classroom
2. Start and end of class (e.g., "Be in your seat and ready to work when the bell rings.")
3. Handing in of assignments, materials, etc.
4. Permissible activities if a student completes seatwork early
5. Leaving the room while class is in session
6. Standards for the form and neatness of one's desk, notebooks, assignments, etc.
7. Supplies and materials to be brought to class
8. Signals for seeking help or indicating a willingness to answer a teacher question addressed to the class as a whole
9. Acceptable noise level in the room
10. Acceptability of verbal and physical aggression
11. Moving around the room to sharpen pencils, get materials, etc.
12. Storage of materials, hats, boots, etc., in the classroom
13. Consumption of food and gum
14. Selection of classroom helpers
15. Late assignments and make-up work

Source: Doyle, W. (1986). Classroom organization and management. In M. C. Wittrock (Ed.), *Handbook of research on teaching* (3rd ed., pp. 392–431). New York: Macmillan.

failure to bring supplies and books to class, inattentiveness, noisiness, callouts, and verbal or physical aggression. Even effective teachers experience student misbehavior, but they manage it differently than less effective teachers. They deal with the misbehavior early before it has a chance to escalate and with the least disruption to the ongoing instruction—for example, by eye contact, physical proximity to the misbehaving student, or "the look." In the words of Walter Doyle, "successful interventions tend to have a private and fleeting quality that does not interrupt the flow of events."[74]

EFFECTIVE PLANNING AND DECISION MAKING

Madeline Hunter defined teaching as "the process of making and implementing decisions, before, during, and after instruction, to increase the probability of learning."[75] If this is true, it is important for the clinical supervisor to help teachers make the most effective decisions possible.

Teacher decisions that are made before and after instruction are commonly referred to as teacher planning. Christopher Clark and Penelope Peterson found in their review of research that teachers' plans influence the content of instruction, the sequence in which topics get taught, and the allocation of time to different topics and subjects.[76] Christopher Clark and Robert Yinger did a research study in which they found that teachers engage in as many as eight different types of planning during the course of a school year.[77] Two of the types—unit planning and lesson planning—involve the content of instruction. The other six types involve planning for different time spans of instruction: daily, weekly, short-range, long-range, term, and yearly. Clark and Yinger also found that planning is not a linear process and that it does not occur at a single point in time. Rather, teachers develop their plans incrementally, starting from a general idea and then gradually elaborating it. The development of their plans is influenced by their reflections on previous plans and experience in the classroom. Clark and Yinger's study involved elementary school teachers, but the findings seem equally applicable to teachers of other grade levels.

Clinical supervisors find that some teachers have difficulty with instruction because they do not plan effectively. One approach to helping these teachers is to ask them to make written lesson plans. However, the research reviewed above suggests that this approach is not sufficient, because it does not acknowledge the incremental, cyclical nature of lesson planning or the fact that other types of planning (e.g., unit, weekly) might be more important to a particular teacher. The writing of structured lesson plans might be a useful starting point for the development of planning skills, but it probably should not be the only focus of clinical supervision.

Besides planning decisions, teachers make decisions during the act of instruction. Called *interactive decisions*, they involve a deliberate choice to act in a specific way while teaching. Clark and Peterson, in their review of research, found that "on the average, teachers make one interactive decision every 2 minutes."[78] This research finding supports Madeline Hunter's characterization of teaching as a process of decision making.

Researchers have discovered several types of effective and ineffective interactive decision making.[79] One of them involves teachers' decision making when they judge students' classroom behavior to be unacceptable. Teachers who are prone to consider alternative teaching strategies to handle the problem, but who decide not to implement them, have lower-achieving classes. These teachers probably have a rigid teaching style. Supervisors need to help them learn how to make on-the-spot changes in teaching strategy to accommodate the circumstantial nature of student behavior in the classroom.

Another finding is that the decisions of effective teachers are more conceptually based, rapid, and simple than the decisions of less effective teachers. This finding suggests that clinical supervisors should recommend to teachers that they learn a conceptual model, or models, of teaching. A starting point might be to have teachers study the models presented in this chapter. An advantage of these models is that they simplify teachers' thinking by focusing their attention on salient aspects of instruction. A limited focus enables quick decisions and changes in actions without disturbing the flow of instruction.

EFFECTIVE IMPLEMENTATION OF CURRICULUM CHANGE

The school curriculum, which in our view also includes instruction and assessment, is constantly changing. The following are just a few examples of curriculum innovations currently being introduced into schools: standards-based instruction, interdisciplinary curriculum, thinking skills instruction, project-based learning, state-mandated standardized tests, and technology-enhanced curriculum. Even the traditional curriculum changes with each new textbook adoption.

The manner in which a teacher implements a curriculum change affects students' learning. For example, suppose a school district changes its mathematics curriculum to put more emphasis on problem solving. Teachers who implement the new curriculum fully will give their students more opportunity to learn mathematical problem-solving skills than teachers who implement it halfheartedly or not at all. As would be expected, researchers have found that students' opportunity to learn a curriculum affects how much of the curriculum they actually learn.[80]

The preceding analysis suggests that one aspect of effective teaching is implementation of curriculum change. Clinical supervisors should be sensitive to this aspect of teachers' work and help teachers who experience difficulty with it. To do this, supervisors need to be knowledgeable about the process of curriculum implementation and factors that affect it. The following discussion focuses on teacher characteristics that affect curriculum implementation. Research on other factors is reviewed in other sources. [81]

One of the supervisor's first tasks is to assess the teacher's level of implementation of the curriculum change. Gene Hall and Shirley Hord's research is relevant to this task.[82] They found that there are eight levels at which teachers can implement curriculum change. The levels are shown in Table 4.9. Hall and Hord developed several interview procedures that supervisors can use to determine at which of the eight levels a teacher is implementing a curriculum change.[83]

Supervisors also need to determine teachers' concerns about using the new curriculum. Hall and Hord found that these concerns follow a predictable progression of stages. (The stages parallel those in Francis Fuller's developmental model of teacher concerns, described in Chapter 2.) The first major stage is self concerns (e.g., "How will using it affect me?"). The second major stage is task concerns (e.g., "I seem to be spending all my time getting materials ready."). The third major stage is impact concerns (e.g., "How is my use of this innovation affecting kids?"). The supervisor can assess these concerns in the conference phase of the clinical supervision cycle. Another approach is to administer the Stages of Concern Questionnaire (SoCQ), a simple paper-and-pencil instrument consisting of 35 rating items.[84]

Walter Doyle and Gerald Ponder identified additional teacher concerns that affect teachers' implementation of a curriculum change.[85] They found that teachers follow a "practicality ethic" in deciding how much of a commitment to make to a curriculum change. The

---

Table 4.9 Levels at which Teachers Implement Educational Change

- *Level 0—nonuse.* The teacher has no knowledge of or involvement with the new curriculum.

- *Level I—orientation.* The teacher is acquiring information about the new curriculum.

- *Level II—preparation.* The teacher is preparing for first use of the new curriculum.

- *Level III—mechanical use.* The teacher is trying to master the basics of the new curriculum.

- *Level IVA—routine.* The teacher's use of the new curriculum is stabilized.

- *Level IVB—refinement.* The teacher varies use of the new curriculum to increase its impact on students.

- *Level V—integration.* The teacher combines his or her own efforts with those of colleagues to maximize the benefits of the new curriculum for students.

- *Level VI—renewal.* The teacher reevaluates his or her quality of use of the curriculum, modifies the new curriculum in a major way to improve its effectiveness, studies new developments relating to the curriculum, searches for new alternatives, and explores new goals for self-improvement or improvement of aspects of the school systems that relate to the curriculum.

Source: Hall, G. E., & Hord, S. M. (2001). *Implementing change: Patterns, principles, and potholes.* (p. 82). Boston: Allyn and Bacon.

practicality ethic involves judgments about whether the curriculum change is (1) clear and specific, (2) congruent with teachers' existing beliefs and practices, and (3) cost-effective in terms of benefits to students relative to teachers' expenditure of energy. Georgea Mohlman, Theodore Coladarci, and N. L. Gage did a research study that confirmed the importance of the practicality ethic in determining the extent to which teachers implement a curriculum change.[86]

A DEFINITION OF EFFECTIVE TEACHING

We invite you to develop your own definition of effective teaching by drawing on the body of research knowledge reviewed above. We undertook this exercise for ourselves and developed the following definition:

Effective teaching involves the ability to:

- provide instruction that helps students develop the knowledge, skills, and understandings intended by curriculum objectives.

- create an instructional climate that causes students to develop positive attitudes toward the teacher's class, the school, and oneself.

- adjust instruction so that all students learn, irrespective of their ability, gender, ethnicity, or other characteristics.

- manage the classroom so that students are engaged in learning all or most of the time.

- make sound decisions and plans that maximize students' opportunity to learn.

- respond to initiatives for curriculum change so that the new curriculum's intents are fully realized.

The research reviewed in this chapter demonstrates that there is a growing body of knowledge about teaching practices that can make teachers' instruction more effective. Because research is an ongoing enterprise, supervisors and teachers should stay informed about new findings. Instructional practices that are supported by research evidence should be viewed as possible alternatives to a teacher's current practices. We make this recommendation based on our view of clinical supervision as a process that involves reflection both on experience (as recorded by an impartial observer) and on research-based knowledge about effective teaching.

ENDNOTES

1. Chall, J. S. (2000). The academic achievement challenge: What really works in the classroom? New York: Guilford Press. Quote appears on p. 180.

2. Schmuck, R. A., & Schmuck, P. A. (2001). *Group processes in the classroom* (8th ed., pp. 292–293). Boston: McGraw-Hill.

3. Rosenshine, B., & Furst, N. (1973). The use of direct observation to study teaching. In R. M. W. Travers (Ed.), *Handbook of research on teaching* (2nd ed., pp. 122–183). Chicago: Rand McNally.

4. The characteristics of an indirect teaching style are described in the next section of this chapter.

5. Onwuegbuzie, A. J., Witcher, A. E., Collins, K. M. T., Filer, J. D., Wiedmaier, C. D., & Moore, C. W. (2007). Students' perceptions of characteristics of effective college teachers: A validity study of a teaching evaluation form using a mixed-methods analysis. *American Educational Research Journal, 44*(1), 113–160.

6. Flanders, N. A. (1970). *Analyzing teaching behavior.* Reading, MA: Addison-Wesley.

7. These studies are reviewed in: Gage, N. L. (1978). *The scientific basis of the art of teaching.* New York: Teachers College Press.

8. Rosenshine, B. V. (1986). Synthesis of research on explicit teaching. *Educational Leadership, 43*(7), 60–68.

9. Hunter, M. (1984). Knowing, teaching, and supervising. In P. L. Hosford (Ed.), *Using what we know about teaching* (pp. 169–192). Alexandria, VA: Association for Supervision and Curriculum Development. See also: Hunter, R. (2004). *Madeline Hunter's mastery teaching* (updated ed.). Thousand Oaks, CA: Corwin.

10. Rosenshine, "Synthesis," p. 60.

11. *Ibid.*, p. 62. Reprinted by permission of ASCD.

12. Bloom, B. S. (Ed.). *Taxonomy of educational objectives: The classification of educational goals.* Handbook 1: Cognitive domain. New York: Longman.

13. Cole, N. S. (1990). Conceptions of educational achievement. *Educational Researcher, 19*(3), 2–7. Quoted text copyright © by the American Educational Research Association. Reprinted by permission of Sage Publishers.

14. *Ibid.*, p. 2.

15. *Ibid.*, p. 3.

16. Gall, J. P., & Gall, M. D. (1990). Outcomes of the discussion method. In W. W. Wilen (Ed.), *Teaching and learning through discussion* (pp. 25–44). Springfield, IL: Charles C. Thomas.

17. Gall, M. D., & Gall, J. P. (1976). The discussion method. In N. L. Gage (Ed.), *The psychology of teaching methods: The seventy-fifth yearbook of the National Society for the Study of Education* (pp. 166–216). Chicago: University of Chicago Press.

18. Winne, P. H. (1979). Experiments relating teachers' use of higher cognitive questions to student achievement. *Review of Educational Research,* 49, 13–49.

19. Redfield, D. L., & Rousseau, E. W. (1981). A meta-analysis of experimental research on teacher questioning behavior. *Review of Educational Research,* 51, 237–245.

20. Rosenshine, B. V. (1976). Classroom instruction. In N. L. Gage (Ed.), *The psychology of teaching methods: The seventy-fifth yearbook of the National Society for the Study of Education* (pp. 334–371). Chicago: University of Chicago Press.

21. Hamaker, C. (1986). The effects of adjunct questions on prose learning. *Review of Educational Research,* 56, 212–242.

22. Brooks, J. G., & Brooks, M. G. (1993). *The case for constructivist classrooms.* Alexandria, VA: Association for Supervision and Curriculum Development. Quote appears on p. 15.

23. Marzano, R. J., Pickering, D. J., & Pollock, J. E. (2001). *Classroom instruction that works: Research-based strategies for increasing student achievement.* Alexandria, VA: Association for Supervision and Curriculum Development.

24. *Ibid.*

25. Windschitl, M. (1999). The challenges of sustaining a constructivist classroom culture. *Phi Delta Kappan, 80,* 751–755.

26. Shulman, L. S., & Quinlan, K. M. (1996). The comparative psychology of school subjects. In D. C. Berliner & R. C. Calfee (Eds.), *Handbook of educational psychology* (pp. 399–422). New York: Macmillan.

27. Ingersoll, R. (1999). The problem of underqualified teachers in American secondary schools. *Educational Researcher, 28*(2), 26–37.

28. Berliner, D. C. (1987). Knowledge is power: A talk to teachers about a revolution in the teaching profession. In D. C. Berliner & B. V. Rosenshine (Eds.), *Talks to teachers* (pp. 3–33). New York: Random House.

29. Borg, W. R. (1980). Time and school learning. In C. Denham & A. Lieberman (Eds.), *Time to learn* (pp. 33–72). Washington, DC: U.S. Department of Education.

30. Fisher, C. W., Berliner, D. C., Filby, N. N., Marliave, R., Cahen, L. S., & Dishaw, M. M. (1980). Teaching behaviors, academic learning time, and student achievement: An overview. In C. Denham & A. Lieberman (Eds.), *Time to learn* (pp. 7–32). Washington, DC: U.S. Department of Education.

31. Cooper, H. (1989). *Homework.* New York: Longman.

32. Bloom, B. S. (1984). The 2 sigma problem: The search for methods of group instruction as effective as one-to-one tutoring. *Educational Researcher, 13*(6), 4–16.

33. Richmond, E. (2009). A high school's leap from so-so to special. Retrieved from http://www.lasvegassun.com/news/2009/jul/27/high-schools-leap-so-so-special

34. These research studies have been the subject of several systematic reviews in recent years: Lauer, P. A., Akiba, M., Wilkerson, S. B., Apthorp, H. S., Snow, D., & Martin-Glenn, M. L. (2006). Out-of-school-time program: A meta-analysis of effects for at-risk students. *Review of Educational Research, 76*(2), 275–313; D'Agostino, J. V., & Murphy, J. A. (2004). A meta-analysis of reading recovery in United States schools. *Educational Evaluation and Policy Analysis, 26*(1), 23–38; Elbaum, B., Vaughn, S., Hughes, M. T., & Moody, S. W. (2000). How effective are one-to-one tutoring programs in reading for elementary students at risk for reading failure? A meta-analysis of the intervention research. *Journal of Educational Psychology, 49*(4), 605–619.

35. Brophy, J. (2001). Introduction. In J. Brophy (Ed.), *Advances in research on teaching: Vol. 8* (pp. 1–23). Oxford: JAI Elsevier; Brophy, J. (1999). *Teaching* (Educational Practices Series No. 1). Geneva: International Bureau of Education.

36. McEwan, E. K. (2002). *10 traits of highly effective teachers*. Thousand Oaks, CA: Corwin.

37. Mack-Kirschner, A. (2004). *Powerful classroom stories from accomplished teachers*. Thousand Oaks, CA: Corwin.

38. King, S. P., & Amon, C. (2008). Assessment data: A tool for student and teacher growth. In E. B. Mandinach & M. Honey (Eds.), *Data-driven school improvement: Linking data and learning* (pp. 71-86). New York: Teachers College Press.

39. *Ibid.*, p. 76.

40. Kizer, M. (2009, November 17). Giving failing schools a new outlook. *The Arizona Republic*. Retrieved from http://www.azcentral.com/arizonarepublic/local/articles/20091115edpueblo1115

41. Marzano, R. (2003). *What works in schools: Translating research into action*. Alexandria, VA: Association for Supervision and Curriculum Development.

42. Williams, T., Kirst, M. W., Haertel, E., et al. (2010). *Gaining ground in the middle grades: Why some schools do better*. Mountain View, CA: EdSource. Retrieved from http://www.edsource.org

43. Krathwohl, D. R., Bloom, B. S., & Masia, B. B. (1964). *Taxonomy of educational objectives. Handbook II: Affective domain*. New York: McKay.

44. Dewey, J. (1938). *Experience and education*. New York: Collier. Quote appears on p. 48.

45. Larkins, A. G., McKinney, C. W., Oldham-Buss, S., & Gilmore, A. C. (1985). *Teacher enthusiasm: A critical review*. Hattiesburg, MS: University of Southern Mississippi.

46. Gage, N. L., *The scientific basis of the art of teaching*, op. cit.

47. Brophy, J. (1981). Teacher praise: A functional analysis. *Review of Educational Research, 51*, 5–32.

48. McKeachie, W. J., & Kulik, J. A. (1975). Effective college teaching. In F. N. Kerlinger (Ed.), *Review of research in education* (Vol. 3, pp. 165–209). Itasca, IL: Peabody.

49. J. P. Gall & M. D. Gall, *op. cit.*

50. This phenomenon was observed in the following study: Mitnick, L. L., & McGinnies, E. (1958). Influencing ethnocentrism in small discussion groups through a film communication. *Journal of Abnormal and Social Psychology, 56*, 82–90.

51. Slavin, R. E. (1989/1990). Research on cooperative learning: Consensus and controversy. *Educational Leadership, 47*(4), 52–54.

52. Brophy, J. (1987). On motivating students. In D. C. Berliner & B. V. Rosenshine (Eds.), *Talks to teachers* (pp. 201–245). New York: Random House. Quote appears on p. 207.

53. Orange, C. (2000). *25 biggest mistakes teachers make and how to avoid them*. Thousand Oaks, CA: Corwin.

54. *Ibid.*, p. 44.

55. *Ibid.*, p. 142.

56. Some of these methods and the theories on which they are based are discussed in Wiseman, D. G., & Hunt, G. H. (2008). *Best practice in motivation and management in the classroom* (2nd ed.). Springfield, IL: Charles C. Thomas.

57. Good, T. L. (1987). Two decades of research on teacher expectations: Findings and future directions. *Journal of Teacher Education, 38*, 32–47.

58. Jackson, G., & Cosca, C. (1974). The inequality of educational opportunity in the Southwest: An observational study of ethnically mixed classrooms. *American Educational Research Journal, 11*, 219–229. The report of the Jackson and Cosca study used the term Anglo to refer to white persons not of Spanish-speaking background. The term Chicano was used to refer to Mexican Americans.

59. *Ibid.*, p. 227.

60. Gall & Gall, "Outcomes of the discussion method."

61. Banks, J. A. (1999). *An introduction to multicultural education*. Boston: Allyn and Bacon.

62. Gay, G. (2000). *Culturally responsive teaching: Theory, research, & practice*. New York: Teachers College Press.

63. Foster, M. (1995). African American teachers and culturally relevant pedagogy. In J. A. Banks & C. A. M. Banks (Eds.), *Handbook of research on multicultural education* (pp. 570–581). New York: Macmillan; see also the set of multicultural competencies identified as important for psychologists serving clients: Hansen, N. D., Pepitone-Arreola-Rockwell, F., & Greene, A. F. (2000). Multicultural competence: Criteria and case examples. *Professional Psychology, 31*, 652–660.

64. Brophy, J. E. (1985). Interactions of male and female students with male and female teachers. In L. C. Wilkinson & C. B. Marrett (Eds.), *Gender influences in classroom interaction* (pp. 115–142). Orlando, FL: Academic Press.

65. Fennema, E., & Peterson, P. L. (1987). Effective teaching for boys and girls: The same or different? In D. C. Berliner & B. V. Rosenshine (Eds.), *Talks to teachers* (pp. 111–125). New York: Random House.

66. *Ibid.*, p. 124.

67. Gardner, H, (1983). *Frames of mind: The theory of multiple intelligences.* New York: Basic Books.

68. See for example: Campbell, L., & Campbell, B. (1999). *Multiple intelligences and student achievement: Success stories from six schools.* Alexandria, VA: Association for Supervision and Curriculum Development.

69. Tomlinson, C. A. (1999). *The differentiated classroom: Responding to the needs of all learners.* Alexandria, VA: Association for Supervision and Curriculum Development.

70. Duke, D. L. (1979). Editor's preface. In D. L. Duke (Ed.), *Classroom management: The seventy-eighth yearbook of the National Society for the Study of Education* (Part 2, pp. xi–xv). Chicago: University of Chicago Press.

71. This research has been the subject of several reviews, including Marzano, R. J., Marzano, J. S., & Pickering, D. J. (2003). *Classroom management that works: Research-based strategies for every teacher.* Alexandria, VA: Association for Supervision and Curriculum Development; Evertson, C. M. (1987). Managing classrooms: A framework for teachers. In D. C. Berliner & B. V. Rosenshine (Eds.), *Talks to teachers* (pp. 52–74). New York: Random House.

72. Evertson, C. M. (1987). Managing classrooms: A framework for teachers. In D. C. Berliner & B. V. Rosenshine (Eds.), *Talks to teachers* (pp. 52–74). New York: Random House.

73. Doyle, W. (1986). Classroom organization and management. In M. C. Wittrock (Ed.), *Handbook of research on teaching* (3d ed., pp. 392–431). New York: Macmillan.

74. *Ibid.*, p. 421.

75. Hunter, M. (1979). Teaching is decision making. *Educational Leadership, 37*(1), 62–67. Quote appears on p. 62.

76. Clark, C. M., & Peterson, P. L. (1986). Teachers' thought processes. In M. C. Wittrock (Ed.), *Handbook of research on teaching* (3d ed., pp. 255–296). New York: Macmillan.

77. Clark, C. M., & Yinger, R. J. (1979). *Three studies of teacher planning* (Research Series No. 55). East Lansing: Michigan State University.

78. Clark & Peterson, "Teachers' thought processes," p. 274.

79. Doyle, W. (1977). Learning the classroom environment: An ecological analysis. *Journal of Teacher Education, 28*, 51–55; Morine. G., & Vallance, E. (1975). *Special study B: A study of teacher and pupil perceptions of classroom interaction* (Technical Report No. 75-11-6). San Francisco: Far West Laboratory for Educational Research and Development; Peterson, P. L., & Clark, C. M. (1978). Teachers' reports of their cognitive processes during teaching. *American Educational Research Journal, 15*, 555–565.

80. Rosenshine & Furst, "The use of direct observation to study teaching."

81. See for example: Fullan, M. (2007). *The new meaning of educational change* (4th ed.). New York: Teachers College Press.

82. Hall, G. E., & Hord, S. M. (2001). *Implementing change: Patterns, principles, and potholes.* Boston: Allyn and Bacon.

83. *Ibid.*, Chapter 5.

84. The SoCQ and scoring procedures are described in chapter 4 and several appendices of Hall and Hord, *ibid.*

85. Doyle, W., & Ponder, G. (1977). The practicality ethic and teacher decision-making. *Interchange, 8*(3), 1–12.

86. Mohlman, G. G., Coladarci, T., & Gage, N. L. (1982). Comprehension and attitude as predictors of implementation of teacher training. *Journal of Teacher Education, 32*, 31–36.

Chapter 5

Using Clinical Supervision in Teacher Evaluation

In developing or redesigning local teacher evaluation systems, we must eventually answer two questions: What do we believe good teaching looks like? What are the processes and procedures that will best fit what we want our system to accomplish?

—Charlotte Danielson & Thomas McGreal[1]

INTRODUCTION

Teacher evaluation has multiple purposes, including the following:

- in preservice education, to determine whether a student is sufficiently competent to earn certification as a professional teacher; in inservice education, to determine whether a teacher's performance is sufficiently strong to warrant tenure or contract renewal.

- in preservice education, to determine whether a student's progress is so weak that a remediation process outside the usual teacher education program needs to be considered; in inservice education, to determine whether a teacher's work performance is so deficient that a remediation process needs to be considered.

- in preservice education, to determine whether a student's performance is so inadequate that dismissal from the program needs to be considered; in inservice education, to determine whether a teacher is so incompetent that dismissal proceedings need to be considered.

- in preservice or inservice education, to recognize extraordinary performance, which might lead to letters of commendation, merit pay increases, special assignments (e.g., a mentorship role), or other rewards.

- in preservice or inservice education, to provide feedback about the current level of performance, which can stimulate the teacher to search for ways to reach a higher level of performance.

- to assure parents, the general public, and legislators that the funds allocated for preservice programs or inservice teaching personnel are buying competent performance.

- in preservice or inservice education, to assure students that they are receiving instruction from competent teachers.

Central to all these purposes for teacher evaluation is the concept of teacher competence. A teacher evaluator must have clearly defined and defensible competence standards and methods for determining whether a teacher's performance on each standard is unsatisfactory, satisfactory, or exemplary.

Standards of teacher competence can be identified by three different methods. One method is to analyze the salient features of teacher work and state each feature as a standard. For example, if we watch teachers at work, we see that they explain new curriculum content, assign seatwork and homework, and create tests and other measures to assess student learning. On the basis of this job analysis, we might claim that teachers are competent if they meet the following standards: they explain new curriculum content well; they assign relevant, appropriate seatwork and homework; and they create performance measures that are well aligned with curriculum content and appropriate to students' developmental level.

Another method for identifying standards of teacher competence is to refer to what we think teachers *should* do in the workplace. For example, we might believe that teachers should strive for social justice in the classroom and incorporate relevant technology in classroom instruction. We might value these teaching practices and use them as evidence of teaching competence, even though they have not yet been adopted as part of teachers' work culture. In a sense, these criteria represent an ideal toward which teachers should aspire.

The third method for identifying standards of teacher competence is to examine theories and empirical research findings about teaching. This is the kind of research and theory that we reviewed in Chapter 4. We can justify standards of teacher competence, such as use of higher-cognitive questions and a high rate of at-task time in the classroom, by referring to empirical evidence that demonstrates their role in promoting some aspect of student learning.

You should be able to refer to one of more of these three methods if you are asked to explain how the standards of teacher competence in your teacher evaluation system were derived. Even if you use standards established by an authoritative organization, such as a state department of education or national professional education association, this is not evidence in itself that the standards are valid. You need to understand the method by which they were derived and whether that method produced defensible standards.

STANDARDS OF TEACHER COMPETENCE

In the following sections, we examine several sources of teacher-competence standards, including those specified in Chapter 4.

State Standards

Many—if not all—state departments of education have established standards of teacher competence and made them easily available, typically by putting them on the Internet. Iowa is a case in point. Its standards are shown in Table 5.1. Specific performance standards (called *criteria* in the table) are organized under eight general standards. Criteria under the first two standards emphasize that the teacher's main role is to promote student learning and that the teacher must have content expertise to perform this role effectively. The criteria under the next four standards (3–6) involve the teacher's performance in the classroom. The final set of criteria (7–8) state that a competent teacher must act as a professional within an organizational setting.

Table 5.1 Iowa Teaching Standards and Model Criteria

The Iowa Teaching Standards appear in Iowa Code section 284.3. The Model Criteria were developed by the Iowa Department of Education with input from stakeholders and adopted by the State Board of Education on May 10, 2002.

Standard 1. Demonstrates ability to enhance academic performance and support for implementation of the school district's student achievement goals.
Model Criteria
The teacher:

    a. Provides evidence of student learning to students, families, and staff.

    b. Implements strategies supporting student, building, and district goals.

    c. Uses student performance data as a guide for decision making.

    d. Accepts and demonstrates responsibility for creating a classroom culture that supports the learning of every student.

    e. Creates an environment of mutual respect, rapport, and fairness.

    f. Participates in and contributes to a school culture that focuses on improved student learning.

    g. Communicates with students, families, colleagues, and communities effectively and accurately.

Standard 2. Demonstrates competence in content knowledge appropriate to the teaching position.
Model Criteria
The teacher:

    a. Understands and uses key concepts, underlying themes, relationships, and different perspectives related to the content area.

    b. Uses knowledge of student development to make learning experiences in the content area meaningful and accessible for every student.

    c. Relates ideas and information within and across content areas.

    d. Understands and uses instructional strategies that are appropriate to the content area.

Standard 3. Demonstrates competence in planning and preparing for instruction.
Model Criteria
The teacher:

    a. Uses student achievement data, local standards, and the district curriculum in planning for instruction.

    b. Sets and communicates high expectations for social, behavioral, and academic success of all students.

    c. Uses student's developmental needs, backgrounds, and interests in planning for instruction.

    d. Selects strategies to engage all students in learning.

    e. Uses available resources, including technologies, in the development and sequencing of instruction.

Standard 4. Uses strategies to deliver instruction that meets the multiple learning needs of students.
Model Criteria
The teacher:

a. Aligns classroom instruction with local standards and district curriculum.

b. Uses research-based instructional strategies that address the full range of cognitive levels.

c. Demonstrates flexibility and responsiveness in adjusting instruction to meet student needs.

d. Engages students in varied experiences that meet diverse needs and promote social, emotional, and academic growth.

e. Connects students' prior knowledge, life experiences, and interests in the instructional process.

f. Uses available resources, including technologies, in the delivery of instruction.

Standard 5. Uses a variety of methods to monitor student learning.
Model Criteria
The teacher:

a. Aligns classroom assessment with instruction.

b. Communicates assessment criteria and standards to all students and parents.

c. Understands and uses the results of multiple assessments to guide planning and instruction.

d. Guides students in goal-setting and assessing their own learning.

e. Provides substantive, timely, and constructive feedback to students and parents.

f. Works with other staff and building and district leadership in analysis of student progress.

Standard 6. Demonstrates competence in classroom management.
Model Criteria
The teacher:

a. Creates a learning community that encourages positive social interaction, active engagement, and self-regulation for every student.

b. Establishes, communicates, models, and maintains standards of responsible student behavior.

c. Develops and implements classroom procedures and routines that support high expectations for student learning.

d. Uses instructional time effectively to maximize student achievement.

e. Creates a safe and purposeful learning environment.

Standard 7. Engages in professional growth.
Model Criteria
The teacher:

a. Demonstrates habits and skills of continuous inquiry and learning.

b. Works collaboratively to improve professional practice and student learning.

(Continued)

Table 5.1 Cont'd

c. Applies research, knowledge, and skills from professional development opportunities to improve practice.

d. Establishes and implements professional development plans based upon the teacher's needs aligned to the Iowa teaching standards and district/building student achievement goals.

Standard 8. Fulfills professional responsibilities established by the school district.
Model Criteria
The teacher:

a. Adheres to board policies, district procedures, and contractual obligations.

b. Demonstrates professional and ethical conduct as defined by state law and district policy.

c. Contributes to efforts to achieve district and building goals.

d. Demonstrates an understanding of and respect for all learners and staff.

e. Collaborates with students, families, colleagues, and communities to enhance student learning.

Source: http://www.iowa.gov/educate/index.php?option=com_content&view=article&id=1684 &Itemid=2486.

The competency standards in Table 5.1 include a statement that they were created by the Iowa Department of Education and stakeholders. There is no description of which of the three methods described above were used to derive them. From our perspective, the standards appear to be based on an analysis of commonalities in teachers' work across grade levels and subject areas and also on commonly accepted notions of what it means to be a professional.

Information at the website for the Iowa Department of Education indicates that the standards are to be used both for teacher evaluation and teachers' professional development. We believe that there is no inconsistency in using the same criteria for both purposes, a point that we will discuss later in the chapter.

School District Standards

School districts might adopt state standards for teacher competence completely or with modifications, or create their own. For example, the San Francisco School District in California lists five standards modified from the California Standards for the Teaching Profession.

- Standard 1: Engaging and supporting all students in learning.
- Standard 2: Creating and maintaining an effective environment for learning.
- Standard 3: Understanding and organizing subject matter knowledge.
- Standard 4: Planning, designing, and delivering learning experiences for all students.
- Standard 5: Assessing student learning.
- Standard 6: Developing as a professional educator.[2]

These standards for teacher competence are similar to those of other school districts in different states that we have examined on the Internet. Also, in most cases, the district standards are derived from state standards.

A school district's standards for teaching competence can be used to create job descriptions. Indeed, it is essential to anchor job descriptions for teachers in these standards. Otherwise, teachers might claim that their evaluation was unfair, because it assessed aspects of their performance that were outside the scope of responsibilities specified in the job description. A particular teaching position might include special responsibilities, in which case they can be included in the job description and specified as standards of performance to be evaluated.

Standards Published by Professional Organizations

Some professional organizations have developed standards of teacher competence. Among them are the National Council on Accreditation of Teacher Education (NCATE), the National Board for Professional Teaching Standards (NBPTS), and the Council of Chief State School Officers' Interstate New Teacher Assessment and Support Consortium (INTASC).

The teacher competence criteria developed by INTASC are particularly interesting, because they specify knowledge, dispositions, and performances as separate types of teacher competence. To illustrate, Table 5.2 shows the knowledge, dispositions, and performances for one of the six standards, called *principles* by INTASC. (Although the standards shown in Table 5.2 were developed for evaluating and supporting the development of new teachers, they appear to be equally appropriate for experienced teachers.) The INTASC standards remind us of the complexity of teaching and that behavioral performance, while important, is not the only framework for viewing teacher competence. Teachers' knowledge and values are important in their own right. Without a solid knowledge base and values that focus on the needs of students, the teacher is a technician, not a full-fledged professional.

Standards Cited in Teacher Dismissal Cases

Edwin Bridges found that courts generally accept standards of competence used by school districts in cases involving disputes about a teacher dismissal.[3] He cites the following standards that have served as bases for dismissals in cases heard at the appellate court level:

1. knowledge of the subject matter
2. ability to impart knowledge effectively
3. ability to obtain the respect of parents and students
4. proper use of corporal punishment
5. willingness to accept teaching advice from superiors
6. adequate academic progress of students
7. ability to maintain discipline
8. physical ability to perform the duties of a teacher
9. emotional stability[4]

Bridges' list reminds us that standards of teacher competence are not just ideals or boilerplate statements in official documents. Rather, they are statements of expectations

Table 5.2 Sample Standard of Teaching Competence Developed by the Interstate New Teacher Assessment and Support Consortium

Principle #6: *The teacher uses knowledge of effective verbal, nonverbal, and media communication techniques to foster active inquiry, collaboration, and supportive interaction in the classroom.*

Knowledge	Dispositions	Performances
The teacher understands communication theory, language development, and the role of language in learning.	The teacher recognizes the power of language for fostering self-expression, identity development, and learning.	The teacher models effective communication strategies in conveying ideas and information and in asking questions (e.g. monitoring the effects of messages, restating ideas and drawing connections, using visual, aural, and kinesthetic cues, being sensitive to nonverbal cues given and received).
The teacher understands how cultural and gender differences can affect communication in the classroom.	The teacher values many ways in which people seek to communicate and encourages many modes of communication in the classroom.	The teacher supports and expands learner expression in speaking, writing, and other media.
The teacher recognizes the importance of nonverbal as well as verbal communication.	The teacher is a thoughtful and responsive listener.	The teacher knows how to ask questions and stimulate discussion in different ways for particular purposes, for example, probing for learner understanding, helping students articulate their ideas and thinking processes, promoting risk-taking and problem-solving, facilitating factual recall, encouraging convergent and divergent thinking, stimulating curiosity, helping students to question.
The teacher knows about and can use effective verbal, nonverbal, and media communication techniques.	The teacher appreciates the cultural dimensions of communication, responds appropriately, and seeks to foster culturally sensitive communication by and among all students in the class.	The teacher communicates in ways that demonstrate a sensitivity to cultural and gender differences (e.g. appropriate use of eye contact, interpretation of body language and verbal statements, acknowledgment of and responsiveness to different modes of communication and participation).
		The teacher knows how to use a variety of media communication tools, including audiovisual aids and computers, to enrich learning opportunities.

Source: Council of Chief State School Officers. (1992). Model standards for beginning teacher licensing, assessment, and development: A resource for state dialogue (pp. 25–26). Washington, DC: Author. http://www.ccsso.org/content/pdfs/corestrd.pdf

for teacher performance that, if not met at a satisfactory level, can have serious negative consequences for a teacher's current job and future career.

Standards Based on Student Learning Gains

Our analysis of state, district, and professional-organization standards for teacher competence indicates that they are based primarily on teachers' performance of customary instructional functions and adherence to principles of professionalism. We have not found sets of standards that are explicitly based on research findings about teaching effectiveness.

The purpose of such research is to identify teaching practices that produce significant gains in student learning, typically measured by standardized tests. In this research, then, the ultimate standard of teaching competence is progress in student learning. Why not then evaluate teacher competence directly by determining how much the teacher's students learn? If we took this approach, there would be no need to evaluate teachers on other types of competence standards, such as those listed in Tables 5.1 and 5.2.

In fact, there is a growing national movement to evaluate teachers by this standard. Its most visible manifestation at the present time is a multibillion-dollar federal project, called the Race to the Top Fund. To be eligible for these funds, states must make certain innovations, including the use of annual teacher evaluations in which the academic achievement gains of the teacher's students serve as one of the primary standards of competence.

Support for this approach comes from a recent research study of middle schools in California with high and low student achievement gains.[5] The sample of middle schools was subdivided into two categories: those serving primarily lower socioeconomic-status (SES) students and those serving primarily higher-SES students. The researchers found that in the former group, principals of schools with greater student achievement gains were more likely to use student progress and achievement data as part of their teacher evaluations. Interestingly, in schools with primarily higher-SES students, principals' use or nonuse of these types of data for teacher evaluation did not affect student achievement gains. A possible interpretation of this finding is that academic achievement motivation is already present in higher-SES schools, so it is not critical to focus on student achievement through the teacher evaluation process. In lower-SES schools, academic achievement motivation perhaps cannot be taken as much for granted, so it makes a difference if the principal highlights the importance of student achievement in various ways, including having it as a key standard of competence in the teacher evaluation process.

"Report cards" are mandated by the national No Child Left Behind Act (see Chapter 13). They indicate whether students are making adequate yearly progress on standardized tests of language arts and mathematics. Report cards can be created for the aggregate of all schools in a state, or its school districts, or for individual schools. Report cards can even be created for individual teachers, and thus become potential data for use in teacher evaluation. This possibility has met with strong resistance from teachers and teacher unions, but others approve of it, including some legislators.

As a clinical supervisor, you might be called on to state your own position on student achievement gains as a criterion of teacher competence. Our own position is that student achievement gains are a worthwhile standard in theory, but difficult to employ in practice. One concern is whether the test used to measure student achievement is valid, reliable, and aligned with the teacher's curriculum. The development of tests that satisfy these requirements is difficult and expensive.

Another concern is that factors other than teacher competence influence student achievement. Consider this point in relation to the medical profession. Suppose doctors were held accountable for their patients' health status. A moment's reflection would tell us that a doctor might prescribe a good treatment plan for a patient, but it will be ineffective if the patient does not follow it. Should we hold the doctor accountable for this patient's health improvement? We think most people would answer no. Suppose, though, that the doctor ignored or did not know about a sound, research-validated treatment plan, and instead prescribed a poor treatment plan, which the patient followed carefully and then experienced a decline in health. Should we hold the doctor responsible for this patient's health status? Most people, we think, would answer yes.

The point of this example is to demonstrate that student achievement outcomes and the outcomes associated with other professions are determined by multiple factors. Therefore, an evaluator needs to identify relevant factors, collect data about them, and draw defensible conclusions from them. It is particularly useful to collect observation data about the teacher's classroom instruction. If they are available, the evaluator and teacher can examine them for indications that the behavior of the teacher and students in class facilitated or detracted from the learning process.

A SYSTEMATIC PROCESS FOR TEACHER EVALUATION

For teacher evaluation to be useful and defensible, teacher education programs, school districts, or other organizations should develop a systematic, well-documented process for it. In our view, this process should include the three main phases of clinical supervision: planning conference, data collection, and feedback conference. We explain each phase in the next sections.

Planning Conference

In clinical supervision a planning process centers around the teacher's concerns and goals for professional improvement (see Chapter 8). In teacher evaluation, however, the planning conference centers around the standards for teacher competence established by the school district or teacher education program. The teacher should have the opportunity to examine these standards prior to the planning conference and to ask questions about them during the conference. Also, the teacher should have the opportunity to state his or her goals for professional development and how he or she has worked toward them since the last formal evaluation of his performance.

The planning conference also should include a review of the procedures that will be used to collect data relating to the standards. At this time the teacher should have an opportunity to state any circumstances that might affect the appropriateness of these procedures. For example, if classroom observation data are to be collected, the teacher should have a say about which class lessons are suitable for this purpose. If observations will focus on how the teacher interacts with students and explains new concepts, it would not make sense for the evaluator to visit the class during a lesson in which students will spend most of their time working on an independent project. If students will be asked to complete a teacher evaluation checklist (see Chapter 13), the teacher needs to be able to examine it to determine whether all the students have the skills and regular class attendance required to complete it.

A planning conference of 45 minutes to an hour or more increases a teacher's understanding of the evaluation process and helps make it less threatening. If the teacher can participate in designing the data collection process, he or she is likely to feel more ownership for it and see it as an opportunity for professional development rather than as just a summary judgment of his or her competence.

Data Collection

The success of a teacher evaluation depends on the quality of the data that are used to judge whether or not he has met specified standards of teacher competence. The teacher should see a clear relationship between each type of data that is collected and the standard of competence to which it relates.

As a general rule, the more data collected about a teacher's performance, the better. If the evaluator can collect observational data on three of the teacher's lessons, that is better than collecting data on one of them. If the teacher can present a portfolio of lesson plans and student work (see Observation Technique 12), that is better than just having a script tape (see Observation Technique 9) of a single lesson. If data are collected from both a student rating scale (see Observation Technique 15) and an observer-administered checklist (see Observation Technique 16), that is better than data from either one alone.

Multiple data sources take time to implement and analyze. Because time is a precious commodity in education, the evaluator must consider how much data about each teacher can be reasonably collected. Sufficient data should be collected to give teachers confidence that the evaluation process is fair and valid. As an example, consider the data collection techniques in Table 5.3. We created them with limited resources in mind and with a focus on collecting data about instructional factors that researchers have found to facilitate student learning (see Chapter 4).

When time for evaluation must be rationed, priority should be given to teachers whose competence has been called into question for one reason or another. For these teachers, multiple types of data and extended data collection periods can be used to develop strong documentation of the teacher's strengths and weaknesses. This documentation then becomes credible evidence for making decisions about certification, tenure within a school district, remediation, or dismissal. The same documentation also can be used to help the teacher design a plan for development of professional skills that do not yet meet standards of competence.

Feedback Conference

In clinical supervision, the primary purpose of a feedback conference is for the participants to reflect on observational data and use those reflections to consider how future clinical supervision cycles or other forms of professional development can improve the teacher's

Table 5.3 Suggested List of Data Collection Techniques for Teachers' Annual Evaluation

1. At-task chart (technique 6 in Chapter 11). An observer completes a seating chart showing students' at-task behavior during one or more lessons. At-task behavior has been found to be associated with student learning, and it is a good indicator of the teacher's ability to manage a classroom so that the available time is used for instruction, not for student behavioral problems.

2. Script tape (technique 9 in Chapter 12). An observer makes a script tape of one or more lessons. In the note-taking part of the script tape, the observer describes teacher and student behavior during the lesson. In the note-making part, the observer describes strengths and weaknesses associated with the behavior that was described in the note-taking part.

3. Achievement test scores (technique 13 in Chapter 13). NCLB report card data for the teacher would be culled from the school district's database, if available. In addition, the evaluator and teacher can use part of the planning conference to identify teacher-made tests and other measures that would be appropriate for assessing how well students are learning. For example, at the upper grade levels, teachers typically give unit tests that measure learning over a period of weeks or months. The teacher can submit a copy of the test, students' scores on it, and an analysis of what the scores demonstrate about their learning gains.

4. Student rating scale (technique 15 in Chapter 13). A person other than the teacher can give students a questionnaire on which they rate the teacher on various factors associated with teaching effectiveness.

5. Curriculum alignment (technique 14 in Chapter 13). The teacher can bring a list of state or district curriculum standards that relate to his classroom curriculum to the planning conference. The teacher and evaluator can consider what kinds of evidence could be submitted to demonstrate that his classroom curriculum is aligned with the state or school curriculum. Possibilities are lesson plans, student worksheets, and homework assignments.

instructional skills. The feedback conference in teacher evaluation can serve these purposes, too, but its main purpose is to give the teacher an opportunity to concur or disagree with the data and the conclusions that the evaluator has reached on the basis of them.

The evaluator must listen carefully to the teacher and consider whether the evaluation report needs to be revised. We ourselves have made revisions to personnel evaluation reports after listening to a teacher's feedback. In some cases, the teacher objects to certain phrases that seem overly harsh or unjustified. In other cases, teachers have explained how poor student performance can be attributed, at least in part, to factors other than the teacher's skills. We revised the report to reflect these factors. A teacher who has had an opportunity to review the evaluation report and the data on which it is based is more likely to view the evaluation process as fair and productive than a teacher who simply receives an evaluation report by mail or other means.

If a preservice or inservice teacher has received a favorable evaluation, the feedback conference can end on a positive, congratulatory note. The teacher and evaluator might discuss the next steps in the teacher's career, including opportunities for new learning that will advance her career and improve her instructional skills. If the evaluation report indicates an unsatisfactory level of competence, the feedback conference will take a different turn. The evaluator will need to discuss the consequences of this judgment with the teacher. We discuss these consequences in the next two sections.

Postconference Consequences for Preservice Teachers

At the preservice level, the consequences of a negative evaluation might involve termination from the teacher education program or additional student teaching and coursework. These consequences are likely to be emotionally distressing for the teacher, particularly if they have a financial impact. For example, if remedial student teaching and coursework are necessary, the teacher might incur substantial tuition costs that he or she did not plan for. The evaluator will need to counsel the teacher through the process of considering his or her options, or ask someone else to perform this role.

In our experience, preservice teachers are willing to accept the consequences of a negative evaluation if they understand the data on which the evaluation was based and accept their validity. Even preservice teachers who are terminated can come to accept this decision if given sufficient time to process it and realize that while the door to a teaching career has been closed, doors to other careers remain open.

Postconference Consequences for Inservice Teachers

At the inservice level, an evaluation report might be mostly positive while mentioning a few minor instructional weaknesses. In this situation, the evaluator and teacher can discuss options for remediating them. The evaluator might recommend that the teacher be given release time to observe the classrooms of teachers who are strong in the instructional skills that the teacher lacks. Other options might be for a school administrator to assign a mentor teacher or a clinical supervisor to help the teacher.

A more negative evaluation report might include a finding that the teacher has failed to meet one or more of the school district's standards of teacher competence. The consequences of such a judgment will depend on three levels of law that ensure a due process for the teacher—contract, state, and constitutional.[6] A teacher relatively new to a school district is likely to be on probationary status, and there might be no legal requirement to renew his or her contract for the following school year; the school district might choose this option or decide to offer remedial assistance and a contract renewal. Removal of a teacher with tenure in a school district is typically a much more difficult matter. There are likely to be legal requirements for due process mandating that before the teacher is summarily dismissed for lack of competence, there must be an effort to help remedy the deficiencies. One way to do this is through an official plan of assistance.

When a plan of assistance is required, often the principal who put the teacher on notice is expected to design it and carry it out. If there is tension between the principal and the teacher, as there often is, it will be difficult to conduct a truly helpful remedial program. Therefore, we recommend the formation of a small committee to assume this responsibility. One member should be a neutral administrator who does not have direct supervisory responsibility for the teacher; another might be a person chosen by the teacher to serve as his advocate. The third person should be someone with special knowledge, expertise, or skill in the standards in which the teacher is deficient. This person should have strong clinical supervision skills.

The committee should reach an agreement on what types of professional development should be included in the plan of assistance, how long it will last, and what will be accepted as satisfactory evidence that the deficiencies have been remedied. The committee can call on other people and resources to carry out the planned activities.

A plan of assistance might not bring a teacher to a satisfactory level of competence. If the teacher has tenure in the school district and does not agree with this judgment, additional processes are almost always necessary—grievances, arbitration, hearings, and even lawsuits. There are several implications for clinical supervision techniques in connection with these occurrences. Consider an observer on the witness stand being cross-examined by the teacher's attorney.

"On what basis were these judgments made?" Systematic observational data recorded in the classroom can help answer this question.

"Did the teacher receive any feedback from these observations?" A record of postobservation conferences is useful.

"Was any help provided to the teacher?" If a plan of assistance was carried out, it needs to be carefully documented.

School administrators tell us that when intensive assistance has been called for, approximately half the teachers recover, a quarter resign voluntarily, and a quarter are dismissed (and usually appeal the decision). In cases where dismissed teachers have been reinstated by an arbitrator or hearing panel, it is usually because the district has failed to provide due process, such as a satisfactory program of assistance. Some of the reasons for an unsatisfactory program include the following:

- setting an unreasonable number of goals for the teacher.
- not providing feedback after observations.
- displaying evidence of prejudice or vindictiveness.
- not providing sufficient time for the program to have an effect.

If you are a clinical supervisor involved in a plan of assistance for a teacher, you will be able to advise colleagues on how to design and carry out a plan of assistance that avoids these pitfalls. The expertise of a clinical supervisor is essential to a plan of assistance that is fair to the teacher and to the school district that has made a financial and emotional investment in the teacher.

PROBLEMS OF PRACTICE IN CLINICAL SUPERVISION

Recent books about designing and implementing an effective teacher evaluation system present many sensible ideas.[7] We believe that our ideas about the role of clinical supervision in teacher evaluation are also sensible. However, teacher evaluation in practice is often more problematic than the ideal practices that we and others espouse. We consider several of these problems below.

The Widget Effect

A report by the New Teacher Project, titled "The Widget Effect," has been widely circulated.[8] The study involved a survey of approximately 15,000 teachers and 1,300 administrators in

12 districts across four states. The study's major finding is this: "[T]eacher evaluation systems, which in theory should serve as the primary mechanism for assessing . . . variations [in the effectiveness of teachers] . . . in practice tell us little about how one teacher differs from any other, except teachers whose performance is so egregiously poor as to warrant dismissal."[9] Some of the more specific findings are these:

- In districts where teachers are rated as satisfactory or unsatisfactory, 99 percent of teachers are rated as satisfactory. In districts with more rating options, 94 percent received one of the top two ratings, and less than 1 percent were rated as unsatisfactory.

- Eighty-one percent of administrators and 58 percent of teachers reported that they know a tenured teacher who is performing poorly, and 43 percent of teachers reported that they know a tenured teacher who should be dismissed for poor performance.

- At least half of the districts have not dismissed a single tenured teacher for poor performance in the past five years.

- Fifty-nine percent of teachers and 63 percent of administrators stated that their district is not doing enough to identify, compensate, promote, and retain the most effective teachers.[10]

The authors of the report characterize these findings as the Widget Effect, which is defined as the tendency of educators to assume that classroom effectiveness is the same from teacher to teacher.

These findings strongly suggest that current teacher evaluation systems are dysfunctional. The systems do not identify exceptionally good teachers who might be rewarded with leadership roles, nor do they identify exceptionally poor teachers who deprive students of the high-quality education they deserve.

The "Widget Effect" study did not identify reasons for the poor quality of current teacher evaluation systems. In our view, one of the main reasons is that teacher evaluation is labor-intensive—and therefore expensive. It becomes even more expensive when a teacher is rated as marginal or incompetent, because then staff time is needed to design and implement a plan of assistance or dismissal hearings. School systems typically operate on tight budgets; teacher evaluation and its aftermath simply do not have the same priority as other needs, such as satisfying legislative mandates.

If this analysis of the problem is correct, legislators, school boards, and others will need to build support for teacher evaluation as a budget priority. Clinical supervisors can play an important role in building this support by contributing their expertise in creating standards of teacher competence, procedures for observing them, and methods for helping teachers improve in competence through repeated cycles of clinical supervision. The alternative is a continuation of current practice, which involves paying lip service to the importance of teacher evaluation but failing to do it in a meaningful way.

The Sting of Teacher Evaluation

Many teachers fear being evaluated. The fear is reasonable, because a negative evaluation report can have fearful consequences for them—denial of initial certification or dismissal from a teaching position. Even if an evaluation report is only slightly negative, it can cause the teacher to become guarded and anxious about possible career consequences, such as denial of opportunities for career advancement or access to desired resources. The teacher also might develop the perception that the workplace is hostile, and this perception can lead to persistent stress. Even if the evaluator proposes paths for remediation and professional development, the teacher might resist them because of fear and loss of trust in the evaluator.

One way to deal with the sting of evaluation is to eliminate evaluation and only provide positive feedback. This approach, of course, is not viable. However, educators need to find ways to lessen the sting of evaluation. One solution is to have clear standards of teacher competence and methods for assessing whether they have been met. Teachers then are able to know precisely what they need to do in order to receive a favorable evaluation report. They still might fear the evaluation process, but this fear is more tolerable than the generalized anxiety that is created when teachers face an unknown or vague evaluation process.

The Competence and Fairness of the Teacher Evaluator

Teachers become anxious and distrustful if they are concerned about the competence or fairness of the individual who is evaluating their performance. One school district in a southern state is a case in point.[11] The district bases its teacher evaluation process on a model that involves a pre-evaluation meeting with each teacher, lengthy observation periods in which the evaluator documents specific instances in which teachers succeed or struggle, and follow-up activities that include coaching on effective instructional methods.

This evaluation process appears sound and is consistent with the teacher evaluation model described in this chapter. However, there are problems with it in practice. One of the district's administrators made this observation:

> I wish there was some way we could train administrators to be more consistent and bring more fidelity to the process . . . Teachers know which administrators take this process seriously, which ones are there to clean house, and which ones don't care.[12]

This observation is supported by the findings of the Widget Project, which we described above. In the 12 school districts that were studied, researchers found that "[e]valuations are short and infrequent (most are based on two or fewer classroom observations totaling 60 minutes or less), and conducted by untrained administrators."[13]

Better training for evaluators and a team approach might ameliorate these problems. As an example of a team approach, one of us (M. Gall) occasionally served as the clinical supervisor for preservice students preparing to be high-school science teachers. In some cases, I could assess the soundness of the student's instructional methods, but not her subject-matter competence. The cooperating teacher and I agreed on a team approach in which I worked with the student teacher on instructional methods and he on subject matter. We jointly evaluated the student teacher, with each of us focusing on standards relating to our expertise.

At the inservice level, specialists in teacher evaluation could evaluate each teacher. The evaluator would present his findings for each teacher to the administrator. Teachers whose competence is judged to be unsatisfactory would then be assessed more thoroughly by a team that included the evaluator, a school administrator, a teacher colleague, and perhaps others as well. A similar approach could be used for a teacher whose performance is considered exemplary and deserving of special rewards, such as a recommendation to serve as a mentor teacher or administrator. The initial judgment of exemplary performance would gain in credibility if it was followed up by a team evaluation.

The Accountability Movement in Education

As we explain in this and other chapters, legislative mandates are increasingly holding teachers and administrators accountable for student learning. As the accountability movement grows, the evaluation of teacher competence will become an increasing focus of concern. Weak teacher evaluation systems, which appear to be widespread, will be a source of embarrassment for educators and make it difficult to request budget increases.

The accountability movement might subside; if not, educators will need to understand it and cope with it. Policy analysts associated with the Hamilton Project have studied teacher evaluation within the current accountability movement in education and made recommendations for improving it.[14] One of their recommendations is for legislators to fund data systems that link each student's achievement test scores to his teacher (or teachers in the case of middle- and high-school students). Another is to evaluate individual teachers by using multiple measures of performance, such as student achievement on tests, observations of student work, and parent ratings. The project authors claim an advantage of this multifaceted approach; "Sound objective and subjective measures of teacher quality are likely to converge, at least for those teachers at the top and bottom of the distribution of teacher quality."[15]

ENDNOTES

1. Danielson, C., & McGreal, T. L. (2000). *Teacher evaluation to enhance professional practice*. Alexandria, VA: Association for Supervision and Curriculum Development. Quote appears on p. 11.

2. These standards are described at http://www.uesf.org/resources/SFTeach.pdf.

3. Bridges, E. (1990). *Managing the incompetent teacher*. Eugene, OR: ERIC Clearinghouse on Educational Management.

4. *Ibid.*, p. 14.

5. Willims, T., Kirst, M. W., Haertel, E., et al. (2010). *Gaining ground in the middle grades: Why some schools do better*. Mountain View, CA: EdSource. Retrieved from http://www.edsource.org

6. Legal aspects of teacher evaluation are described in Ribas, W. B. (2005). *Teacher evaluation that works!* (2nd ed.). Westwood, MA: Ribas Publications.

7. Among these books are Danielson, C., & McGreal, T. L. (2000). *Teacher evaluation to enhance professional practice*. Alexandria, VA: Association for Supervision and Curriculum Development; Lawrence, C. E. (2005). *The marginal teacher: A step-by-step guide to fair procedures for identification and dismissal* (3rd ed.). Thousand Oaks, CA: Corwin; Peterson, K. D. (2006). *Effective teacher evaluation: A guide for principals*. Thousand Oaks, CA: Corwin; Ribas, W. B. (2005). *Teacher evaluation that works!* (2nd ed.). Westwood, MA: Ribas Publications.

8. Weisberg, D., Sexton, S., Mulhern, J, & Keeling, D. (2009). *The widget effect: Our national failure to acknowledge and act on differences in teacher effectiveness*. Brooklyn, NY: The New Teacher Project. Retrieved from http://widget-effect.org/downloads/TheWidgetEffect_execsummary.pdf

9. *Ibid.*, p. 2.

10. *Ibid.*, p. 4.

11. Sawchuk, S. (2009, June 1). Study finds teacher evaluations usually rosy. *Education Week*. Retrieved from http://www.edweek.org/ew/articles/2009/06/01

12. *Ibid.*

13. Widget effect, p. 4.

14. Staiger, D. O., Gordon, R., & Kane, T. J. (2006). *Identifying effective teachers using performance on the job*. Washington, DC: The Brookings Institution. Retrieved from http://www.brookings.edu/papers/2006/04education_gordon.aspx

15. *Ibid.*, p. 19.

Chapter 6

Problems of Practice
in Clinical Supervision

*In real-world practice, problems do not present themselves to the practitioner as givens.
They must be constructed from the materials of problematic situations which are puzzling,
troubling, and uncertain . . . He must make sense of an uncertain situation that initially
makes no sense.*
—Donald Schön.[1]

INTRODUCTION

In Units 3 and 4 of this book we describe specific techniques that are useful in clinical
supervision. However, we do not mean to imply that clinical supervision is reducible to a
set of techniques that can be applied in cookbook fashion. Clinical supervision, like most
human enterprises, is too complex for cookbook solutions. Knowledge of conferencing and
observation techniques is helpful, but so is creativity.

Our purpose in this chapter is to develop your awareness of problems that commonly
arise in clinical supervision and approaches for analyzing and solving them. We primarily
present problems that we and our colleagues have experienced in clinical supervision. We
also present an analysis of each problem, realizing that others might analyze it differently
and with an equally sound, or better, rationale.

You will note that we use the phrase "problems of practice" often in this chapter. It is
not our phrase alone. Our search of the electronic database (http://www.eric.ed.gov) for
Education Resources Information Center (ERIC), conducted in April 2010, yielded 72 bibliographic citations in which this phrase occurs. We like the phrase, because it reminds us that
educational practice, including the practice of clinical supervision, is anything but routine.

As we explain in Chapter 1, clinical supervision involves various educators in different
roles. To avoid confusion, we will use certain terms to refer to these roles:

- *Preservice teacher*. A student enrolled in a teacher education program either at the
  undergraduate or graduate level.
- *Student teacher*. A preservice teacher who is serving an apprenticeship in a school
  setting for a period of weeks or months. For the preservice teacher to be labeled

a "student teacher," the apprenticeship must involve responsibility for teaching at least one class of students for a period of weeks or months. A preservice teacher who is in a school to observe teaching or to tutor selected students is not considered a student teacher in this chapter. Some teacher education programs have briefer periods of student teaching, typically called practicums, and longer periods called student teaching. In both cases, the preservice teacher is considered a student teacher if the apprenticeship involves the requirements we stated above.

- *Cooperating teacher.* A teacher who has a teaching license, classroom teaching responsibilities, and supervisory responsibility for a student teacher who will fulfill student teaching responsibilities in his classroom.

- *University supervisor.* A college or university employee who supervises a student teacher. This employee might be a professor or an educator (e.g., a retired teacher) who has been hired to supervise student teachers. In each case, the university supervisor represents the university and is responsible for ensuring that the student teacher satisfies the requirements of the university's teacher education program.

- *Inservice teacher.* A teacher who is working for a school and has regular classroom teaching responsibilities. Some inservice teachers might be enrolled concurrently in a teacher education program, but if they are employed by a school to teach students, we consider them to be inservice teachers in this chapter.

TEACHERS WHO HAVE CONFLICTING PRIORITIES

A retired elementary teacher who had served as a cooperating teacher for many student teachers told us about a student teacher who created a particular problem for her. The student teacher needed to prepare and teach a one-week unit as one of her practicum requirements.

The student teacher prepared the unit, and the cooperating teacher selected a school week during which she would teach it. As the week approached, the student teacher received an offer from a family friend to join the family for a vacation the same week that she had agreed to teach the unit. The cooperating teacher told her that the professional thing to do was to teach the unit, but that she would not insist on it. The student teacher chose to go on the vacation.

In another case, a cooperating teacher complained to a university supervisor that her student teacher arrived at the school at the last minute and scurried around the teachers' work area copying and organizing instructional materials. As a consequence, the cooperating teacher did not have time to provide feedback to the student teacher about his instruction or to help him plan upcoming lessons.

The university supervisor talked to the student teacher about this problem, and he acknowledged that the cooperating teacher's observations of his behavior were valid. As an excuse, the student teacher stated that he had many things on his plate, and it was difficult to get all of them done in a timely manner. He did not express an awareness that student teaching should be his top priority and therefore should take precedence over his other responsibilities.

Analysis: Preservice teachers might not realize that teacher education programs are professional preparation programs, not academic majors. They are not in the same situation as students in an academic major, who might decide to skip classes for various reasons with no negative consequences.

To avoid this misperception, the faculty of teacher education programs needs to make explicit statements to their students that they are preparing for a professional role and therefore must act like professionals. The faculty might expand on this point by preparing a list of professional expectations that students should live up to and the consequences for not doing so.

If these expectations were presented to everyone associated with the student teaching program (including cooperating teachers), the above-mentioned cooperating teachers might have solved the problems that their student teachers created for them by referring the student teachers to the list of expectations and consequences for not following them.

TEACHERS WHO HAVE DIFFICULTY TRANSLATING INSIGHTS INTO ACTION

A university supervisor asked a colleague to help him with a difficult student teaching situation. The student teacher had responsibility for several high-school science classes and was experiencing classroom management problems. Nothing that the supervisor had suggested was effective in helping the student teacher with these problems.

The consulting university supervisor (hereafter called "consultant") introduced himself to the student teacher and explained that he was there by invitation of the regular university supervisor and with permission of the cooperating teacher. He asked the student teacher if she was aware that students in her classes were occasionally disruptive, and she acknowledged the problem, but did not think it was serious.

The consultant observed several of the student teacher's lessons, each time making anecdotal records (see Observation Technique 9) about incidents of classroom disruption and what the student teacher said and did in response to the disruption. If the student teacher said nothing, the consultant made a note of that, too.

It quickly became apparent to the consultant that the student teacher had a pattern of reacting to a student's disruptive behavior by making comments like, "If you do that again, I'm going to have to send you to the principal" or "If that happens again, you'll have extra homework." However, the student teacher did not follow through on her stated plan of action when the student engaged in disruptive behavior again.

The consultant presented his notes to the student teacher in a feedback conference and asked her to look at them to see what they said about her teaching. With some prompting, she was able to see that she stated consequences for disruptive behavior, but did not follow through on them. The consultant asked if she had any ideas about why this pattern of behavior occurred. The student teacher offered several ideas, but the primary idea was that she was afraid that students would not like her or resent her if she punished them.

After more discussion in the feedback conference, the student teacher stated that she would follow through with her stated consequences if a student's disruptive behavior warranted it. The consultant observed the next class and, in fact, the student teacher did send a student to the principal following disruptive behavior. The consultant continued making anecdotal records based on his observations of student conduct.

Fortunately, in the next feedback conference, the consultant and student teacher were able to find evidence in the notes that the class was better behaved for the rest of the period after she had followed through on consequences. Unfortunately, she reverted to her habit of not following through on consequences when the consultant and regular university supervisor observed her classes over the next few weeks.

Over time, the consultant collected more data, including data on what students whispered to each other as he sat near them. He learned that some of the students were talking about difficult family situations that quite possibly would detract them from their schoolwork. The student teacher was not aware of these situations and did not take any particular interest in them when given observational data by the consultant.

Analysis: One way to analyze the problem of practice that this student teacher created for the consultant and regular university supervisor is to consider the fact that teaching requires an interest both in the curriculum and in students as individuals with diverse needs. The student teacher we described above had a strong interest in the curriculum she was teaching and liked the students she was teaching, but was somewhat disengaged from them, even afraid of them. She did not engage students before or after class to get to know them as individuals and to ask how she might assist their learning.

One solution to this problem of practice might be to continue working with the student teacher over a substantial period of time, perhaps asking her to do student teaching again the next semester or quarter. Just as school-age students learn at different rates, so some adults learn the teacher's role quicker than others.

It might be that, over time, the student teacher whom we described would become adept at managing both the curriculum and students. Another possibility is that she might conclude that her interests and talents do not lend themselves well to the teaching profession. A student teacher who comes to this conclusion need not view her lack of success in the classroom as a defeat, but as an experiment that did not produce the results she wished. The things that she learned about herself during student teaching might lead her to explore other professions that would be more fulfilling.

TEACHERS WHO HIDE FROM THE SUPERVISOR

It is customary for university supervisors to visit student teachers soon after they have begun their student teaching experience. In one situation, however, a student teacher stalled for time before agreeing on a visit from her university supervisor. The supervisor would call her to make an appointment, but the student teacher would say things like, "I'm not ready for you to come out yet," "Everything's going fine right now, so I'd rather you come a few weeks from now," and "I'm working with my cooperating teachers, and that's going fine, so let's wait awhile before you come out."

The university supervisor agreed to these requests in the belief that the student teacher was being honest and also out of a desire to avoid a conflict that might hamper the supervisory relationship. After about four weeks, though, the supervisor felt that he could wait no longer and insisted that the student teacher allow him to meet and then visit one of her classes and make some observations.

The supervisor arrived at the student teacher's high school and took a seat in one of the student teacher's social studies classes to collect data by script taping (see Observation Technique 9). He found that the teacher barely had the class under control. He learned, too, that the cooperating teacher was not only a social studies teacher, but a football coach as well. Some of his football players were in the student teachers' classes. These students seated themselves together in the back of the room or off to the side. Although they were not unruly, they tended to talk to each other and have a low percentage of at-task time.

The university instructor inferred from the students' behavior that they did not respect the student teacher's authority. They were slow to respond to her directions for each class activity and would ask questions that implied criticism of the value of the activity.

The university supervisor insisted on observing several more class sessions and then met with the student teacher in a feedback conference. The student teacher expressed her belief that all was well with her instruction and was somewhat resistant to examining the supervisor's observational data. The supervisor patiently kept bringing her attention back to the data, and finally the student teacher admitted that there was a problem. It seemed to the supervisor that the student teacher was afraid to acknowledge problems in her instruction, because that might convey weakness and invite a negative evaluation of her teaching effectiveness.

Analysis: We find that some teachers avoid acknowledging problems in their instructional practice, because they view it as a sign of weakness. The supervisor can help these teachers by commenting that it is actually a sign of strength to acknowledge problems in one's instruction. The teacher who has identified and labeled a problem has taken the first step to solving the problem and becoming a more effective teacher.

The university supervisor came to the realization that he should have had a planning conference and made observations much earlier in the school term. He had not done this because his other student teachers generally observed the cooperating teacher's classes and did small instructional tasks (e.g., assisting individual students, grading papers, organizing instructional materials) for three or four weeks before taking full responsibility for a class.

In the case of this student teacher, however, the cooperating teacher had pressing demands on his time, mostly involving spring training for the football team. Therefore, he had turned his classes over to the student teacher before she was ready to begin teaching them. When the student teacher, the cooperating teacher, and the university supervisor met in a joint conference, the cooperating teacher acknowledged that he had not spent sufficient time in preparing the student teacher to take over his classes. He then offered to meet with the classes and prepare them to accept the student teacher as their regular teacher with full authority for their learning and assessment. Also, he worked with the student teacher to create a new seating chart that would break up the clique of football players and a few other cliques so that they could not get each other off task.

This intervention involving the trio of the cooperating teacher, the student teacher, and the university supervisor proved to be effective. The student teacher had a successful experience and was subsequently employed as a teacher in a nearby school district the following year.

INCOMPATIBILITIES BETWEEN STUDENT TEACHERS AND COOPERATING TEACHERS

We have found that teacher educators try their best to match student teachers with an appropriate cooperating teacher. For example, they will place a student who is learning to be a high-school mathematics teacher with a cooperating teacher who works in a high school and teaches different levels of mathematics. If teacher educators are concerned about the teaching ability of a student, they might try to match him with a cooperating teacher who takes a developmental approach to working with student teachers.

In some cases, teacher educators make what they think are good placements, only to find an unanticipated incompatibility between the student teacher and cooperating teacher. One case that we know about involved a woman from a Spanish-speaking country who had been a successful high-school teacher there for many years. She married an American citizen and moved to this country with the intent of teaching Spanish at the high-school level. The teacher licensing agency in her state did not recognize her teaching credentials, so she needed to enroll in a state-approved teacher education program.

It happened that her cooperating teacher did not have nearly her level of skill in Spanish and also had a different teaching style. Conflicts arose when it came time for the student teacher to take responsibility for several of the cooperating teacher's classes. The cooperating teacher objected to some parts of her curriculum and teaching methods. He was not swayed by the student teacher's argument that she was a native speaker of Spanish and also had taught successfully for many years. The student teacher became very upset with the situation and asked the university supervisor to intervene.

In another case, the coordinator of student teaching placements assigned a male student teacher to a female cooperating teacher. They appeared to be well matched with respect to subject-matter interests and teaching style. However, as the school term progressed, their ability to communicate with each other broke down. Finally, the student teacher confided to the university supervisor that the cooperating teacher reminded him of his former wife. He felt that the cooperating teacher, like his former spouse, made unreasonable demands on him and talked down to him.

Analysis: In both cases, an incompatibility between the student teacher and the cooperating teacher created a major roadblock for the student teacher's professional development. The tension between the two of them, rising at times to mutual antagonism, made it impossible for the university supervisor to make effective use of the conferencing and observation techniques of clinical supervision.

These problems of practice need to be resolved, so that the student teaching experience is productive. In both cases, the university supervisor appealed to the director of student teaching placements for the university's teacher education programs. This individual analyzed the problem as one of an unfortunate incompatibility that did not necessarily involve incompetence on the part of either the student teacher or the cooperating teacher.

In each case the placement director decided to ask whether the stakeholders—the student teacher, the cooperating teacher, and the university supervisor—would be willing to have a meeting with him. Everyone agreed with the plan, because they realized that they had reached an impasse using their own resources. At the meeting, the placement director stated that the student teacher and university supervisor were guests in the cooperating teacher's classes and that he would seek another placement for the student teacher if the conflicts could not be resolved.

With this said, the cooperating teacher in each case felt that any threat to their authority and competence was removed, and they became willing to consider how the student teaching placement could continue to a successful conclusion. In both cases, the conflict was resolved by a mutual decision for the cooperating teacher to move into the background during the time that the student teacher had responsibility for his classes. It also was mutually decided that the university supervisor would visit the student teacher's classes more frequently, provide regular feedback to both the student teacher and cooperating teacher, and alert the cooperating teacher if the classes were getting out of hand. This decision was facilitated by the fact that, in both cases, the university supervisor was a successful former teacher who was respected by the cooperating teacher.

We know a cooperating teacher who avoids the problem of incompatibility by making her expectations explicit to university supervisors and faculty. She will only accept student teachers who are willing to follow her philosophy of multicultural education and her teaching style. Furthermore, she insists that her student teachers meet with her for at least four or five Saturdays early in the placement so that she can teach them about her approach to multicultural education and model certain teaching techniques that she uses in her classes. Her reason for these expectations is that she does not want her students to have to make a major shift during the school year from her instructional approach to a different and possibly incompatible instructional approach used by the student teacher.

Because this teacher's colleagues and former student teachers highly respect her, the university's placement director is quite willing to accommodate her expectations. Prospective student teachers are told about this cooperating teacher's expectations, and they are free to ask for another placement or to request a placement with her. This approach has proved successful over a period of years in avoiding any problem of incompatibility between the cooperating teacher and her student teachers.

EXPERIENCED TEACHERS WHO ARE IN A RUT

We find that many teachers go from one year to the next without having a clinical supervisor or teacher development specialist observe their instruction. They consider themselves to be effective teachers, because students and the students' parents do not complain about their instruction. In fact, these teachers are effective in a certain way: They are not so ineffective that others complain about them, but they are not sufficiently effective that others recognize them as master teachers. The problem of practice here is how to help these teachers get out of this rut, so that they improve their instruction without threat to their professional self-image and the addition of more tasks to their already full work schedules.

A doctoral student who was a former teacher and school principal found an appealing solution to this problem.[2] For his dissertation research, he asked for teachers to volunteer for a professional development activity that would increase their level of enthusiasm while teaching. When he had formed a group of volunteers, he went into each teacher's classroom and videotaped their lesson. Most of the volunteers had previously worked with the doctoral student as a teacher colleague or as a teacher in the school where he had been the principal.

The doctoral student then offered a brief workshop on the importance of enthusiasm in teaching and observable indicators of enthusiasm. (These indicators, developed by Mary Collins, are listed in the description of Conference Technique 2.) He had the teachers practice these behaviors among themselves by having them teach brief lessons and giving each other feedback about their use of the indicators. Also, he invited the volunteers to practice incorporating these indicators of enthusiasm in their classroom instruction. Several weeks later, he videotaped another one of their lessons to determine whether their enthusiasm level had changed from the level observed in the initial videotaped lesson.

Most of the teachers made substantial progress, becoming more dynamic, expressive, and emotionally responsive to students' comments. One teacher in particular impressed us when we observed his initial and follow-up videotaped lessons. In his initial lesson, his delivery was clear, but flat. He mostly stood in one place in the classroom, made few gestures, and had a static facial expression. In the follow-up lesson, he was much more energetic and varied in his gestures, facial expressions, and movement around the classroom. He seemed to be enjoying himself. Indeed, he told the doctoral student that he felt freed up and more connected to the students whom he was teaching.

Analysis: This example of teacher development suggests several ideas about how to work with experienced teachers who have become complacent about their instruction or resigned to the view that this was the best that they could do for their students. First, it seems reasonable that teachers will be more responsive to examining their instruction if the process is voluntary. Second, teachers will be more willing to work with someone if they respect this person. Third, they will pay more attention to data that have been collected in their own classroom and that they consider to be relevant to their teaching effectiveness. Fourth, they will experience satisfaction with the process if they can observe genuine gains over time in their teaching effectiveness.

This analysis does not make specific reference to clinical supervision. However, it does fit the clinical supervision model that we describe in this book. The individual with special expertise about some aspect of teaching, such as enthusiasm, can be thought of as the clinical supervisor. The sharing of this expertise with the teacher can be done through brief planning conferences. The collection of classroom observation data and providing it as feedback to the teacher are, of course, integral features of clinical supervision.

Helping experienced teachers through this process has one important advantage over other models for helping them move from acceptable instruction to excellent instruction. The advantage is that clinical supervision is not highly time-consuming for the teachers. The planning and feedback conferences can be relatively brief, and it takes no additional time for teachers to be observed while they are engaged in classroom instruction. Of course, there are costs to the school district in making clinical supervisors available to their teachers. These costs can be readily justified if teachers make instructional gains that benefit the district's students.

ENDNOTES

1. Schön, D. A. (1983). *The reflective practitioner: How professionals think in action*. New York: Basic Books. Quote appears on p. 40.

2. Denight, J. A. Effects of teacher enthusiasm training on at-task behavior and attitudes of students in high school. *Dissertation Abstracts International: Section A. Humanities and Social Sciences*, *48*(11), 2845.

Unit Three

Conferencing Techniques

Chapter 7

Interpersonal Communication in Clinical Supervision

Take my advice: don't give advice.
—Anonymous

INTRODUCTION

Everyone has their own way of communicating with others. If you plan to be a clinical supervisor, you need to reflect on your communication style, because it will greatly affect the success of your work with teachers. In particular, you should consider the effects that you wish to achieve or avoid. For example, you would not want to communicate in a manner that makes the teacher defensive or anxious. Those are effects that impede communication and the teacher's ability to develop instructional skills. Instead, you would want to communicate in such a way that the teacher trusts you and feels that you are supporting his efforts to become more effective.

A clinical supervision cycle includes three phases: a planning conference, classroom observation, and a feedback conference. In this chapter, we consider communication techniques that facilitate the two conference phases, both of which involve face-to-face interaction between the supervisor and the teacher.

COMMUNICATION TECHNIQUE 1: EMPHASIZE AN INDIRECT STYLE OF CONVERSING WITH THE TEACHER

Ned Flanders differentiated two styles of teaching—a direct teaching style (i.e., lecturing, directing, criticizing) and an indirect style (i.e., accepting feelings, encouraging, acknowledging, using student ideas).[1] Arthur Blumberg used similar categories to distinguish communication styles in clinical supervision, and he gathered research evidence that teachers prefer an indirect style of supervision.[2] The following communication behaviors form a continuum, from more indirect to more direct: expressing and accepting feelings; praising; acknowledging and using others' ideas, asking questions; lecturing or otherwise engaging in monologue; directing; criticizing, even antagonizing.

We have found that when teachers are given a choice of supervisors, some choose one who is known to be quite direct, whereas others prefer one who tends to be indirect.

Teachers who prefer the direct approach may say, "I know where she stands" or "He tells it like it is" or "I'm tired of people 'bouncing everything off the wall.'" Those who like an indirect style may say, "I feel more comfortable with Mary; she doesn't act like she has all the answers" or "Fred helps me do my own thinking and treats me like a colleague" or "I've had enough of the 'hard sell' approach."

The distinction between direct and indirect styles of communicating is similar in certain respects to Douglas McGregor's distinction between two styles of management—Theory X and Theory Y.[3] Theory X applies to traditional business management and the assumptions underlying it. Theory Y is based on assumptions derived from research in the social sciences.

Three basic assumptions of Theory X are:

1. The average human being has an inherent dislike of work and will avoid it if possible.
2. Because of this human dislike of work, most people must be coerced, directed, and threatened with punishment to get them to put forth adequate effort toward the achievement of organizational objectives.
3. The average human being prefers to be directed, wishes to avoid responsibility, has relatively little ambition, and wants security above all.

McGregor indicates that the "carrot and the stick" theory of motivation fits reasonably well with Theory X. External rewards and punishments are the motivators of workers. The consequent direction and control does not recognize intrinsic human motivation.

Theory Y is more humanistic and is based on six assumptions:

1. The expenditure of physical and mental effort in work is as natural as play or rest.
2. External controls and the threat of punishment are not the only means for bringing about effort toward organizational objectives. Human beings will exercise self-direction and self-control in the service of objectives to which they are committed.
3. Commitment to objectives is a function of the intrinsic rewards associated with their achievement.
4. The average human being learns, under proper conditions, not only to accept but also to seek responsibility.
5. The capacity to exercise a relatively high degree of imagination, ingenuity, and creativity in the solution of organizational problems is widely, not narrowly, distributed in the population.
6. Under the conditions of the modern organization, the intellectual potential of the average human being is only partially utilized.

McGregor saw these assumptions leading to superior-subordinate relationships in which the subordinate would have greater influence over the activities in his or her own work and also have influence on the superior's actions. Through participatory management, greater creativity and productivity are expected, and also a greater sense of personal accomplishment and satisfaction by the workers.

Flanders and Blumberg's concept of a direct style of communicating appears similar to the Theory X approach to management of workers. Conversely, their concept of an indirect style appears similar to the Theory Y approach. Theory X and Theory Y are applicable to clinical supervision in that they occur in a workplace setting, and the supervisors have a management-like role relative to teachers. In our view, the assumptions underlying Theory Y are more applicable to clinical supervision than those of Theory X.

In this chapter, we describe communication techniques usually regarded as indirect, or in other words, teacher-centered. If your communication style is naturally indirect, you might already be using them. If your communication style is direct, we invite you to consider whether incorporating some of these techniques into your conferences with teachers would enhance your ability to gain and hold their trust, and also their willingness to listen carefully to your comments and questions.

COMMUNICATION TECHNIQUE 2: LISTEN MORE, TALK LESS

Some clinical supervisors dominate the conversation in planning and feedback conferences. The teacher has little chance to identify goals and objectives, analyze and interpret information, or reach decisions about future actions. In clinical supervision as we envision it, a good ratio might be the teacher taking up approximately two-thirds of the talk time and the supervisor one-third.

If the teacher talks more, the supervisor will need to listen more. Active listening, of course, is desirable. It can be demonstrated by staying in close proximity to the teacher, maintaining eye contact, and nodding at appropriate times. These behaviors communicate to the teacher that he is being heard and appreciated as a fellow professional.

COMMUNICATION TECHNIQUE 3: ACKNOWLEDGE, PARAPHRASE, AND USE WHAT THE TEACHER SAYS

Observers who insert an "I understand" or "I know what you mean" in the course of a supervisory conference indicate that they are paying close attention to what the speaker is saying. Accurate paraphrases also show that they understand the teacher. Using the teacher's ideas can be even more convincing than merely acknowledging (hearing) or paraphrasing (comprehending) them. Applying an idea to a different situation is but one example; pointing to a logical consequence is another.

Paraphrasing can backfire if it is too similar to the teacher's comment. For example, if a teacher says, "I had a hard time getting the class to settle down today," responding with "It sounds like the class was restless" does not contribute to the conference. An effective paraphrase must be a genuine effort to communicate that we understand what the other person is getting at. For example, the supervisor might say, "It seems like the class did not start the way you wanted it to." Another option is to use or extend the teacher's comment in some way—for example, by asking a question like "Is getting this class to settle down a frequent problem?" or making a statement like, "You're not alone. Getting students to settle down at the start of class is a problem that other teachers struggle with." A more directive extension of the teacher's comment might be, "If getting the class to settle down is a real problem for you, perhaps we can explore whether there are some effective ways to get a class ready to start learning right away when you start your lesson."

COMMUNICATION TECHNIQUE 4: ASK CLARIFYING QUESTIONS

The teacher's statements often need to be probed to clarify the observer's understanding and to get the teacher to think carefully about inferences and decisions. "Tell me what you mean by that" or "Can you say a little more about that?" are some examples. Another is "What would you accept as evidence that . . . ?"

If we do not clarify, miscommunication often results. Occasionally someone will say, "You're absolutely right! Moreover, . . ." and then the person proceeds to say the exact opposite of what you thought you said. Of course, that could be a conscious strategy or a case of not listening at all, but a clarifying question helps avoid unintentional misunderstandings.

An example of paraphrasing and asking clarifying questions took place in a high school where the principal gave the faculty an administrator appraisal form to fill out anonymously. After analyzing the compiled responses, the principal said in a faculty meeting, "What you seem to be telling me in this survey is that I'm not as accessible as you would like." Several teachers asked a clarifying question, almost in unison, "Could you tell us what 'being accessible' would look like?" To which the principal replied: "Well, I'd keep my door open more and welcome 'drop-in' chats. And if you stopped me in the hall and asked a question, I'd try to answer it briefly instead of pointing out that I was on my way to a meeting."

Having announced and clarified his intentions in public, he was destined to become "Mr. Accessible" in the next few months. Of course, he had some help from wags on the faculty who could not resist asking, "Are you feeling accessible?"

Several points can be made with this example: (1) the paraphrase translated a statistic into flesh-and-blood behavior; (2) the clarifying question checked the perceptions of the principal and his observers; and (3) the public announcement of a resolution to change virtually ensured success. Note that the principal had objective data, analyzed and interpreted the data, responded to a clarifying question, and received verbal support in his resolve to change. These are exactly the steps we should follow in helping teachers improve their teaching.

COMMUNICATION TECHNIQUE 5: GIVE SPECIFIC PRAISE FOR TEACHER PERFORMANCE AND GROWTH

Saying "That was a nice lesson" is not specific praise. Saying "That was an excellent answer you gave to Billy" or "Removing Fred from the group was an effective way to handle the problem" makes the approval explicit. It is especially important to note positive instances where the teacher has shown growth toward a stated goal.

There is some possibility that an observer's comments will create more behavior change than was bargained for. A workshop leader received this comment from a participant on the post-workshop evaluation: "Stopping the tape recording to explain what was happening was really helpful." So the leader stopped the tape about 20 times during their next workshop, until someone sent this note: "Why don't you let the tape play long enough for us to hear what's going on?"

Again, an elderly lady who had never eaten apple pie remarked that when she was a girl, she turned down her first opportunity to do so and gained considerable attention: "Imagine that! Carrie doesn't eat apple pie." The attention was such that in subsequent situations, she felt compelled to continue her refusal, although she confessed, "I always thought I might have liked it."

However, in our experience, the possibility of too little praise for teachers is much more likely than too much. Teaching often seems a thankless task to those who toil in the schools of our nation. They seldom lack critics, however.

COMMUNICATION TECHNIQUE 6: AVOID GIVING DIRECT ADVICE

This technique does not mean to imply that a supervisor should never give direct advice. Rather, the suggestion is to just wait awhile. Let teachers analyze and interpret first. Often the decisions they reach will be very similar to yours. For most teachers, having their ideas for change reinforced by someone they respect is more likely to produce results than being expected to carry out someone else's idea. On the other hand, there are times when it is better to say what we think rather than let indirectness become manipulative. If a teacher makes clear that she wants to know your views about a lesson that you observed, it probably is better to comply with the request than to refuse it. After sharing your views, you can ask a question like, "Does that square with the way you see your lesson?" This type of question puts the conversation back in the teacher's court.

Some people are naturally compliant, submissive, and obedient; perhaps they enjoy being told what to do. Nevertheless, our experience with teachers indicates that most of them prefer to feel responsible for their own actions. People who choose teaching as a career expect to be in charge of their classes; they expect to make professional decisions about goals, subject matter, materials, methodology, evaluation, and other aspects of the educational process.

As we explain in Chapter 4, there is a knowledge base about effective teaching that exists independently of the clinical supervisor and teacher. It is a resource that both can draw on to analyze observational data and generate ideas for instructional improvement. As a clinical supervisor, it might well be appropriate for you to share this chapter, sections of it, or resources mentioned in it with the teacher. If you do this, you should be able to avoid giving the impression that the knowledge base is necessarily authoritative or better than the teacher's knowledge. Instead, you should convey to the teacher that research-based knowledge about effective teaching is another source of data that can stimulate her thinking about her instructional practices.

COMMUNICATION TECHNIQUE 7: PROVIDE SUPPORT IN EMOTIONAL SITUATIONS

Some of the problems that administrators identify as deterrents to instructional improvement by their teachers have their basis in personal aspects of the teacher's life—for example, apathy, lack of organization, or the tendency to get angry when students engage in misbehavior. It would be convenient if we could exclude these personal problems from a discussion of techniques to use in conducting conferences, but they often enter the discussion despite all efforts to stay on a professional level. In fact, some clinical supervisors have had the experience of a teacher crying at some point in a conference. Analyzing behavior is an intensely personal process that defies a scientific or cold-blooded approach.

Hence, we need ways of dealing with emotional situations as they arise. It does not seem reasonable for an observer to be in tears along with the teacher, yet some expression of sympathy or empathy is in order. If the problems seem to be medical or psychiatric, the course of action is clear: Seek help by referring the teacher to an appropriate specialist. If the problem is not at this level of severity, a sympathetic listener can often help a person work through it. A clinical supervisor told us about a university student who told him: "You're the first one around here who has helped me!" This student had sought aid from several advisers in solving a personal problem. The supervisor took the time to listen to the particulars and then said, "It seems to me you've identified several possible alternatives. You could drop out of school and work full-time for a while, or you could take a reduced load and work part-time; and you also need to decide whether to get married now or wait." With his own alternatives outlined, the student said, "I see now what I need to do. Thank you." (He did not share his decision with the supervisor.)

The level of trust that two people have established is a major variable in how helpful a supervisor can be to a teacher with a personal problem that may be interfering with classroom effectiveness. Several factors influence trust building. We tend to trust those who trust us. We tend to trust those whose competence we respect. One way to build a teacher's confidence in our competence as observers is to demonstrate our ability to provide useful feedback and verbal support when the teacher is experiencing emotional distress.

Clinical supervisors occasionally work with inservice teachers who are on a plan of assistance because of serious instructional weaknesses. Obviously, the tone of conferences will be different than that of conferences with teachers whose instruction is generally satisfactory or exemplary. Yet the supervisor does not have to turn from Dr. Jekyll into Mr. Hyde. A skillful parent serves as both a supportive counselor and a disciplinarian and can do so in a consistent style. Supervisors, too, should be able to fulfill both aspects—professional development and evaluation—of their role skillfully.

We each have an externally perceived self and an internally perceived self. We develop discomfort when we become aware of a discrepancy between what we believe to be "the real me" and what "the perceived me" is seen to be doing in others' eyes or in the information collected through systematic observation. For example, perhaps a teacher who believes that teachers should smile a lot feels that he smiles a lot; if he views videotapes of himself that show no smiles, he has dissonance. This dissonance can be reduced in several ways, such as

1. "The videotape is wrong."
2. "It was a bad day, I was nervous."
3. "It isn't really that important to smile so often."

In other words, he can (1) deny the information, (2) reduce the importance of the information, or (3) reduce the importance of the behavior. Another possibility is that he can resolve to make the perceived self more like the "real" or ideal self. That requires changing his behavior.

The goal of supervision for instructional improvement is to get teachers to change their behavior in ways that both they and their supervisors regard as desirable. In some cases only the observer (and not the teacher) sees a suggested change as desirable. Now the observer experiences dissonance. Among the options for reducing this dissonance are the following:

1. "You'll do it my way, or I'll send you to Siberia."
2. "Let's look at some more data about what is happening."
3. "Let's work on something you are concerned about."

In other words, the observer may (1) reduce dissonance by forcing compliance from the teacher, or (2) and (3) attempt to achieve consonance through increased understanding of what is on the teacher's mind.

COMMUNICATION TECHNIQUE 8: ACKNOWLEDGE AND USE NONVERBAL COMMUNICATION

When a child attempts to do something difficult and says, "I can't," a typical parental response is, "Of course you can!" The response is intended to be positive, but it denies feelings. It might not hurt to say, "It's difficult, isn't it, but you'll get it."

Researchers have found that feelings are seldom acknowledged verbally in the classroom.[4] Acknowledgment of feelings in conferences is less well documented, but we suspect that it is too seldom done. When the goal is to change behavior, affective aspects cannot be ignored. The emotions that can be expressed in a conference range from rage to despair, from exhilaration to depression. Clinical observers should not ignore these emotions any more than they would ignore important statements.

Emotions typically are expressed through nonverbal communication. Therefore, clinical supervisors need to be sensitive to teachers' nonverbal messages and interpret them appropriately. They also need to be aware of the nonverbal messages that they communicate to teachers. Of course, they will want these messages to communicate support, concern, and caring about the teacher's needs for professional growth.

Nonverbal communication has been studied extensively by researchers.[5] They have found that individuals use a variety of nonverbal cues to communicate with each other. The major nonverbal cues are listed in Table 7.1, accompanied by questions that you can ask yourself to interpret what particular nonverbal cues mean—both those that the teacher communicates and those you communicate in your role as clinical supervisor. In studying the table, you might note that nonverbal cues send two general kinds of messages. One type involves messages about how the teacher feels about the clinical supervisor (or vice versa). The other type of nonverbal cue reveals how the person feels about himself. By studying nonverbal cues of this type, you can get a sense of whether the teacher views himself positively or negatively and whether he sees himself as a professional.

You also can compare the teacher's nonverbal and verbal messages to determine whether they are congruent with each other. Incongruent messages need to be interpreted, as they might indicate barriers to effective clinical supervision. For example, we recall situations where a student teacher made statements indicating that all was going well in her classroom, but nonverbal cues suggested a desire to avoid interacting with the clinical supervisor. Careful, supportive communication with several of these teachers revealed that they were having problems in managing their classroom, but felt that they would face

Table 7.1 Nonverbal Cues in Interpersonal Communication

Nonverbal Cue	Points to Consider
Clothing	A person's clothes can indicate how he feels about himself and also how he chooses to relate to others. Is the clothing neat, possibly indicating a positive self concept and concern for others? Is it appropriate for the setting? Does it make a statement about the person's life style?
Cosmetics	A person's hair, hair coloring, make-up, and jewelry can make a statement about how she feels about herself and how she chooses to present herself to others. Are the person's cosmetic features appropriate to the setting? Do they reflect a positive self-image?
Gestures	Gestures can involve the entire body or parts of the body—hands, arms, eyes, and facial muscles. Does one person touch the other, perhaps for the purpose of emotional support? Does a person roll his eyes, possibly indicating disbelief about what the other has said? Does a person avoid eye contact? Does a person frown or smile? Is a person's arms crossed or open?
Physical space	The amount of space two people put between themselves can express how each feels about the other. Close proximity suggests trust and intimacy. Distance might suggest fear, distrust, or a desire for formality.
Posture	Does each person lean forward, indicating attentiveness to what the other person is saying? Does each person lean back, indicating possible lack of interest or distrust of the other person?
Time	Is each person punctual in keeping appointments? Is the meeting rushed or relaxed? Does each person's rate of speech indicate that he is calm, excited, or anxious?
Tone of voice	Is the person's tone of voice calm, angry, sarcastic, confident, enthusiastic, happy? Is the voice level soft or loud?

negative consequences, such as termination of their student teaching placement, if these problems became public.

One way to respond to teachers who appear to be conveying negative emotions is to describe what you are observing: "You appear to be quite angry about that" or "This seems to make you anxious." Don't be surprised if the teacher's response is "Oh, no, I'm not really angry" or "Who's anxious? I'm not anxious." We tend to deny negative feelings, as if it were a sign of weakness to have them, particularly in a teaching situation.

Expressing feelings can be healthy and helpful. After an especially satisfying performance before a large class of graduate students, the instructor was told by one student, "I enjoyed seeing that you were relishing the experience." That is a good observation to share. Telling a teacher "You appeared to be enjoying the responses you were getting" or "I shared your apprehension when Dickie volunteered" can have a desirable effect on the tone of the discussion.

COMMUNICATION TECHNIQUE 9: RESPECT CULTURAL NORMS WHILE COMMUNICATING

Effective communication between individuals is always a challenge. Even close friendships involve a process of learning how to talk to each other and what constitutes acceptable topics for conversation. Misunderstandings and hurt feelings can occur, even though friends basically like each other. Communication between clinical supervisors and teachers is similar. A learning process is involved, and it can be especially challenging if the persons come from different cultural and socioeconomic backgrounds.

Researchers have examined challenges to communication between individuals from different cultures in a field of inquiry sometimes called *intercultural communication.*[6] These researchers have learned that members of different cultures have different ways of transmitting and interpreting messages. For example, silence during a conversation in U.S. Caucasian culture might mean that the participants have run out of things to say to each other. In another culture, silence might mean that the participants are actively reflecting on what has been said and coming to some conclusion about it.

Prejudice about another person's culture obviously can deter effective communication. The effects of prejudice can be especially harmful if the persons talking to each other represent cultures that have had histories of domination and oppression. For example, the country of one person's culture might have much greater wealth as a result of conquest of another person's culture. This type of power and wealth inequality can enter into a clinical supervision conference, such that one of the participants feels that he is right because he comes from a majority culture or another person feels defensive and weak because he comes from a minority culture.

All participants in a clinical supervision process need to become aware of these prejudices and do the best they can to overcome them. This is not an easy goal to accomplish, but one helpful step is for each participant to learn about the other person's culture, including its cultural achievements and history. Another helpful step is to learn how the other person's culture perceives your own culture. This knowledge can help you understand how the other person in the clinical supervision relationship perceives you. You might become aware of things you might say or do that will be perceived as troublesome for the other person.

One of the theories used to understand intercultural communication is communication accommodation theory.[7] According to this theory, individuals can shape their verbal and nonverbal messages in order to emphasize or minimize their differences. For example, if a teacher wishes to emphasize her professional similarity to a clinical supervisor, she will engage in a process of convergence, meaning that she will shift her style of verbal and nonverbal communication to match the supervisor's style. Conversely, if a teacher wishes to emphasize her cultural difference from the supervisor, she will engage in a process of divergence, meaning that she will convey verbal and nonverbal messages that are characteristic of her own cultural group. A teacher or supervisor might engage in divergent communication if he feels threatened by the other person's culture or if he feels that adopting a convergent style of communication would threaten his cultural identity.

Communication accommodation theory exposes the thorny issues that can arise when a clinical supervisor and teacher come from different cultures, especially cultures that have had antagonistic histories in relation to each other. Supervisors and teachers should be aware of convergent and divergent intercultural communication and consider whether either style is interfering with the use of clinical supervision to promote the teacher's professional growth. In addition, they should consider the merits of adopting a style of interpersonal communication commonly shared by professionals across various fields. Among the salient elements of this style are respect for those being talked about (e.g., students and their parents), avoidance of swearing, formal diction, and the various communication techniques described in this chapter.

If the supervisor feels that her efforts might threaten the student's cultural identity, she will need to raise this issue in a sensitive manner so that both she and the student can examine it in a safe, mutually respectful manner. This approach should lead the student to realize that it is possible to engage in both professional and culturally distinct communication, each in its own appropriate setting.

Communication researchers use the term *code-switching* to refer to this shifting of communication styles. Code-switching can involve moving from a formal to an informal style of interpersonal communication. Or if the supervisor and teacher speak the same multiple languages (e.g., English and Spanish), they might find it helpful to code-switch occasionally from one language to the other. Perhaps they feel that they can convey certain ideas and feelings better in one of the languages, particularly if that language is closely associated with their family upbringing and cultural heritage.

COMMUNICATION TECHNIQUE 10: USE A MENTORING STYLE WHEN APPROPRIATE

In Chapter 3, we described mentoring as an increasingly popular method of professional development for new teachers. In fact, an educator might be asked to serve in both roles—serving as a mentor for novice teachers while also providing clinical supervision to improve their skills. We believe that the communication techniques used in clinical supervision are well suited for either role. In addition, communication techniques recommended specifically for mentoring can be helpful for both roles. A list of specific mentoring techniques is presented in Table 7.2.

Table 7.2 Effective Communication Techniques in Mentoring

- Mentors recognize that mentoring is a process of enabling another to act, and of building on the mentee's strengths rather than imposing ideas and information from the outside.
- Mentors not only focus on teaching techniques but also on the development of the mentee as an individual in interaction with students.
- The mentoring relationship allows frustration, anger, and other emotions to be expressed.
- Mentors are storytellers who relate back to their own beginning teaching to gain a deeper understanding of what the mentee is experiencing.
- Mentors make provision for thinking to be shared between meetings through the use of e-mail and the telephone.
- Mentors are aware of their own feelings so that any inclination to maintain status does not take precedence over the needs of the mentee.
- Mentors participate in classroom activity as a way of understanding better what the mentee is doing and feeling.

- Mentors talk about the books they've read, the plays and movies they've seen, and their other interests and encourage the mentee to do the same.
- Mentors establish an atmosphere in which the mentee feels free to take risks.
- Mentors raise questions that go beyond issues of day-to-day survival.
- Mentors encourage the mentee to find professional stimulation from others, such as Critical Friends groups, colleagues, and educational organizations.
- Mentors are open to learning from mentees who may have strengths they do not have. At times, the mentorship is a process of mutual appropriation rather than a simple transmission of knowledge.
- Mentors encourage the mentee to look inward by keeping a log and also maintain logs for themselves.
- Mentors recognize that mentees are at different levels of development and adjust their approach accordingly.
- Mentors avoid overidealizing their own past experience and are aware of the changing reality of the present.
- Mentors express their values regarding such current trends in education as standards-based curriculum, the implementation of business practices, and the use of vouchers.
- Mentors serve as cheerleaders, modeling enthusiasm and optimism and providing support at times of discouragement.
- Mentors help others such as school administration to recognize the mentee's worth.
- Mentors believe in the importance of listening and giving total attention as the mentee works toward becoming a skilled professional.

Source: Trubowitz, S., & Robins, M. P. (2003). *The good teacher mentor: Setting the standard for support and success* (pp. 115–116.) New York: Teachers College Press.

ENDNOTES

1. Flanders, N. A. (1970). *Analyzing teaching behavior.* Reading, MA: Addison-Wesley.

2. Blumberg, A. (1974). *Supervisors and teachers: A private cold war.* Berkeley, CA: McCutchan.

3. McGregor, D. (1960). *The human side of enterprise.* New York: McGraw-Hill.

4. Amidon, E., & Flanders, N. (1967). Interaction analysis as a feedback system. In E. J. Amidon & J. B. Hough (Eds.), *Interaction Analysis: Theory, Research, and Application* (pp. 122–124). Reading, MA: Addison-Wesley.

5. Burgoon, J. K. (2010). *Nonverbal communication.* Boston: Longman; Knapp, M.L., & Hall, J. A. (2010). *Nonverbal communication in human interaction.* Boston: Wadsworth.

6. Matsumoto, D. (2010). *APA handbook of intercultural communication.* Washington, DC: American Psychological Association.

7. Giles, H., & Coupland, N. (1991). *Language: Contexts and consequences.* Pacific Grove, CA: Brooks/Cole.

Chapter 8

The Planning Conference

I mean to suggest that the preobservation conference is a time for Teacher and Supervisor to reach explicit agreements about reasons for supervision to occur in the immediate situation and about how supervision should operate.
—Robert Goldhammer[1]

INTRODUCTION

A planning conference provides an opportunity for the teacher and supervisor to identify the teacher's concerns and translate them into observable behavior. It also results in a decision about the kinds of instructional data that will be recorded during classroom observation, which is the next phase of the supervisory cycle. Furthermore, a planning conference is an opportunity for the teacher to communicate with a fellow educator; it breaks down the isolation that teachers feel as a result of working alone in a self-contained classroom. These conferences are especially important to student teachers who might have no one other than the supervisor with whom to share personal concerns and emerging understandings about what it means to be a teacher.

The success of a planning conference depends in large part on how much trust the teacher places in the supervisor. Trust refers to the teacher's confidence that the supervisor has the teacher's interests at heart. A supervisor might be technically proficient; but unless he also instills trust, supervision is likely to be ineffective.

Planning conferences need not be long. Twenty to 30 minutes is usually sufficient for the first planning conference, unless the teacher has a particularly difficult problem to discuss or unless the teacher and supervisor are strangers to each other. Later planning conferences might require only five to 10 minutes, especially if there has been no change in the teacher's goals for improvement since the preceding clinical supervision cycle of planning-observation-feedback. The conferences are best held on neutral territory (e.g., the school cafeteria) or in the teacher's classroom. Going into a supervisor's office for a conference might make the teacher feel like he or she is being "called on the carpet."

This chapter presents various techniques that help to ensure a successful planning conference. In a sense, they constitute a set of agenda items for the conference. Therefore, you might find it helpful to prepare for a planning conference by recording certain of the techniques as your written agenda. Keep in mind, though, that the techniques are not prescriptive. You will need to use judgment in incorporating them into your supervisory style and applying them to each supervisory situation.

CONFERENCE TECHNIQUE 1: IDENTIFY THE TEACHER'S CONCERNS ABOUT INSTRUCTION

The major goal of clinical supervision is to help teachers improve their instruction. One step toward this goal is to use the planning conference to identify areas of instruction in which the teacher needs improvement.

A supervisor might directly ask the teacher the specific areas in which he or she would like to improve, but some teachers have not formulated self-improvement goals and feel put on the spot when asked to do so. If this is the case, the supervisor will need to assist the teacher in identifying concerns. Asking questions like these can be helpful: "How has your teaching been going?" "Do you find you are having more success in one area than another?" "My goal is to help you do the best possible teaching. What aspects of your teaching should we take a look at?"

In asking these questions, the supervisor should be intent on helping the teacher reveal true concerns without feeling threatened. A threatened teacher is likely to clam up or reveal only "safe" concerns. For example, some teachers have told us that "individualization of instruction" is a safe concern, but discipline is not. They believe teacher who mentions discipline problems might be perceived as incompetent, whereas a teacher who mentions individualization is likely to be perceived as well along the road toward being a master teacher.

Some teachers insist that they have no concerns—their class is running beautifully. In some instances this may be an accurate perception by the teacher, but we would suggest that there is always room for improvement in one's teaching. A good teacher can always get even better.

When a teacher insists that he or she has no concerns, the supervisor probably should take the statement at face value. The supervisor might then suggest using a "wide-lens" observation technique such as video recording (see Observation Technique 10), so that they can look together at the teacher's instruction. An appropriate tone can be set by asking, "How about making a videotape of one of your lessons so that we can see what aspects of your teaching you're satisfied with?" After the video recording has been made and reviewed in the feedback conference, the teacher is likely to become aware of areas needing improvement that were not previously apparent.

Teachers sometimes find it helpful to examine a checklist or other instrument that will be used to evaluate their teaching performance. In showing the checklist to a teacher, the supervisor might ask, "Which of these areas do you think you're strong in? Which of these areas do you think we might take a closer look at as areas for improvement?" Figure 8.1 presents one of the best known of these instruments—the Teacher Concerns Checklist, developed by Frances Fuller.[2] The items represent different levels of teacher concerns, which we described in our presentation of Fuller's model of teacher development in Chapter 2.

Figure 8.1 does not include several preliminary items in the Teacher Concerns Checklist that solicit general information about the teacher (e.g., name and age). If you wish, you can write your own items soliciting this type of information. Figure 8.1 also does not include the five-point scale adjacent to each item (1 2 3 4 5). In reproducing the checklist, you

DIRECTIONS: This checklist is designed to explore what teachers are concerned about at different points in their careers. There are, of course, no right or wrong answers; each person has his or her own concerns.

We consider you to be "concerned" about a thing if *you think about it frequently and would like to do something about it personally.* You are not concerned about a thing simply because you believe it is important—if it seldom crosses your mind, if you are satisfied with the current state of affairs, do not say you are concerned about it. You may be concerned about problems, but you may also be concerned about opportunities which could be realized. You may be concerned about things you are not currently dealing with, but only if you anticipate dealing with them and frequently think about them from this point of view. In short, you are concerned about it if you *often think about it* and would like to do something about it.

On the following pages, you will find statements about some things related to teaching.

Read each statement. Then ask yourself: When I Think about my teaching, How much Am I concerned about this?

If you are *not concerned* about that now, circle "1."
If you are *a little concerned*, circle "2."
If you are *moderately concerned*, circle "3."
If you are *very concerned*, circle "4."
And if you are *extremely concerned*, circle "5."

Read each statement, then ask yourself: When I think about my teaching, how much am I concerned about this?

Lack of respect of some students
Standards and regulations set for teachers
Selecting and teaching content well
The mandated curriculum is not appropriate for all students
Whether students are learning what they should
Whether the students really like me or not
Increasing students' feelings of accomplishment
The nature and quality of instructional materials
Where I stand as a teacher
Motivating students to study
Working productively with other teachers
Lack of instructional materials
Rapid rate of curriculum and instructional change
Feeling under pressure too much of the time

The routine and inflexibility of the situation
Becoming too personally involved with students
Maintaining the appropriate degree of class control
Acceptance as a friend by students
Understanding the principal's policies
The wide range of student achievement
Doing well when a supervisor is present
Meeting the needs of different kinds of students
Being fair and impartial
Diagnosing student learning problems
Getting a favorable evaluation of my teaching
Being asked personal questions by my students
Too many noninstructional duties

Figure 8.1 Teacher concerns checklist[1]

Ensuring that students grasp subject matter fundamentals	Chronic absence and dropping out of students
Working with too many students each day	Lack of academic freedom
Challenging unmotivated students	Teaching required content to students of varied backgrounds
The values and attitudes of the current generation	Student use of drugs
Adapting myself to the needs of different students	Feeling more adequate as a teacher
Whether students can apply what they learn	Guiding students toward intellectual and emotional growth
Understanding the philosophy of the school	Being accepted and respected by professional persons
Students who disrupt classes	Adequately presenting all of the required material
Instilling worthwhile concepts and values	Slow progress of certain students
How students feel about me	My ability to present ideas to the class
Student health and nutrition problems that affect learning	Helping students to value learning
The psychological climate of the school	Whether each student is getting what he needs
Clarifying the limits of my authority and responsibility	Increasing my proficiency in content
Assessing and reporting student progress	Recognizing the social and emotional needs of students
	The wide diversity of student ethnic and socioeconomic backgrounds

Figure 8.1 (*Continued*)

Source: Fuller, F. F. (1978). Teacher Concerns Checklist. Austin: Research and Development Center for Teacher Education, The University of Texas at Austin.
[1]This is version B3 of the Teacher Concerns Checklist

simply would add this scale next to each item. Also, you can add items that express concerns not in the checklist.

Another way to help teachers gain awareness of their concerns about instruction is to show them a list of concerns that other teachers have expressed. An example is the list compiled by Simon Veenman, based on more than 80 studies of the perceived problems of beginning teachers.[3] He listed each problem, counted the number of times it was mentioned across the studies, and then ranked the items by frequency of mentions. The problems and their rank, in order from the most frequently mentioned to the least frequently mentioned, are shown in Table 8.1. Tom Ganser followed up on Veenman's review by surveying a sample of student teachers and inservice teachers. He found that the problem rankings were different for his sample.[4]

Table 8.1 Perceived Problems of Beginning Teachers

Rank	Problem
1	Classroom discipline
2	Motivating students
3	Dealing with individual differences
4.5	Assessing students' work
4.5	Relations with parents
6.5	Organization of class work
6.5	Insufficient materials and supplies
8	Dealing with problems of individual students
9	Having teaching load resulting in insufficient prep time
10	Relations with colleagues
11	Effective use of different teaching methods
13	Awareness of school policies and rules
14	Determining learning level of students
16	Knowledge of subject matter
16	Burden of clerical work
16	Relations with principals/administrators
18	Inadequate school equipment
19	Dealing with slow learners
20	Dealing with students of different cultures and deprived backgrounds
21	Effective use of textbooks and curriculum guides
22	Lack of spare time
23	Inadequate guidance and support
24	Large class size

Source: Veenman, S. (1984). Perceived problems of beginning teachers. *Review of Educational Research,* *54*(2), 143–178. (Table appears on pp. 154–155.) Copyright © 1984 by the American Educational Research Association. Reprinted by permission of Sage Publishers.

CONFERENCE TECHNIQUE 2: TRANSLATE THE TEACHER'S CONCERNS INTO OBSERVABLE BEHAVIORS

Helping a teacher translate concerns about teaching into observable behaviors is one of the most important techniques in clinical supervision. It is similar to a doctor's diagnostic work. The doctor's first task is to translate the patient's complaints into medical terms. The doctor does this by asking questions: "What are the specific problems you've been having?"

"What does the discomfort feel like?" "How long have you felt this way?" These questions help the doctor create a clear picture of the medical problem and then to prescribe a treatment.

The clinical supervisor similarly needs to function as a diagnostician in the planning conference. Suppose a student teacher says, "I'm not sure I have the confidence to be a teacher." The teacher's expressed concern is lack of confidence, but the supervisor needs to probe further. Confidence might mean something different to the teacher than it does to the supervisor.

In translating concerns into observable behaviors, the supervisor needs to listen for teacher statements that contain abstract or ambiguous words, as in these examples:

"I'm afraid I'm a dictator."

"I can't get this class of students interested in learning about geography."

"There's just not enough time to cover everything I want to get across."

"Some of my students are like wild animals."

"I'm afraid I don't project warmth."

"I wonder if I'm too critical of students."

"These kids just aren't able to understand basic algebra."

As a supervisor, your task is to clarify these concerns so that they are stated in observable form. Here are examples of questions that might help the teacher state a concern more concretely:

"Do you know a teacher who projects warmth? What does she do?"

"What kinds of things do you do that make you think you're too critical of students?"

"How would you know if a student understands or doesn't understand?"

"To help me understand how much content you're trying to cover, can you start by telling me the most important information and ideas you want students to learn?"

In listening to a teacher's responses to such questions, you can ask yourself this question: "Is the teacher providing sufficient information for me to clearly observe her concern as it is expressed in her classroom?" Another helpful question to ask yourself is "Do the teacher and I mean the same thing when we use the term _____?"

Research studies have been done to clarify the meaning of key concepts in teaching. For example, Andrew Bush, John Kennedy, and Donald Cruickshank conducted research to determine the observable referents of teacher clarity.[5] They asked students to list five behaviors performed by their clearest teacher. They were able to identify the following observable behaviors underlying the concept of clarity:

- gives examples and explains them.
- repeats questions and explanations if students don't understand them.
- lets students ask questions.
- pronounces words distinctly.
- talks only about things related to the topic he or she is teaching.
- uses common words.
- writes important things on the blackboard.

- relates what he or she is teaching to real life.
- asks questions to find out if students understand what he or she has told them.

This list is not exhaustive, but it can help teachers and supervisors work together to improve the clarity of the teacher's instruction.

Nonverbal aspects of teaching, such as teacher enthusiasm, also can be made observable through careful analysis. Mary Collins identified the following observable referents for enthusiasm by reviewing previous research on this variable, doing her own analysis of this concept, and consulting other teacher educators.[6]

Observable Referents for Enthusiasm

- *Vocal Delivery:* great and sudden changes from rapid excited speech to a whisper; varied, lilting, uplifting intonations; many changes in tone, pitch.
- *Eyes:* dancing, snapping, shining, lighting up, frequently opened wide, eyebrows raised, eye contact with total group.
- *Gestures:* frequent demonstrative movements of body, head, arms, hands, and face; sweeping motions; clapping hands; head nodding rapidly.
- *Movements:* large body movements; swings around, changes pace, bends body.
- *Facial Expression:* appears vibrant, demonstrative; changes denoting surprise, sadness, joy, thoughtfulness, awe, excitement.
- *Word Selection:* highly descriptive, many adjectives, great variety.
- *Acceptance of Ideas and Feelings:* accepts ideas and feelings quickly with vigor and animation; ready to accept, praise, encourage, or clarify in a nonthreatening manner; many variations in responding to pupils.
- *Overall Energy:* explosive, exuberant; high degree of vitality, drive, and spirit throughout lesson.

Using this list as a guide, Collins and others were able to help teachers significantly improve their level of enthusiasm in the classroom.[7]

Chapters 9–12 present more examples of observable referents for specific teacher concerns, and also methods for recording classroom data about them.

CONFERENCE TECHNIQUE 3: IDENTIFY PROCEDURES FOR IMPROVING THE TEACHER'S INSTRUCTION

The first two techniques described in this chapter are intended to help the teacher identify concerns and translate them into observable behaviors. What happens next in a planning conference?

If the teacher has successfully identified some observable concerns, the stage is set for thinking about possible changes in instructional behavior. For example, consider a teacher who is worried that he comes across as dull and unenthusiastic. As the supervisor helps this teacher identify observable behaviors that comprise enthusiasm (perhaps with the help of the list in the preceding section), the teacher is likely to ask, "I wonder how I could get myself to do those things?" The supervisor can facilitate this process by thinking aloud with the teacher about procedures that can be used to acquire new teaching skills.

The simplest procedure is for the teacher to practice the behaviors independently. The supervisor might say, "Why don't you make a list of these enthusiasm behaviors on a 5x8 card and keep it near you when you teach? In a week or so, I'll come in and make a video recording so you can see how you're doing."

Some procedures are more involved. For example, a teacher's concern might be how to use learning centers in his or her classroom. This involves a whole set of instructional skills. To acquire them, the teacher might need to read articles and books and attend workshops on learning centers.

If a teacher's concern is about changing student behavior, a sequence of procedures is needed. To illustrate, suppose the teacher is concerned that students do not pay attention during class discussions. The supervisor first helps the teacher to define "attention" as a set of observable student behaviors—answering teacher's questions thoughtfully, looking at other students as they speak, initiating relevant comments and questions, and so forth. The teacher's next task is to develop instructional procedures that will bring about these desired "attending" behaviors. Finally, the teacher will need to practice these instructional procedures until they are mastered.

The following is an excerpt from a planning conference in which the goal was change in the attending behavior of second-grade children:

TEACHER: I'd like you to come in and take a look at Randall and Ronald. They don't do anything but play and talk.

SUPERVISOR: Are Randall and Ronald the only ones you want me to observe?

TEACHER: No. I have a real immature group this year. You might as well observe all of them.

SUPERVISOR: What do you mean by "immature"?

TEACHER: Oh, they have very short attention spans, haven't learned to settle down, and they just talk without permission.

[*At this point, teacher and supervisor decided to focus on one problem behavior— talking without permission. The dialogue continues.*]

SUPERVISOR: Can you give an example of a situation where they talk without permission?

TEACHER: Well, when I have them in a small reading group, and I ask one of them a question, any of them will speak up if they think they have the answer. Sometimes they don't even listen to the question, they just say what's on their mind. And it doesn't matter whether another child is already talking. They'll just ignore him and speak at the same time.

SUPERVISOR: I think I have a pretty clear idea of what's happening. What do you think you can do so that only the child you call on responds, and so that if another child has something to say, he waits his turn?

TEACHER: I guess I could teach them some rules for participating. Like raising their hands when they wish to speak and remaining quiet when another child is speaking.

The teacher and supervisor proceeded to discuss possible methods of teaching these rules to the children. The teacher took notes on the procedures and agreed to practice using them the following week. In addition, the supervisor suggested that the teacher try praising or otherwise rewarding children when they obey participation rules in the reading group. In making this suggestion, the supervisor discovered that the teacher was unfamiliar with the reinforcement principles underlying the use of praise and other rewards in classroom teaching. The supervisor therefore suggested that the teacher might benefit from enrolling in an upcoming workshop on classroom management in which these principles would be discussed.

CONFERENCE TECHNIQUE 4: ASSIST THE TEACHER IN SETTING INSTRUCTIONAL-IMPROVEMENT GOALS

In the preceding section, we presented the example of a teacher concerned about students speaking out of turn. The supervisor helped the teacher identify several observable behaviors of students that reflected this concern and also aided the teacher in identifying procedures for changing these behaviors. It seems apparent that the teacher's goal is to improve students' verbal participation behaviors in reading groups. The clinical supervision process is facilitated by making this goal explicit. By doing so, teacher and supervisor both develop a clear understanding of the direction in which the clinical supervision process is headed. It also prevents a state of confusion, with the teacher thinking, "I wonder what the supervisor expects me to be doing?"

The supervisor or the teacher can state the goal, but whoever does so should check that the other person has the same understanding of the goal and agrees with it. In the example we have been considering, the goal formulation process might occur as follows:

SUPERVISOR: To review, then, one of the things you're concerned about is students speaking out of turn. You've picked out a number of behaviors you'd like to see your students engage in. Given that, is there a goal you would set for yourself?

TEACHER: Yes. My first goal is to reduce the incidence of students' speaking out of turn. My other goal is to have my students engage in more positive behaviors, like listening to one another and raising their hands when they have something to say.

SUPERVISOR: Those are worthwhile goals, and I'll do what I can to help you with them.

This type of interchange gives structure and focus to the planning conference.

For teachers who are working on growth goals (rather than deficiency needs), goal-setting can be teacher-centered. Teachers who are on plans of assistance or have little insight into the teaching process might require supervisor-centered goal-setting. If the supervisor discusses his or her reasons for setting a particular instructional-improvement goal, the teacher is more likely to view it as reasonable rather than arbitrary or as the supervisor's personal philosophy of teaching. If the discussion process is open and there is a climate of trust, we have found that most teachers will gradually "own" the goal.

CONFERENCE TECHNIQUE 5: ARRANGE A TIME FOR CLASSROOM OBSERVATION

After talking about the teacher's concerns and instructional-improvement goals, the supervisor and teacher can turn their attention to planning for observation of the teacher in his or her classroom.

The first step in planning for observation is to arrange a mutually convenient time for the supervisor to visit the classroom and observe a lesson. The major criterion for selecting a lesson to observe is that it should present opportunities for collecting data on instances of the teacher's concerns and solutions to those concerns. If the teacher's concern is students' responses in a classroom discussion, there is no point in observing a lesson in which students are engaged in independent learning projects.

It is important to arrange a mutually convenient time for classroom observation. Teachers are resentful when supervisors come to their room unannounced. Indeed, our experience indicates that few things disturb teachers more than unannounced visits by a supervisor or other individual in a position of authority. Teachers need to feel that the supervisor respects them as professionals and as people with first-line responsibility for their classrooms. They are not likely to feel this way if a supervisor pops in anytime he or she wishes to do so.

Arranging a mutually convenient time is particularly important for student teachers. They can be put into a state of constant tension if they know that the supervisor can enter their class unannounced at any time. Arranging a time for observation beforehand enables the student teacher to prepare instructionally—and emotionally—for the supervisor's visit. It also gives the student teacher a sense of control over the supervisory process. Having this sense of control increases the likelihood that the student teacher will use supervision for self-improvement, rather than feel used by it.

CONFERENCE TECHNIQUE 6: SELECT AN OBSERVATION INSTRUMENT AND BEHAVIORS TO BE RECORDED

Teachers' comments in a planning conference primarily reflect their own perceptions of their instruction. These perceptions might differ from what actually transpires. (The theory of action, described in Chapter 1, concerns this type of discrepancy in professional practice.) Observational data provide an objective check on the teacher's perceptions and also a record of instructional phenomena that might have escaped the teacher's perception.

A wide range of observation instruments are described in Unit 4. Also, the Appendix lists these instruments and some of the teaching techniques that can be observed by their use. You will need to become familiar with these instruments in order to help the teacher select one that is appropriate for his or her instructional concerns. For example, if a teacher is concerned about nonverbal behavior, a video recording (Observation Technique 10) might be appropriate. If the concern is about a problem child in the classroom, an anecdotal record (Observation Technique 9) can be helpful. Or if a teacher is concerned about the level of commotion in his or her classroom, a record of students' movement patterns (Observation Technique 8) might yield useful data for instructional improvement.

If the teacher and supervisor use the conference only to talk about instruction, the conversation might drift into vague generalities and abstractions. Selecting an observation instrument brings the teacher "down to earth" by focusing attention on the observable realities of classroom instruction. If the teacher is unfamiliar with methods of classroom observation, the supervisor can introduce particular instruments and emphasize that they are used to collect objective data, not to pass judgment on the teacher. Once teachers become familiar with the range of instruments, they should be encouraged to initiate suggestions about which is most appropriate for their concerns.

CONFERENCE TECHNIQUE 7: CLARIFY THE INSTRUCTIONAL CONTEXT IN WHICH DATA WILL BE RECORDED

Instructional behavior does not occur in a vacuum. It occurs in a context that must be understood if the observational data are to be interpreted properly. A supervisor cannot expect to gain this understanding by walking into a teacher's classroom "cold." Instead, we recommend that you allow time in the planning conference to ask the teacher a few questions about the instructional context of the behaviors to be observed. Because the usual instructional context is a lesson that the teacher plans to teach, you might wish to ask the teacher questions such as these:

"What content will you be teaching in the lesson that I'll be observing?"

"What are your students like, and how diverse are they?"

"What do you expect the students to learn in this lesson?"

"What teaching methods and materials will you be using?"

"Is there anything I should be aware of as you teach this lesson?"

Asking these questions indicates to the teacher that you wish to understand the teacher's classroom from his perspective. Also, when you actually visit the classroom, your presence during the lesson will be tolerated better, because you and the teacher have a shared understanding of what the lesson is about.

ENDNOTES

1. Goldhammer, R. (1969). *Clinical supervision: Special methods for the supervision of teachers*. New York: Holt, Rinehart & Winston. Quote appears on p. 60.

2. Fuller, F. F. (1978). *Teacher Concerns Checklist*. Austin: University of Texas, Research and Development Center for Teacher Education.

3. Veenman, S. (1984). Perceived problems of beginning teachers. *Review of Educational Research, 54*(2), 143–178.

4. Ganser, T. (1999). *Reconsidering the relevance of Veenman's (1984) meta-analysis of perceived problems of beginning teachers*. Retrieved from ERIC database. (ED429964)

5. Bush, A. J., Kennedy, J. J., & Cruickshank, D. R. (1977). An empirical investigation of teacher clarity. *Journal of Teacher Education, 28*, 53–58.

6. Collins, M. L. (1978). Effects of enthusiasm training on preservice elementary teachers. *Journal of Teacher Education, 29*, 53–57.

7. Klinzing, H. G., & Jackson, I. (1987). Training teachers in nonverbal sensitivity and nonverbal behavior. *International Journal of Educational Research, 11*(5), 589-600; Denight, J. A. (1987). Effects of teacher enthusiasm training on at-task behavior and attitudes of students in high school. *Dissertation Abstracts International: Section A. Humanities and Social Sciences, 48*(11), 2845; Bettencourt, E. M., Gillett, M. H., Gall, M. D., & Hull, R. E. (1983). Effects of teacher enthusiasm training on student on-task behavior and achievement. *American Educational Research Journal, 20*, 435–450.

Chapter 9

The Feedback Conference

Perhaps the best measure of whether a [feedback] conference has been useful, in Teacher's framework, is whether it has left him with something concrete in hand, namely, a design for his next sequence of instruction.
—Robert Goldhammer[1]

INTRODUCTION

Before a successful feedback conference can occur, the teacher and supervisor should have completed a planning conference in which they

- establish a climate of mutual trust.
- determine the teacher's concerns and self-improvement goals.
- translate the concerns and goals into observable behaviors.
- select an observation instrument and types of classroom behavior to be recorded.
- discuss relevant contextual features of the classroom lesson that is to be observed.

Also, the supervisor will need to have collected—and, if appropriate, summarized—the observational data. If these things have been done, the supervisor will have laid the groundwork for a successful feedback conference.

In the feedback conference itself, the supervisor and teacher review the accuracy of the observational data. Next, they interpret the data, looking for significant patterns—especially those involving the teacher's instructional behavior and its effect on students. They also try to explain the patterns, possibly invoking values, beliefs, and formal theories of teaching and learning. Finally, the teacher and supervisor consider future action, including experimenting with alternative teaching strategies, changing curriculum objectives, treating particular students differently, or setting goals to learn new instructional skills. Also, the teacher and supervisor might agree on the need for more observational data of the same or a different type. In fact, the feedback conference that completes one cycle of clinical supervision often initiates the planning phase of the next cycle. In that case, the next planning conference might occur immediately after the feedback conference, or it can be scheduled for a later time.

These procedures are useful only if the supervisor's purpose is to help the teacher become a reflective, self-regulating individual focused on personal professional growth. Unfortunately, this is not always true of actual clinical supervision. Miriam Ben-Peretz and Sarah Rumney observed feedback conferences between student teachers and their cooperating teachers in Israeli teacher-education programs and discovered that the conferences were

> in most cases very one-directional, the teacher making comments and the trainee agreeing. The majority of remarks concerned shortcomings of the student teachers. For instance, the teacher would say: You should have taught this in a different way, or I do not agree with your explanation of this word, or Why didn't you follow my instructions?[2]

Ben-Peretz and Rumney concluded from these and other research findings that "cooperating teachers perceive the student teachers not as novice professionals but as 'students' whose primary duty is to listen and learn."[3] They also found that feedback conferences led by cooperating teachers were quite brief. Ten to 20 minutes was the typical duration. Feedback conferences led by university supervisors were substantially longer (30 to 40 minutes); there was also more reciprocal communication and more generation of alternative ideas for teaching. Although Ben-Peretz and Rumney's research was limited to Israeli teacher education, research indicates that the same situation exists in the United States and elsewhere.[4]

Finding time for the feedback conference—and other parts of the supervisory cycle—is no easy task. Nonetheless, finding time should be a major priority, given that teachers' professional growth is at stake.

CONFERENCE TECHNIQUE 8: PROVIDE THE TEACHER WITH FEEDBACK USING OBJECTIVE OBSERVATIONAL DATA

Many teachers feel defensive as they enter the feedback conference, because they see it as an evaluation of their competence. Their defensiveness will worsen if they perceive the observational data to be subjective, inaccurate, or irrelevant. Therefore, an objective record of classroom events—such as is provided by videotaping, audiotaping, or selective verbatim transcript—is crucial. Teachers might be surprised by what the data reveal, but they generally will accept the data as valid and instructive.

Observational records are never perfect. For example, videotaping provides an excellent record of classroom events, but it cannot capture everything. Furthermore, the judgment, skill, and biases of the person operating the video camera will affect the recording. A teacher might be tempted to dismiss the observational record because of these imperfections. As a supervisor, you can acknowledge the teacher's concerns, but also note that, while all data are imperfect, some data are better than others. If the data achieve a certain level of objectivity, there is much to be learned from them. You might wish to invoke the time-honored saying, "Let's not throw the baby out with the bathwater."

We have found it best to present the observational record to the teacher as soon as possible in the feedback conference. A statement like, "Let's look at the data we have collected," is usually sufficient. If the data are numerical or involve the use of symbols, you first might need to refresh the teacher's memory of what they mean.

While the teacher reviews the observational record, you can ask him to *describe*—not *evaluate*—what the record reveals about the lesson. For example, suppose a teacher looks at a video recording and says, "Wow. It took me too long to get the class settled down."

Your response might be, "Let's see how many minutes passed from the time the bell rang to the time instruction began." Once the minutes are known, the supervisor and teacher can discuss whether the time required to settle the class down is excessive and what a reasonable time limit might be.

As another example, consider the teacher who examines a selective verbatim transcript (see Chapter 10) and says, "I didn't explain the Malthusian theory of population growth very well." As a supervisor, your response might be, "You're not happy with your explanation. But before we make any judgments about it, let's try to understand how you went about explaining the theory to the class. So, looking at the selective record, would you walk me through your explanation?" By asking the teacher to focus on description, the supervisor demonstrates that understanding, not evaluation, is the priority.

Interpretation of the observational record follows naturally from a careful descriptive analysis of it. The teacher and supervisor together can look for possible causes and consequences of observed teacher behavior. For example, observation of students' at-task behavior during a class period might show their interest in an instructional activity waning after 20 minutes. The teacher might interpret these data as indicating a weakness in the activity or as a normal consequence of students' limited attention span. Depending on the interpretation, decisions for change will vary. If the activity is judged inappropriate, it can be modified in future lessons. If it is interpreted as appropriate but too long for students at this developmental level, it might merely need to be shortened.

Deciding what changes to make in future instruction can take many forms. Decisions can relate to any of the instructional elements discussed in the planning conference. For example, the conferees might conclude that one or more of the following should be changed: the objectives of the lesson or unit; what the teacher does during the instruction; what students do during instruction.

Decisions vary in magnitude. At one extreme, the teacher might decide to leave teaching as the result of systematic observational feedback. (We have seen instances of this.) At the other extreme, the teacher might decide not to change a thing. (This has not happened, in our experience; teachers who believe they are perfect must be very rare.) More often, teachers think of several aspects of their instruction that can be improved. We recall a teacher who studied a seating chart on which an observer had recorded which students were responded to by the teacher and what kind of response was given. She then began to understand why some students had felt "turned off," and she began to plan activities that would create opportunities to respond in positive ways to those students. Many teachers who have analyzed charts of their direct and indirect behaviors using Flanders's Interaction Analysis System (see Observation Technique 17) have modified their indirect-direct ratio. Teachers who have had access to verbal flow patterns on seating charts (see Observation Technique 7) have been stimulated to experiment with different seating arrangements.

Occasionally a teacher reaches a decision as the result of viewing data without having made any comments during the feedback conference. We recall one teacher, whose communication style was low-key during a videotaped lesson, display a very dynamic style during the next observed lesson (also videotaped). The supervisor asked about the obvious and abrupt change in teaching style, a matter that had not been mentioned in the previous conference. The teacher replied, "It wasn't until after I saw that first tape that I realized how undynamic I was. I swore I'd try something much different the next time!"

Time for collecting observational data and providing feedback is always limited. One way to deal with this problem is for the teacher to collect some of the data. This can be done by such methods as teacher-made video or audio recordings (see Chapter 12) or check-lists completed by students (see Chapter 13). If the teacher has collected and analyzed these data, the feedback conference can be more efficient. Furthermore, the performance of these tasks can be a learning experience for teachers, because it focuses their attention on particular aspects of their instruction.

CONFERENCE TECHNIQUE 9: ELICIT THE TEACHER'S INFERENCES, OPINIONS, AND EMOTIONS

One way for a supervisor to open the feedback conference is to ask, "How do you feel your lesson went?" In response, cautious teachers might hesitate to say, "Great!" for fear the supervisor will contradict or disagree. A less threatening opening question, after the teacher has had a chance to inspect the information, is to ask, "What aspects of the data do you want to talk about first?"

Eliciting the teacher's reactions to the data requires skill and patience. There is always a temptation to jump to conclusions about what has been recorded and observed before the teacher has had an opportunity to reflect on it. A conversation move that works well is to ask the following questions:

"What do you see [or hear] in the observational record that you would repeat if you taught this lesson again?"

"What would you change?"

"What would a student want changed?"

We have asked these questions of hundreds of teachers—primary, intermediate, sec-ondary, and college—who have examined observational data on their teaching behavior. No one has answered all the questions with "I wouldn't change a thing." With respect to the third question, the teacher can be asked to view his instruction from the perspective of different students—say, one who usually has difficulty understanding and one who is usu-ally ahead of the rest.

Because these questions are phrased in a relatively nonthreatening manner, most teachers are able to respond openly and with insight. In response to the third question, the following interchange between the teacher (T) and supervisor (S) occurred:

T: "Which student?"

S: "What do you mean, which student?"

T: "Well, the slowest, the brightest, the least interested?"

S: "OK, the slowest."

T: "All right. What I see that teacher doing is talking too fast, using vocabulary I don't understand, discussing topics that don't affect me. I don't think she likes me; she almost never calls on me even when I know the answer."

This was a good insight for the teacher to develop.

For most teachers, the steps in the feedback conference are reasonable and appropri-ate: providing objective data, analyzing and interpreting it, and drawing conclusions with the teacher taking equal part in a collaborative process. Unfortunately, some supervisors reverse the process. They provide their own conclusions and then search the observational record for evidence to substantiate them. Alternative interpretations might not even be considered.

For a small percentage of teachers, a "conclusions first" conference approach might be justified. For example, it might be more effective to say, "You've been late for work 12 times this month. This has got to stop, or there will be serious consequences!" rather than to say, "Here are some data about your punctuality. Do you find anything of interest?" An alternative move might be to ask, "What do you propose to do about this record of tardiness?"

Most teachers experience emotions as they teach and also as they examine the observational record of their teaching. While teaching, they might experience distress when students spin out of control or when a planned lesson ends well before the end of the class period. They might feel burned out at the end of the school year or after years of a stressful school environment or insufficient intellectual stimulation. They might experience joy when they see students get excited by a teaching activity or experience an insight. They might experience disappointment when the observational record presents them with data very discrepant from their image of themselves as a teacher. Or they might experience elation when the observational record demonstrates improvement in a troublesome aspect of their teaching behavior.

It is important for you as a supervisor to be aware that teachers have emotions, to bring the teacher's emotions into the feedback conference as appropriate, and—most importantly—to accept, without judgment, whatever a teacher might tell you about these emotions. For example, we have had preservice teachers whose field placements are not going well. They often are fearful that they will fail the placement, and so they react to observational data with fear about what the data might reveal. Also common among preservice teachers is anxiety about standing up in front of a class of students and having sole responsibility for their instruction.

A moderate level of anxiety can facilitate positive changes in teaching behavior. If the anxiety is too severe, though, the teacher might "freeze" and be unable to process the observational data and learn from it. In this situation, it is helpful for the supervisor to surface the teacher's anxiety and discuss it. This process by itself can relieve the teacher's anxiety. Also, a frank discussion about the anxiety can suggest solutions that the teacher to eliminate the problem that is producing the anxiety. For example, we have had student teachers who were very anxious about how they were perceived by the class for which they were about to assume responsibility. Once this anxiety was out in the open, we were able to work with the student teacher and the cooperating teacher so that the latter could better prepare the class to accept the student teacher's legitimacy as its instructor.

CONFERENCE TECHNIQUE 10: ENCOURAGE THE TEACHER TO CONSIDER ALTERNATIVE METHODS AND EXPLANATIONS

Supervisors often have a strong inclination in the feedback conference to say something like, "Here's what I would do if I were you." This short-circuits the supervision process. If teaching were a straightforward physical skill, then viewing the performance and giving advice like "Keep your eye on the ball," might be effective. Translated to advice about teaching, this tends to become "Be firm, fair, and consistent." This is undoubtedly good advice, but it does not tell what to be firm about (discipline? curriculum standards?) or what is fair and consistent (activities for the physically handicapped? individualized academic assignments?). Moreover, there are always reasonable alternatives for teaching anything, so any prescriptive advice might make the teacher question the supervisor's expertise.

When change is desired, the supervisor should encourage the teacher to generate several alternatives for improving her instruction and choose the one she considers most promising. Once the teacher has made suggestions, the supervisor can add to them. Having the opportunity to speak first helps the teacher feels heard and increases receptivity to what the supervisor has to say.

The ability to generate alternative explanations for behavior in the classroom is equally important to a teacher's potential to grow as a professional. Without this ability, teachers can get into a rut or become rigid in their thinking. In reality, human behavior is complex and is affected by many factors. Therefore, any one explanation for classroom behavior is likely to identify some relevant factors, but ignore others. By constantly considering alternative explanations, the teacher is likely to develop a richer understanding of students, themselves, and their colleagues.

As a case in point, we recall working with an inexperienced teacher at the middle-school level. The teacher was struggling with several students who would not do any seat work. His explanation was that these students were experiencing the turbulence of adolescence, one manifestation of which was rebellion against adult authority. We recommended that the teacher talk individually with each student to see whether their reluctance to do seat work might have other explanations. The teacher learned, to his surprise, that one student was earning a failing grade and figured there was no point in doing any more work in the class; his fate was sealed. Another student said that she was troubled by problems at home and could not focus on her studies. Needless to say, these alternative explanations caused the teacher to think about the students in a different way and to consider new methods for motivating them.

Some teachers hold the implicit belief—below the level of conscious awareness—that their behavior is "fixed." Even if their teaching methods do not produce the results they wish, they do not believe their behavior is amenable to change. By encouraging teachers to consider alternative methods for achieving an instructional objective or other goal, you help them question this belief.

As we explained in Chapter 1, Chris Argyris and Donald Schön claim that professional practitioners have "espoused theories" and "theories-in-use" that guide their work. If these theories are not questioned, the practitioner is likely to develop a set of work routines that do not change over time, even if they are ineffective. One way to help professional practitioners—including teachers—break out of these routines is to have them generate ideas about alternative methods of behaving in a certain situation and then test them in actual practice.

For example, one of us worked with a team to help a group of secondary teachers consider new ways of teaching their curriculum. Observational data revealed that the teachers, in general, required students to learn a great deal of isolated facts and skills. The teachers had used this approach for so long that they could imagine no other way of approaching the curriculum. The team introduced the teachers to an alternative method of teaching curriculum content, which is called *concept-based teaching*, among other names.[5]

Some teachers were skeptical about this teaching method. They thought it would be difficult to implement and would wind up confusing students. However, as they tried the method (with staff-development support), they found that they could continue teaching facts and skills they considered important, but now organized in a meaningful conceptual framework. Some students who formerly learned by rote, if at all, now had better comprehension of the curriculum and were willing to expend more effort on learning.

CONFERENCE TECHNIQUE 11: PROVIDE THE TEACHER WITH OPPORTUNITIES FOR PRACTICE AND COMPARISON

Some supervisors play a more direct role in the supervisory process by suggesting and demonstrating a particular method or technique in a classroom setting. Curriculum specialists in particular are often asked to do such demonstrations. In this situation, the teacher becomes the observer and can record data to be analyzed and interpreted in the feedback conference. For example, an elementary teacher was experiencing difficulty explaining the mathematical meaning of *pi* and the formulas for circumference and area. She asked a mathematics specialist to take over a lesson while she observed the explanation and recorded student responses and questions. During the feedback conference, information about the specialist's lesson was considered alongside information taken from the teacher's experience and plans.

Gerald Elgarten conducted an experiment to determine whether modeling by the supervisor facilitates the development of experienced mathematics teachers.[6] In one of the experimental conditions, a supervisor observed the teacher's lesson and identified teaching behaviors that needed to be introduced or changed.[7] The supervisor then taught the same lesson to the teacher's next class while modeling the strengths of the teacher's lesson and also the targeted teaching behaviors. The teacher observed the lesson and responded to three questions:

1. What do I [supervisor] do that you don't do too often?
2. What do we both seem to do?
3. What good things do you do that I don't seem to do?

These three questions served as the focus of the feedback conference. At the end of the conference, the teacher left with a list of teaching behaviors to practice and internalize. In another experimental condition, the teachers received similar supervision, except that the supervisor did not model the desired changes in teaching behavior by teaching a lesson. The results of this experiment revealed that the teachers who had the opportunity to see their supervisor teach a model lesson implemented more of the desired changes than teachers who participated in clinical supervision without this feature.

One explanation for the effectiveness of supervisor modeling is that it gives teachers the opportunity to observe good teaching techniques in a real-world context, not just hear about them. Also, supervisors undoubtedly gain credibility in the eyes of teachers if they can "practice what they preach."

Another effective strategy is to suggest that one teacher observe another in order to compare teaching styles, strategies, and techniques. If the observing teacher has some knowledge of systematic observation and recording, the feedback conference can result in a mutual sharing of ideas and perspectives. In a small group that takes turns sharing videotaped examples, the observers can learn about their own teaching vicariously while watching others. This type of collaborative observation and feedback by teachers is a feature of several of the professional development methods described in Chapter 3, particularly peer consultation and peer coaching.

The Gates Foundation announced in 2009 that it plans to post online videos of exemplary teachers during their classroom instruction.[8] If this plan comes to fruition, the online videos would be an excellent resource for teachers to observe exemplary teachers' instructional practices and compare them with their own practices. Many videos of exemplary teachers are already available through various professional organizations. For example, the Association for Supervision and Curriculum Development (ASCD) has a long history of creating videos illustrating exemplary use of various teaching strategies. The videos typically are accompanied by guides for use in workshops or self-study.

Many books that describe general teaching principles or specific teaching strategies are available. Supervisors should consider having a collection of these resources to make available to teachers. Reading them can help the teacher identify ideas for teaching beyond those that are already in their repertoire. We recommend that you start your search for these resources by noting the books and articles that we cite in Chapter 4. Most of them describe teaching methods that have been demonstrated by researchers to improve student learning.

ENDNOTES

1. Goldhammer, R. (1969). *Clinical supervision: Special methods for the supervision of teachers.* New York: Holt, Rinehart & Winston. Quote appears on pp. 69–70.

2. Ben-Peretz, M., & Rumney, S. (1991). Professional thinking in guided practice. *Teaching & Teacher Education, 7*, 517–530. (Quote appears on p. 519.) Copyright © 1991 by Elsevier. Reprinted by permission of Sage Publishers.

3. *Ibid.*, p. 525.

4. Graybeal, N. D. (1984). Characteristics of contemporary classroom supervisory process. *Dissertation Abstracts International: Section A. Humanities and Social Sciences, 45*(07), 2071.

5. Erickson, H. L. (2002). *Concept-based curriculum and instruction: Teaching beyond the facts.* Thousand Oaks, CA: Corwin.

6. Elgarten, G. H. (1991). Testing a new supervisory process for improving instruction. *Journal of Curriculum and Supervision, 6*, 118–129.

7. The experiment had four experimental conditions, but we describe only the two of that are relevant to this chapter.

8. Pierce, D. (2009, January 27). Gates Foundation to show excellent teaching. *eSchoolNews.* Retrieved from http://www.eschoolnews.com/news/top-news/?i=56948

Unit Four

Classroom Observation Techniques

Chapter 10

Selective Verbatim Transcription

Except in special instances in which some quality of timing or of sound or of sight evolved as a salient supervisory issue, written data have proven most useful and most wieldy to clinical supervisors. Perhaps the greatest advantage of a written record . . . is that Teacher and Supervisor can assimilate it most rapidly and most easily; the eye can incorporate, almost instantaneously, evidence that took a relatively long time to unfold in the lesson.
—Robert Goldhammer[1]

INTRODUCTION

The primary goal of clinical supervision is to help teachers become better at facilitating students' learning. Accomplishing this goal requires that the supervisor and teacher have a shared vision of what learning means. The learning process is extremely complex, but we believe that there are some essential elements that all educators would acknowledge, including the following six principles:

1. For learning to occur, students' attention must be directed to the information to be learned.
2. For learning to occur, students must interact with the information so that it becomes personally meaningful.
3. For learning to occur, students must be appropriately motivated.
4. For learning to last, students must practice using the information so that it becomes stored in long-term memory and can be retrieved for subsequent use.
5. Various group processes in the classroom can facilitate or hinder students' learning.
6. The content of students' learning depends on whether the teacher emphasizes lower or higher forms of knowledge (e.g., facts versus concepts) and lower or higher intellectual operations (e.g., recall versus synthesis and prediction).

You will find in this chapter that a teacher's verbal communication patterns can facilitate students' learning if they incorporate these learning principles. Therefore, as a clinical supervisor, you can help teachers improve their instruction by careful observation and analysis of their communication patterns. An observation technique called *selective verbatim transcription* is useful for this purpose.

In the planning conference, the supervisor and teacher select beforehand the particular types of classroom talk to be transcribed. It is in this sense that the verbatim record is "selective." In this chapter we focus on verbal behaviors that reflect effective or ineffective teaching and that are amenable to the selective verbatim technique. You can refer to the Appendix for a comprehensive list of effective teaching techniques and information about which ones are well-suited for this type of observation.

The classroom talk that is the focus of selective verbatim should be word-for-word. For example, suppose the supervisor is recording a teacher's questions, and the teacher asks, "What do we call animals that live exclusively off plants . . . you know, we have a certain name for these animals . . . does anyone know it?" If the supervisor writes, "What is the name of animals that live exclusively off plants?" this is not a verbatim transcription. It misses certain features of the communication that might affect students positively or negatively.

A selective verbatim is usually made while the teacher's class is in progress, but this is not a requirement. If an audio or video recording of a class session is available (see Chapter 12), the selective verbatim can be made from the recording.

ADVANTAGES OF SELECTIVE VERBATIM TRANSCRIPTS

Selective verbatim transcripts have several advantages as a classroom observation technique. We describe four of them here.

First, providing teachers with a selective verbatim transcript focuses their attention on particular aspects of what they say to students or on what students say to them. In this way they become sensitized to the verbal process in teaching. All other types of communication are screened out by the transcript.

Second, compared to a complete transcript, a selective verbatim transcript focuses teachers' attention on just a few verbal behaviors. Teachers who are trying to improve their instruction are more successful if they do not try to change many aspects of their communication behavior at once.

The third advantage of selective verbatim is that it provides an objective, nonjudgmental record of the teacher's behavior. While in the act of teaching, many teachers get so caught up in the process that they do not listen to what they are saying. Even if teachers do listen, the verbal events are so fleeting that they are unable to reflect on the impact of these events. Selective verbatim solves this problem by holding up a "verbal mirror" to teachers, which they can examine at their convenience.

Finally, selective verbatim has the advantage of being simple to use. Supervisors only need a pencil or pen and a pad of paper—or they can use a laptop computer, if they wish. Also, the verbatim transcript can be made while the supervisor is observing the teacher's classroom. The transcript might need to be typed if the supervisor's handwriting is illegible, but no other transformation of the data is needed.

DRAWBACKS OF SELECTIVE VERBATIM

Selective verbatim is a powerful tool for classroom observation, but a teacher who knows in advance what verbal behaviors will be recorded might become self-conscious about using them. For example, just knowing that a supervisor will observe verbal praise might increase a teacher's use of this behavior. We find, though, that teachers generally do not become self-conscious when a selective verbatim transcript is made. Even if this should happen, the teacher might gradually internalize the technique of verbal praise and use it whether the supervisor is present or not.

Another problem with selective verbatim arises from its "selectivity." The larger context of classroom interaction is lost if the teacher and supervisor focus too narrowly on verbal behavior. For example, a teacher might look at a selective verbatim transcript of praise statements and dismiss them with, "Oh, I see I used verbal praise 10 times. I guess that's pretty good." The analysis needs to go further to explore such questions as whether the praise was given to students who deserved it and whether it overemphasized extrinsic motivation for learning. In-depth analysis of this kind requires that the supervisor to record, at least mentally, the entire flow of the lesson. A skillful supervisor is one who simplifies the teaching process by focusing the teacher's attention on a few aspects of teaching, yet is able to relate these aspects to the total context in which instruction occurred.

A selective verbatim transcript is not useful if the teacher or supervisor select trivial aspects of verbal communication for observation. To avoid this problem, the supervisor and teacher should explore why each identified type of verbal behavior is worth recording and analyzing. If a satisfactory rationale cannot be given, they must consider whether scarce supervisory time should be used to record that particular type of verbal behavior.

Supervisors occasionally find that they cannot keep up with recording relevant verbal interactions. They simply go by too fast. When this happens, we recommend that supervisors use a symbol, such as a line, to indicate where they temporarily stopped recording. It is generally better to record a few verbal statements word for word than to paraphrase them or not indicate where omissions occurred.

The following sections describe various kinds of verbal communication in teachers' lessons that can be recorded by means of selective verbatim transcription.

OBSERVATION TECHNIQUE 1: TRANSCRIBING TEACHER QUESTIONS

Asking questions is one of the most important aspects of teaching. In fact, Mary Jane Aschner called a teacher a "professional question maker."[2]

Researchers have found that teachers rely on question-asking as a staple of their teaching repertoire. Almost a century ago, R. Stevens discovered that high school teachers asked almost 400 questions during an average school day.[3] Unbelievable as this figure might seem, this level of question-asking frequency has been observed in more recent studies.[4] Question-asking also takes up a significant amount of class time. S. J. Doneau found that teachers' oral questions consume from 6 to 16 percent of classroom time, depending on the grade level and subject being taught.[5] Also, Kenneth Sirotnik found that the most common form of verbal interaction between teachers and students is the traditional recitation—a series of rapid-fire teacher questions to test students' mastery of facts, typically those covered in a textbook.[6]

Asking a lot of questions during a lesson might seem unjustified, but research suggests otherwise. Barak Rosenshine found that asking many questions during a recitation is more effective than asking few questions.[7] This finding makes sense if we consider that the criterion in research on teaching effectiveness typically is student performance on achievement tests that assess the amount of information and skills that students have learned. Asking more questions allows the teacher to have students rehearse more information and skills than asking fewer questions would.

The centrality of questions in the instructional process leads us to recommend that if a teacher and a supervisor can observe only a single aspect of classroom interaction, it should be the teacher's question-asking behavior.

Procedure for Recording Teacher Questions

The supervisor's task is to make a written record of each question asked by the teacher. (Another approach is to use a checklist, such as that shown in Figure 13.6 in Chapter 13.) Because teachers typically ask many questions, the supervisor might ask the teacher to estimate the length of the lesson. Then the supervisor can use time sampling, which means that the supervisor observes samples of the lesson (e.g., every other three minutes of the lesson). Obviously, if you are planning to observe the teacher's use of questions, you will want to select a lesson in which this verbal behavior occurs with some frequency.

It seems a simple matter to decide what is or is not a question. "How many kilometers are in a mile?" is obviously a question. But how about "Johnny gave a good answer, didn't he?" or "Sue, won't you stop fidgeting in your seat?" or "I'd like someone to tell me how many kilometers there are in a mile." The latter example is a declarative statement, not an interrogative, yet it clearly has the intent of a question. To avoid confusion, we suggest a simple rule: if the teacher's statement is asked in a questioning manner or has the intent of a question, include it in the transcript. There is no harm in including ambiguous examples, but omitting them might cause a teacher to overlook a significant aspect of his question-asking behavior.

Figure 10.1 shows selective verbatim transcripts based on observation of two fifth-grade teachers. The teachers assigned students to read the same brief handout on the behavior patterns and environment of wolves, followed by a question-and-answer session to help the students review and think about what they had just read.

Analyzing Data about Teacher Questions

As teachers examine selective verbatim transcripts of their questions, you can ask them to focus on one or more of the following aspects of question-asking behavior.

Purpose for Asking Questions

It is worth asking the teacher what his purpose was in asking questions in the observed lesson. Perhaps he will state one of the following purposes, each of which reflects sound learning principles:

- Questions can focus students' attention on what is to be learned. In other words, the teacher's question serves as a cue to students that the information required to answer the question is important. This attention-directing is necessary, because students are often exposed to a lot of information in their curriculum materials, and they

Teacher 1

1. Now, what do we know about this animal? What do you know about the wolf? You can refer back to this little ditto, if you'd like. Jeff?
2. Next?
3. Mike?
4. Heather?
5. Now Jeff just said that sometimes livestock . . . people or farmers hate them because they kill their livestock. Would livestock be small animals? What do you think?
6. Terry?
7. John?
8. Mike?
9. Terry, again?
10. Jeff?
11. Jerry?
12. Who said that, Jerry? Was there a quote or something in that article?
13. Do you remember the man's name?
14. Do you know something? Last night, after we read this article, after school, Jeff said, "Gee Mr. Edwards, I think I've seen that name, or something." He went right down to the library and brought back this book, and it's by the same man. Jeff, did you have a chance to look at that last night?
15. Jeff, does it concern itself with the wolf?
16. Does anyone have anything else to say about what we already know?

Teacher 2

1. What do you know about the Arctic and that kind of area that would lead you to believe that a dog would have to be more strong there than he would have to be, say, here? Dana?
2. Pam?
3. What kind of work does he have to do?
4. Terry?
5. Karen?
6. Why do the dogs work harder in the north than they work here? John?
7. Why don't our dogs have to work?
8. What don't we need done here?
9. Allen?
10. Doug?
11. Why do you suppose the Eskimos don't have machines? Joey?
12. Do you think so? Does anyone have another idea about why they don't, 'cause there's probably more than one idea?
13. Why would they be primitive? Pat?
14. Wanda?
15. It mentioned in the stories that wolves traveled in packs, in groups. Why do you suppose they do? What do you suppose is their reason for doing this? Joe?

Figure 10.1 Selective verbatim transcripts of fifth-grade teachers' questions.

might not be able to determine which of it is most important. The relevant learning principle, as we stated above, is this: "For learning to occur, students' attention must be directed to the information to be learned."

- Teachers can use questions to motivate students to engage in learning. In a study of middle-school U.S. history classes, Ed Hootstein asked students what techniques a teacher could use to make this subject interesting.[8] One of the most-mentioned techniques was, "Use thought-provoking questions."[9] The relevant learning principle is this: "For learning to occur, students must be appropriately motivated."

- Teachers can use questions to get students to process new information and put it into their own words, so that it becomes meaningful. Questions also get students to practice using the new information. These related purposes reflect two key learning principles: "For learning to occur, students must interact with the information so that it becomes personally meaningful; and they must practice using the information so that it becomes stored in long-term memory and can be retrieved for subsequent use."

As teachers examine their selective verbatim transcript in relation to these and other purposes for asking questions, you can expect that they will become more reflective about using questions in a purposeful manner to promote students' learning.

Cognitive Level of Questions

A simple way of classifying questions is to put them into two categories: "fact" and "higher cognitive." Fact questions require students to recall information stated in the curriculum materials. In contrast, higher cognitive questions (also called "thought" questions) require students to think about the information they have studied and to state their own ideas. If the teacher and supervisor wish, questions can be analyzed into additional categories using Bloom's taxonomy[10] or another question classification system.

The research literature we reviewed in Chapter 4 does not demonstrate unequivocally that higher cognitive questions are superior to fact questions. The available evidence suggests instead that an emphasis on either type of question can be effective depending on the teacher's objectives for the lesson. This view of the evidence is consistent with one of our learning principles: "The content of students' learning depends on whether the teacher emphasizes lower or higher forms of knowledge (e.g., facts versus concepts) and lower or higher intellectual operations (e.g., recall versus synthesis and prediction)."

Fact questions and higher cognitive questions are not always easy to distinguish from one another. For example, a student might be asked to recall a fact stated in the assigned reading. The student might not be able to recall the fact, but can deduce it by using higher cognitive processes and other information he or she knows. A question that is higher cognitive in form (e.g., a "why?" question) might actually be a "fact" question if the student simply repeats an idea heard or read elsewhere.

It appears that the first teacher in Figure 10.1 is emphasizing fact questions, as indicated by phrases like "What do we know about . . . ?" "Who said that?" and "Did you have a chance to look at that last night?" In contrast, the second teacher focuses on higher cognitive processes, as indicated by phrases like "What . . . would lead you to believe . . . ?" "Why . . . ?" and "Does anyone have another idea?" One of these teachers is not necessarily more effective than the other. The first teacher might have had good reasons to emphasize fact questions, and the second teacher might have had equally good reasons to emphasize higher cognitive questions. The supervisor can identify these reasons by conferencing with the teachers about the thinking that went into their lessons.

Amount of Requested Information

Fact questions can be classified into "narrow" and "broad," depending on the amount of information called for in the question. For example, the first teacher in Figure 10.1 asked, "What do you know about the wolf?" This is an example of a broad fact question. "Do you remember the man's name?" is an example of a narrow fact question, because it asks for only one bit of information. Teachers sometimes ask a series of narrow fact questions—a teacher-centered practice that uses up class time unnecessarily—when one broad question might be sufficient.

Academic and Personal Questions

Teachers' questions often focus on academic knowledge and thinking. For example, in teaching about a novel, a teacher might ask such questions as, "What is the main conflict facing the hero?", "What symbols does the author use?", and "How does the setting affect the actions of the characters?" These questions reflect the traditions of literary analysis and criticism established by academic scholars.

It is also possible to ask questions that are more personally engaging, for example, "How do you think the hero will respond to this challenge?" Martin Nystrand and Adam Gamoran call these *authentic questions*, because they invite students to express their own ideas and feelings.[11] Bracha Alpert studied a high school teacher who made extensive use of such questions.[12] Here is a sample of them:

- "Why is the [literary character] so angry . . . think of what kinds of things make you angry, really angry?"
- "Do you feel sorry for any of the characters?"
- "Did you see his way as somewhat less worthwhile than hers?"

Alpert found that authentic questions motivated students to engage in classroom interaction, because their personal feelings and opinions were legitimated as part of the curriculum. Students of other teachers whom Alpert studied were more reluctant to participate in discussion because of a nearly exclusive emphasis on academic knowledge and thinking skills. The value of personal questions is supported in the learning principle: "For learning to occur, students must interact with the information so that it becomes personally meaningful."

Redirection

Teachers can call on one student to answer each question, or they can ask several students to respond. That is, they can "redirect" the question. Redirection is a useful technique for increasing student participation and eliciting a variety of ideas for students to consider. Higher cognitive questions are redirected more easily than fact questions, because the former usually do not have a single correct answer.

Both teachers in Figure 10.1 used the technique of redirection by naming the student they wished to respond to their question. Redirection also can occur by nonverbal acknowledgment of a student who has his hand raised or by establishing eye contact with a student. These instances of redirection will not show up in a selective verbatim transcript. If you wish to record these instances, you can do so by writing an *R* or other symbol whenever they occur. Or instead, the names of the students can be recorded, if you know them.

Probing Questions

Probing questions are follow-up questions designed to help students improve or elaborate on their initial response to the teacher question. They are not easy to detect in a selective verbatim transcript unless you make special note of them, perhaps by placing a *P* beside each one. The following is a complete verbatim transcript of the events that transpired when the second teacher in Figure 10.1 asked Questions 6 and 7.

TEACHER: Why do the dogs work harder in the north than they work here? John?

JOHN: Well, most of the dogs here don't really have to work hard.

TEACHER: Why don't our dogs have to work?

JOHN: They're house pets, and we do most of the work ourselves, and we don't need stuff like they do up there.

TEACHER: What don't we need done here?

JOHN: We don't need dogs to pull things here. We have cars, but the Eskimos don't, so they use dogs.

The teacher's two probing questions helped John give a more complete and specific answer to the initial question.

Teachers sometimes are unaware that they accept or overlook poor responses to their questions. A transcript of their probing questions provides one indication of whether this is happening. An absence of probing questions suggests lack of attention to student responses, whereas liberal use of this technique suggests that the teacher is listening carefully to what students say and is challenging them to do their best work.

Multiple Questions

The practice of asking several questions in a row can be spotted easily in a selective verbatim transcript. Note that the first teacher begins his lesson by asking two questions in succession: "Now, what do we know about this animal? What do you know about the wolf?" The same teacher also asks multiple questions in the fifth and 12th recorded statements. The second teacher asks multiple questions in the 12th and 15th recorded statements.

Teachers usually engage in this behavior when they are "thinking on their feet." They may try various phrasings and ideas before they hit upon the question they want to ask. Teachers for whom this is habitual practice should reflect on whether it is distracting or confusing to students. Teachers can avoid asking multiple questions by preparing questions in advance of the actual lesson.

Teachers also engage in multiple question-asking when they literally repeat their question. They probably do this either because they think students did not hear them the first time they asked the question or because they believe that students need several prompts to get them to respond. The problem is that repeating the question might condition students not to listen carefully to the teacher the first time he or she asks a question.

OBSERVATION TECHNIQUE 2: TRANSCRIBING CONSTRUCTIVIST DIALOGUE

As we explained in Chapter 4, educators are increasingly interested in a theory of learning known as *constructivism*. According to this theory, individuals learn by "constructing" their own understanding of the world. Some theorists—most notably, Jean Piaget—focus on how individuals come to understand the world by experimenting with it and developing progressively more sophisticated cognitive structures. Other theorists—most notably, Lev Vygotsky—focus on how individuals interact with each other to develop a shared understanding of the world. This theoretical approach is sometimes called *social constructivism*. In teaching methods based on social-constructivist theory, the teacher and students work together to develop a shared understanding of curriculum content.

Higher-cognitive questions, which we discussed above, also stimulate students to think. However, the thinking is less sustained than in constructivist teaching, and higher-cognitive questions generally do not require students to rigorously test their thinking. The sustained nature of constructivist question-asking is sometimes characterized as *constructivist dialogue* or *collaborative dialogue*. An example of constructivist dialogue is shown in Figure 10.2. (Additional features of constructivist teaching are described in Chapter 13).

The situation is a first-grade math lesson on measurement and equivalency. Children were asked to use a balance to determine how many plastic links equaled one metal washer in weight. The teacher is interacting with one of the children, a girl named Anna.

T: How many links does it take to balance one washer?
S: (After a few minutes of experimenting) Four.
T: If I placed one more washer on this side, how many more links do you think we would need to balance it?
S: One.
T: Try it.

Anna placed one more link in the balance tray and noticed that balance was not achieved. She looked confused and placed another link in the tray and then a third. Still no balance. She placed one more link in the tray. Balance was achieved. She smiled and looked at the teacher.

T: How many cubes did it take to balance one washer?
S: Four.
T: And how many to balance two washers?
S: (counting) Eight.
T: If I put one more washer on this side, how many more links will you need to balance it?
S: (Pondered and looked quizzically at the teacher) Four.
T: Try it.
S: (after successfully balancing with four links) Each washer is the same as four links.
T: Now, let me give you a really hard question. If I took four links off of the balance, how many washers would I need to take off in order to balance it?
S: One!

Figure 10.2 Selective verbatim transcript of a constructivist dialogue.
Source: Brooks, J. G., & Brooks, M. G. (1993). *The case for constructivist classrooms.* (pp. 73–74) Alexandria, VA: Association for Supervision and Curriculum Development.

Jere Brophy compared research on teaching, including constructivist dialogue, in different school subjects.[13] He found that the nature of these dialogues varied from one subject to another. Figure 10.3 shows Brophy's synthesis of these discourse variations. Studying these variations will help supervisors know what to expect in constructivist lessons taught in different subjects.

Language Arts
- Discussion of the meanings of text (especially narratives) and of individuals' reactions to it.
- Discussion to enrich students' understanding of content and appreciation of literature.
- Analysis of examples of writing genres to develop understanding of the nature of their features and how these might be included in one's own writing.

Mathematics
- Mathematical argumentation: using problem contexts for developing mathematical ideas, representations, and procedures.
- Geometric inquiry, sensemaking, and problem solving within a classroom discourse that establishes ideas and truths collaboratively.

Physical Sciences
- Biological inquiry framed within the constructivist model of learning and ideas about biology as a domain.
- Analysis of physics problems and negotiation of potential approaches and solutions.
- Discussion to stimulate students to construct understandings, concept maps, and mental models of chemical phenomena in problem solving or laboratory debriefing contexts.
- Engaging in the dialectic between evidence and explanation or observation and theory that occurs in extended inquiry activities in earth system science (more in small-group than in whole-class settings).

Social Studies
- Analysis and response to historical events, with focus not just on establishing what happened but on considering connections to other events and implications for personal or civic policy decisions.
- Negotiation of learning accomplished through field studies, map-based instruction, and simulation work in geography (during subsequent debriefings).
- Thoughtful discourse around big ideas in culture studies.
- Value-based discussion of social and civic issues, especially controversial issues.
- Economics-based discussion occurring in the context of concept teaching, inquiry, or debriefing following experiential learning or simulations.

Figure 10.3 Discourse variations across school subjects.
Source: Adapted from: Brophy, J, (Ed.). (2001). *Advances in research on teaching* (Vol. 8, pp. 454–455). Oxford: JAI Elsevier.

Procedure for Recording Constructivist Dialogues

Constructivist discourse is not a routine feature of teaching, nor is it typically found in all school subjects. You are most likely to have the opportunity to make a selective verbatim transcript of constructivist dialogue during a science or math lesson of a teacher who has had some preparation in constructivist theory and methodology.

As the lesson unfolds, you should make notes about any materials, media, or raw data that were used as part of the process to develop students' understanding about a concept or principle. If students took notes or made drawings, consider collecting samples to analyze with the teacher in the feedback conference. Most important, record all teacher questions and student responses or statements relating to efforts to achieve an understanding of the curriculum content.

As an alternative to this selective verbatim technique for recording data about constructivist teaching, you can consider the checklist technique presented in Chapter 13.

Analyzing Data about Constructivist Dialogues

Because constructivist teaching usually involves many questions, you and the teacher might look at other aspects of question-asking that we discuss in this part of the chapter. However, the main focus of analysis should be on the distinctive features of constructivist teaching.

In a constructivist dialogue, the teacher often helps students understand the abstract concepts of science, mathematics, and other disciplines by making reference to concrete representations of these concepts. You and the teacher can examine the selective verbatim transcript to determine whether teacher questions and student statements were centered around primary source data, manipulatives, or other materials. In Figure 10.2, we see that the interactions between the teacher and student focused on a balance tray.

If a student does not understand a concept or cannot answer a question, the teacher might be tempted to offer an explanation. The alternative is to ask a question that encourages the student to keep interacting with primary source data or other materials in a search for understanding. If the selective verbatim transcript reveals instances of preemptive explanations, you and the teacher can explore ways that questioning could be used instead.

One of the most effective types of questions is a request for the student to make a prediction based on the student's existing understanding of the concept, and then to test it with the materials or primary source data. For example, in Figure 10.2, we see that the teacher asks the student to make a prediction about what will happen if one more washer is put on the balance tray; the student makes a prediction, and then the teacher says, "Try it."

OBSERVATION TECHNIQUE 3: TRANSCRIBING TEACHER FEEDBACK STATEMENTS

Researchers have found that teacher feedback can facilitate students' learning (see Chapter 3). For example, if we are learning a new skill, we need feedback to know how well we are performing the skill. Without feedback, we might simply practice bad habits or terminate the learning process too soon.

Praise and criticism probably are the most common types of teacher feedback. Sincere praise encourages students to learn and to keep trying if obstacles arise. Harsh criticism has the opposite effect. This aspect of verbal communication, then, is relevant to the learning principle that we stated earlier in the chapter: "For learning to occur, students must be appropriately motivated."

Procedure for Recording Teacher Feedback Statements

As the supervisor, you need to arrange with the teacher to observe a lesson in which there is frequent verbal interchange between the teacher and students. During instruction, you will record the teacher's verbal feedback statements. It also is useful to record the immediately preceding student remark or action that prompted the feedback. Another option is to make note of the affective content: Was the verbal feedback enthusiastic in tone? Neutral? Hostile?

As with question classification, it is not always easy to decide whether a particular teacher remark is an instance of verbal feedback. You will need to rely on your judgment to decide whether a teacher's remark will be perceived by a student as feedback on her behavior. Your judgment will be sound to the extent that you closely observe students' reactions and the total instructional context.

Figure 10.4 presents a selective verbatim transcript of a junior high school teacher's feedback statements and the context in which they occurred. The lesson was organized around an article about population explosion that the students had been asked to read. Reading this transcript, you might wonder whether or not to include probing questions, which we described earlier in the chapter, as instances of teacher feedback. Consider, for example, the second and third teacher utterances in Figure 10.4. We classified them as probing questions because they were intended to elicit a more specific answer from the student. At the same time, the fact that the teacher asked the questions is feedback to the students that the answer can be improved. At least, that is our view of the situation. As an observer of classroom instruction, you will need to make your own judgment about whether to include probing questions in a selective verbatim of teacher feedback.

Analyzing Data about Teacher Feedback Statements

The teacher and supervisor can examine a selective verbatim transcript of feedback statements for their frequency, variety, and specificity.

Frequency of Teacher Feedback

The simplest analysis of a selective verbatim transcript of teacher feedback statements is to determine their frequency. Some teachers provide little or no feedback to their students. Their instructional style usually is more direct than indirect, and their primary concern is to impart knowledge—perhaps with insufficient concern about whether students are "receiving" the knowledge.

Other teachers make extensive use of feedback. They tend to be more responsive to students and to encourage teacher-student interaction. In Figure 10.4, we counted 10 instances of teacher feedback—a fairly high frequency for this amount of transcription.

T: All right. Could someone tell me what the report was about? Ann?
S: Well. It was about birth control.
T: Birth control?
S: Uh, population explosion.
S: It was about the population explosion, but it was also about limits. It made a lot of predictions, like we won't have room to get around, and there's not going to be any room to plant crops.
T: *I'm glad you remembered that the author said that these were "predictions."* Why do you think I'm glad you remembered that the author used the word "predictions?"
S: I also heard that they're going to have a farm under the sea, for sea-farming.
T: *Who's "they"?*
S: Well . . . the scientists.
S: And as the years go by, cars will get better and better.
T: *Are you sure?*
S: Well. I'm not certain, but pretty sure.
T: *Pretty sure. This is kind of what I wanted you to get out of this article. These are your opinions, your predictions of what might happen. And they sound pretty good to me, and I'll bank on them to a certain extent, but something might happen to the automobile industry so that your predictions wouldn't come true.*
T: Who made that statement that was quoted in the article?
S: Professor Kenneth E. F. Watt.
T: *Professor Kenneth E. F. Watt is saying it.* Do we know that what he's saying is worthwhile?
S: Well, Professor Kenneth E. F. Watt isn't the only one that is making these predictions. There's probably thousands of people making these predictions.
T: *Yes, that's a good point, Rodney. We can have some faith in what he's predicting because others are making similar predictions.*
T: Why, throughout the whole world, are there so many people having so many children? Did you ever stop to think about it? Steve?
S: When the children grow up, they want children. Then when those children grow up, then they get more children, and that goes on and on.
T: *Steve, I'm not sure I'm following you. Could you clarify your idea a bit? Why do people want to have so many children?*
T: (concluding remark.) *I thought the ideas you had to contribute were a lot more interesting than the article itself.*

Figure 10.4 Selective verbatim transcript of teacher feedback.

Variety of Teacher Feedback

John Zahorik did a study of teachers' feedback behavior and found that it tended to be lacking in variety.[14] Only a few kinds of feedback were used regularly. Zahorik found that the most frequent form of feedback to students was simply to repeat the student's answer to a question. An illustration of this practice is the eighth teacher utterance in Figure 10.4. A teacher whose feedback is constricted in this manner can be encouraged to consider other types of feedback for facilitating students' learning.

Ned Flanders found that a particularly effective form of feedback is to acknowledge students' ideas by building on them.[15] He identified the following ways in which to build on student ideas:

1. *Modifying* the idea by rephrasing or conceptualizing it in the teacher's own words.
2. *Applying* the idea by using it to reach an inference or take the next step in a logical analysis of a problem.
3. *Comparing* the idea with other ideas expressed earlier by the students or the teacher.
4. *Summarizing* what was said by an individual student or group of students.

The sixth teacher utterance in Figure 10.4 is an example of acknowledgment by applying students' ideas to reach an inference.

Research conducted by Flanders and others indicates that teachers seldom acknowledge students' feelings, even though educators generally agree that feelings—and other aspects of the affective domain—are an important part of the instructional process. Flanders found that even a small increase in feedback that acknowledges students' feelings can have a noticeable positive effect on students' motivation and the emotional climate of the classroom. The supervisor and teacher can discuss this type of feedback and look for instances of it in the selective verbatim transcript.

Specificity of Teacher Feedback

Teachers tend to give simple, nonspecific forms of feedback, such as, "Good," "Uh-huh," or "OK." Jere Brophy, among other educators, suggests that teachers should develop the habit of making their praise or criticism more specific.[16] Below is a list of guidelines that he developed for this purpose.[17] The guidelines are for praise statements, but they also can be applied to criticism and other forms of feedback (rewards, assignments to remediate academic weaknesses, etc.). You will note that Brophy's guidelines concern not just the phrasing of the praise statement, but also the characteristics of students, especially their motivational state.

Effective Praise

1. is delivered contingently.
2. specifies the particulars of the accomplishment.
3. shows spontaneity, variety, and other signs of credibility; suggests clear attention to the student's accomplishment.
4. rewards attainment of specified performance criteria (which can include effort criteria, however).
5. provides information to students about their competence or the value of their accomplishments.
6. orients students toward better appreciation of their own task-related behavior and thinking about problem solving.

7. uses students' own prior accomplishments as a context for describing present accomplishments.

8. is given in recognition of noteworthy effort or success at difficult (for this student) tasks.

9. attributes success to effort and ability, implying that similar successes can be expected in the future.

10. fosters endogenous attributions (students believe that they expend effort on the task because they enjoy the task and/or want to develop task-relevant skills).

11. focuses students' attention on their own task-relevant behavior.

12. fosters appreciation of and desirable attributions about task-relevant behavior after the process is completed.

Ineffective Praise

1. is delivered randomly or unsystematically.

2. is restricted to global positive reactions.

3. shows a bland uniformity, which suggests a conditioned response made with minimal attention.

4. rewards mere participation, without consideration of performance processes or outcomes.

5. provides no information at all or gives students information about their status.

6. orients students toward comparing themselves with others and thinking about competing.

7. uses the accomplishments of peers as the context for describing students' present accomplishments.

8. is given without regard to the effort expended or the meaning of the accomplishment (for this student).

9. attributes success to ability alone or to external factors, such as luck or an easy task.

10. fosters exogenous attributions (students believe that they expend effort on the task for external reasons—to please the teacher, win a competition or reward, etc.).

11. focuses students' attention on the teacher as an external authority figure who is manipulating them.

12. intrudes into the ongoing process, distracting attention from task-relevant behavior.

OBSERVATION TECHNIQUE 4: TRANSCRIBING TEACHER STRUCTURING STATEMENTS

The use of structuring statements is one of the nine characteristics of effective teaching that Barak Rosenshine and Norma Furst identified in their review of the research literature (see Chapter 3).[18] Structuring statements are teacher comments that help focus students' attention on a lesson's purpose, organization, and key points. Common types of structuring statements include:

- previews of what students will learn in the lesson.
- summaries of what was taught in the lesson.
- comments that signal transitions in the lesson.
- directions for doing seat work and other tasks.

Several elements of Madeline Hunter's model of effective teaching (see Chapter 3) directly involve the use of structuring statements—namely, anticipatory set, stating of objectives, and closure.[19]

Procedure for Recording Structuring Statements

A teacher's structuring statements usually need to be observed in the context of a complete lesson. Most such statements occur at the beginning and end of the lesson, so you need to be especially observant at these times.

Structuring statements and classroom management statements, which we cover in the next section of this chapter, sometimes appear similar. You can distinguish between them in this way: structuring statements focus on the academic content of the lesson, whereas classroom management statements focus on classroom procedures and students' personal behavior. Using this rule of thumb, we would classify the following statements as examples of structuring statements: "When you're done with the textbook problems, you can read a story silently," and "Be sure to insert page numbers when you type your project report in the computer lab." In contrast, we would classify the following statements as examples of classroom management statements: "If you talk to your neighbor one more time, I'll have to call your parent," and "Be sure to clear your desk of all objects when the bell rings." Some teacher statements might be classified one way or the other; if in doubt, it's probably better to record the statement than to pass over it.

Figure 10.5 presents a composite of teachers' structuring statements in various lessons. We used this approach, rather than presenting the selective verbatim of one teacher, to show the variety of forms that these verbal comments can take.

Analyzing Data about Structuring Statements

The teacher and supervisor can examine the selective transcript of structuring statements for their frequency and whether each type (preview, summary, transition signals, directions) was included in the lesson. Another important aspect of structuring statements is their clarity. Students can get off task or misdirect their learning if they do not understand what the teacher is saying. Not surprisingly, Rosenshine and Furst, among other researchers, have found that students learn better when they have teachers who make clear verbal statements. This finding makes sense in terms of one of the learning principles that we listed at the start of the chapter: "For learning to occur, students' attention must be directed to the information to be learned." A corollary of this principle is that students will have a difficult time maintaining attention if the information provided by the teacher is unclear, if it comes at students too quickly, or if the teacher digresses or jumps back and forth from one point to another.

1. The report we're going to read today is about apartheid in South Africa.
2. The film we just saw on how glass is made illustrates very well some of the points that were covered in the book we're using in this class.
3. Yes, electric cars are one of the really important ways we might be able to control air pollution in the future. You might want to remember that when you write your science-fiction stories.
4. Okay. Today I've shown you three different ways you can do calculations. First, you can use your hand calculator. Second, you can use the calculator that's on most computers. And third—does anyone remember what the third method is?
5. Get out your graphic organizer on social customs and, as you're reading the story, write down things relating to music, food, and clothing in Kenya.
6. We've gone through the characteristics of the preterite tense and past tense in Spanish. Now let's compare those characteristics to see how the two tenses differ.
7. Be sure to color in the object in your picture first. Then you can cut the object out and tape it on the big board. Make sure you put the picture right above the notecard that spells out the name of the object

Figure 10.5 Selective verbatim statements involving structuring.

OBSERVATION TECHNIQUE 5: TRANSCRIBING CLASSROOM MANAGEMENT STATEMENTS

Classroom management is the greatest concern of many teachers (see Chapter 4) and therefore a major focus of clinical supervision. Classroom management has two major aspects: (1) ensuring that students learn and follow classroom rules and procedures; and (2) handling student misbehavior, which can be viewed as noncompliance with classroom rules and procedures. One way in which teachers get students to follow rules and procedures is by giving directions during the lesson. Directions are similar to structuring statements in that they focus students' attention. Teacher statements when students misbehave also serve to refocus their attention by reminding them of the learning task to be performed and consequences for not doing so.

Procedure for Recording Classroom Management Statements

The supervisor writes each teacher statement that involves a classroom rule, procedure, or remark directed at a student (or group of students) for misbehavior. Figure 10.6 shows a selective verbatim transcript of a student teacher's classroom management statements in a ninth-grade science class. Most of the statements reflect efforts to refocus students' attention to the learning task. Some are intended to get a student to stop engaging in inappropriate behavior (e.g., statements 6, 17, and 21).

Analyzing Classroom Management Statements

Classroom management statements can be viewed as a reflection of how well rules and procedures have been taught. In a well-managed classroom, there should be relatively few statements of this sort. However, it is unlikely that there will be no such statements, because

1. Guys, you need to settle down.
2. Attention, get out your notebooks.
3. Attention. The quicker we get through this review, the more time you'll have to look at how your plants are doing.
4. Loosen up, guys.
5. Guys, I need for things to be quiet.
6. This is not appropriate. This is your first warning of the day.
7. Bill . . . (Teacher is trying to quiet him down)
8. Loosen up, guys.
9. You have three more minutes.
10. Guys, you should be finishing up.
11. I need everybody to go back to their regular seat now. We have to do review.
12. Listen up, guys.
13. The quicker we get through this, the more time you'll have for your bottle. Get back to your seats.
14. Alyssha . . . everybody . . . let's look at the study sheet, so we'll have time for the bottle experiment.
15. It's up to you to figure out how to finish. Ssshh.
16. If we spend the whole time reviewing, you won't have time to look at your bottles. Sshh.
17. Sshh. Guys, this is not the time to be doing this.
18. Sam, this is your warning.
19. Ryan!
20. Guys!
21. Justin . . . Teresa . . . turn around!
22. Mark! Kelly! Sam!
23. Mark, you can't be writing notes now!
24. Sshh. Guys, it really needs to be quiet in here. Kelly!
25. Guys, everybody needs to be quiet.
26. Sam, I'm calling your parents after class.
27. Guys, listen up. You're preventing people from learning.

Figure 10.6 Selective verbatim transcript of classroom management statements.

some students occasionally will misbehave even if they know the teacher's rules and procedures and the consequences for not following them.

When observing a teacher's classroom management behavior, you should determine the teacher's management model in the planning conference. A common feature of most models is to specify conseqnuences for inappropriate behavior, explain those consequences to students, and follow through on them when inappropriate behavior persists. Statement 26 in Figure 10.6 is an example of stating a consequence for inappropriate behavior. Conferencing with the student teacher whose selective verbatim transcript is shown in Figure 10.6 revealed that she did not follow through with this consequence or other stated consequences. The supervisor helped the student teacher see a relationship between the escalating misbehavior in her lessons and the failure to put consequences into effect.

Teachers can analyze their management statements about rules and procedures to determine their clarity and whether or not they achieved their purpose. Management statements about student misbehavior can be analyzed for their level of severity and effectiveness. The first five statements in Figure 10.6 seem fairly mild. The sixth statement is more severe. Statement 22 and several others with exclamation points indicate even greater severity. (The supervisor used the exclamation point to indicate a sharp tone of voice or actual shouting.) In Chapter 4, we reviewed researchers' findings that effective teachers correct misbehavior unobtrusively and before it has a chance to escalate.

ENDNOTES

1. Goldhammer, R. (1969). *Clinical supervision: Special methods for the supervision of teachers.* New York: Holt, Rinehart & Winston. Quote appears on p. 84.

2. Aschner, M. J. (1961). Asking questions to trigger thinking. *NEA Journal, 50*, 44–46.

3. Stevens, R. (1912). The question as a measure of efficiency in instruction: A critical study of classroom practice. *Teachers College Contributions to Education*, No. 48.

4. Floyd, W. D. (1960). An analysis of the oral questioning activity in selected Colorado primary classrooms. *Dissertation Abstracts International: Section A. Humanities and Social Sciences, 46*, C22, 46; Moyer, J. R. (1966). An exploratory study of questioning in the instructional processes in selected elementary schools. *Dissertation Abstracts International, Section A. Humanities and Social Sciences, 27*(01), 147; Schreiber, J. E. (1967). Teachers' question-asking techniques in social studies. *Dissertation Abstracts International: Section A. Humanities and Social Sciences, 28*(02), 523.

5. Doneau, S. J. (1985). Soliciting in the classroom. In T. Husén & T. N. Postlethwaite (Eds.), *The international encyclopedia of education: Research and studies* (pp. 407–413). Oxford: Pergamon.

6. Sirotnik, K. A. (1983). What you see is what you get—consistency, persistency, and mediocrity in classrooms. *Harvard Educational Review, 53*, 16–31.

7. Rosenshine, B. V. (1987). Explicit teaching. In D. C. Berliner & B. V. Rosenshine (Eds.), *Talks to teachers* (pp. 75–92). New York: McGraw-Hill.

8. Hootstein, E. W. (1993). Motivational strategies and beliefs of social studies teachers in a U.S. history course for middle school students. *Dissertation Abstracts International: Section A. Humanities and Social Sciences, 54*(04), 1216.

9. *Ibid.*, p. 56.

10. Bloom, B., Engelhart, M., Furst, E., Hill, W., & Krathwohl, D. (1956). *Taxonomy of educational objectives: The classification of educational goals. Handbook 1: Cognitive domain.* New York: David McKay.

11. Nystrand, M., & Gamoran, A. (1991). Instructional discourse, student engagement, and literature achievement. *Research in the Teaching of English, 25*, 261–290.

12. Alpert, B. (1991). Students' resistance in the classroom. *Anthropology & Education Quarterly, 22*, 350–366.

13. Brophy, J. (Ed.). (2001). *Advances in research on teaching* (Vol. 8). Oxford: JAI Elsevier.

14. Zahorik, J. A. (1968). Classroom feedback behavior of teachers. *Journal of Educational Research, 62*, 147–150.

15. Flanders, N. A. (1970). *Analyzing teaching behavior.* Reading, MA: Addison-Wesley.

16. Brophy, J. (1981). Teacher praise: A functional analysis. *Review of Educational Research, 51*, 5–32.

17. *Ibid.* Copyright © 1981 by the American Educational Research Association. Reprinted by permission of Sage Publications.

18. Rosenshine, B. V., & Furst, N. (1973). The use of direct observation to study teaching. In R. M. W. Travers (Ed.), *Handbook of research on teaching*, (2nd ed., pp. 122–183). Chicago: Rand McNally.

19. Hunter, M. (1979). Teaching is decision making. *Educational Leadership, 37*, 62–67.

Chapter 11

Seating Chart Observation Records

These seating chart techniques look simple, but they're not. True, all the supervisor gives you to look at is a seating chart with lines and arrows all over it. But they tell you a lot about what happened in your lesson. You can see that your teaching is following a definite pattern. Then the question you need to ask yourself is, "Is this a good or a bad pattern, something I want to change or something I want to keep on doing?"

—Comment of a high-school teacher

INTRODUCTION

Several techniques for observing teacher and student behavior are collectively called *Seating Chart Observation Records (SCORE)*, because each of them uses a classroom seating chart to record data. Teachers regularly use seating charts in their work, thus making it easy for them to interpret SCORE data.

SCORE techniques enable the supervisor to condense a large amount of information about classroom behavior on a single sheet of paper. They can be created on the spot to address a teacher's concerns and to record aspects of classroom behavior that reflect effective or ineffective teaching. The appendix lists effective, research-validated teaching techniques that are well-suited for observation by SCORE techniques.

In using SCORE techniques, the supervisor and teacher should keep in mind that the classroom is a primary site for students' development of the knowledge, skills, and understandings they need to lead productive, meaningful lives. To use classroom time effectively for this purpose, teachers need to understand the learning process—in particular, the six learning principles that we stated at the beginning of Chapter 10. In summary form, the principles state that learning is affected by:

1. students' level of attention.
2. students' level of motivation.
3. opportunities for students to find personal meaning in the curriculum.
4. opportunities for students to practice newly learned information.
5. group processes among classroom members.
6. whether the curriculum's focus is lower-cognitive or higher-cognitive.

The SCORE techniques that we present in this chapter highlight some of these aspects of the learning process. You might wish to develop SCORE techniques of your own to highlight other aspects.

OBSERVATION TECHNIQUE 6: RECORDING AT-TASK BEHAVIOR

The at-task technique was developed in the 1960s by Frank MacGraw at Stanford University.[1] He devised a system of classroom observation that used a 35-mm remotely controlled camera with a wide-angle lens. From the front corner of the room the camera took a photo of the total class every 90 seconds. After the photos were developed and enlarged, they were arranged in chronological order so that a person could see how the classroom changed over a given time period (e.g., 20 pictures to represent a 30-minute lesson).

Some photo sets showed students gradually moving from a position of sitting erect at their desks to a position of sleeping with their heads on their desks, then back to sitting and looking attentive. Other photo sets showed students working feverishly on matters that had nothing to do with the task at hand, vacant from their seats talking to their neighbors, or engaged in activities that the teacher regarded as inappropriate.

While the photo sets provided valuable information about students' at-task behavior, they were expensive and time-consuming to produce. After some experimentation, MacGraw developed a simple paper-and-pencil technique that provided much the same data as the 35-mm camera. This paper-and-pencil technique has come to be known as an at-task seating chart. A completed at-task chart is shown in Figure 11.1.

Researchers have found a relationship between students' at-task behavior and their learning (see Chapter 4). The higher the rate of students' at-task behavior, the more they learn. This finding comes as no surprise if we consider the learning principles summarized at the start of the chapter. If students are at-task, they are directing their attention to the information to be learned and are engaged in practicing it so that it gets into long-term memory. Furthermore, if students are at task, it suggests that they view the new information and instructional activities as meaningful. Conversely, if students are off task, it suggests that the information and activities are unclear or not meaningful to students.

Researchers have studied at-task behavior (sometimes called *engaged time* or *on-task time*) by various methods: self-report questionnaires, direct observations, work sample analysis, and case studies.[2] We describe here a technique that involves direct observation and seating charts. In Chapter 13, we describe a self-report questionnaire, the Patterns of Adaptive Learning Scales, which measures cognitive and motivational aspects of student at-task behavior.

An at-task percentage is calculated as the average amount of time that students are at task divided by the amount of classroom time in which data was collected. For example, suppose an observer collected at-task data for a 50-minute lesson. The observer would record the number of minutes that each student was at task, sum the at-task time for all the students, and divide by the number of students to get the average at-task time. Suppose that the average is 42 minutes. Dividing 42 by 50 equals 84 percent, meaning that the students as a whole were at task for 84 percent of the lesson.

A large-scale study of elementary-school students conducted in the 1970s found at-task rates between 70 percent and 75 percent.[3] This means that for every hour of instructional time, students typically were at task for 45 minutes and were off task for 15 minutes. Off-task behavior included interim activities (e.g., sharpening pencils and turning in papers),

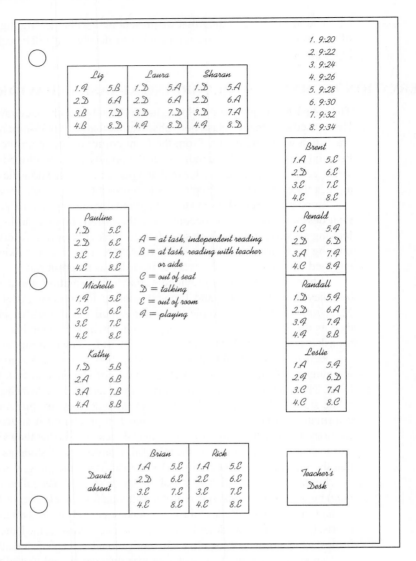

Figure 11.1 At-task seating chart.

waiting for help from the teacher, socializing, daydreaming, and misbehaving. Students had a higher at-task percentage when they were in teacher-led groups (84 percent) than during seat work (70 percent).[4]

We have found similar at-task rates in middle and high schools. However, an effective teacher can achieve at-task percentages of 90 percent or better. To achieve this goal, teachers need to get the lesson started quickly and give students an engaging task for the last few minutes of the period. Assigning learning activities that are interesting and achievable is also essential.

Procedure for Recording At-Task Rates

The intent of at-task observation is to provide data on whether individual students actually are doing the tasks that the teacher indicates are appropriate. Therefore, before using this technique, you must be acquainted with what the teacher expects the students to be doing during a given classroom period. In other words, the teacher—not the supervisor—defines what constitutes at-task behavior. Typical at-task behaviors are reading, listening, answering questions, doing seat work, and working cooperatively to complete a group project.

Lessons in which all students work on the same task at the same time usually present no problem for recording SCORE data. Lessons in which different students are working on different tasks at the same time are more challenging for the observer. If the variety of tasks is too complex, the teacher and supervisor might choose to limit the observation to one or a few groups of students. If classroom events speed up too much, the observer might need to temporarily stop collecting data, but should make a note of the points in time when data collection stopped and resumed.

A record of students' at-task behavior can be made in several ways. In the procedure we use, the supervisor completes the following seven steps:

1. Stations herself in a section of the room where she is able to observe all students.

2. Constructs a chart that includes a separate box for each student and the position of that box within the classroom seating pattern.

3. Writes each student's name, gender, or some other characteristic in his or her box. The purpose is to guide subsequent analysis of the data to determine whether certain categories of students act or are treated differently.

4. Creates a legend to represent at-task behavior and each type of inappropriate behavior observed. A typical legend might include the following:

   A: At task

   S: Stalling

   R: Schoolwork other than that requested by the teacher

   O: Out of seat

   T: Talking to neighbors

5. Systematically examines the behavior of each student for a few seconds in order to determine whether the student is at task—that is, doing what the teacher considers appropriate. If so, the supervisor indicates this by marking *1.A* in the box on the seating chart meant to represent the student. Figure 11.1 indicates that this is the first observation; the letter *A* refers to at-task behavior. Suppose instead that the student is chatting with a classmate. The supervisor would write *1.T* in the box.

6. Repeats step 5 at 3- or 4-minute intervals for the duration of the lesson. The supervisor uses the same letter legend to indicate observed behavior, but changes the number to indicate the sequence of observations. For example, *3.A* in a box indicates that the student was at task during the supervisor's third observation.

7. Indicates the time at which each set of observations was made. This is marked somewhere on the chart (e.g., see upper right-hand corner of Figure 11.1). The supervisor also might find it helpful to record the classroom activity that the teacher was conducting at each time of observation.

We recommend against creating more than five categories for observation (see Step 4, above). Adding more categories complicates the observation process greatly, and the teacher will find it increasingly difficult to interpret the resulting data. In many classroom observations, two categories are sufficient: at task and off task.

Observation of at-task behavior requires a moderate degree of inference. The expression on a student's face might be interpreted as thoughtful reflection about what the teacher is saying or as daydreaming. We suggest you think probabilistically. If you believe it is more likely that the student is engaged in thoughtful reflection than in daydreaming, use the at-task category. It is helpful to tell the teacher that the completed chart is subjective to an extent. Thus, the teacher should look for general patterns rather than question the accuracy of a few isolated observations.

The at-task chart in Figure 11.1 has one box for each student in the class. The students are identified by name on the chart. If the feedback conference occurs fairly soon after the observation, the teacher should have no difficulty matching students with the boxes, even without names. However, if the feedback conference is delayed, you should consider putting students' names in the appropriate boxes of the seating chart. If you do not know their names, you can ask the teacher to have students say their names aloud at the beginning of the class period while you jot them down.

To illustrate these procedures, we refer to an elementary-school principal who observed a first-grade teacher's reading class. The decision to do an at-task seating chart grew out of a planning conference, part of which is reproduced below:

TEACHER: Would you come in and do an at-task in my classroom? Randall and Ronald do nothing but play and talk. I would like to see just how much they really work.

PRINCIPAL: Are Randall and Ronald the only ones you want me to observe?

TEACHER: No. I have a real immature group this year. You might as well observe all of them.

PRINCIPAL: What do you mean by "immature"?

TEACHER: Oh, they have short attention spans, haven't learned to settle down, and they are all talking without permission. In other words, this first grade doesn't really know how to settle down and do some work.

PRINCIPAL: Do they seem to understand what you have planned for them?

TEACHER: Yes, but they have a hard time settling down to work. Ronald moans and groans most of the time or plays.

PRINCIPAL: What kinds of behavior should I observe for the at-task? What categories should I use?

TEACHER: Before I forget, remember some of my children are out of the room for music at the time you're coming.

PRINCIPAL: That's right. I'll put it on my checklist so I won't forget it.

TEACHER: Check to see if they're out of their seats, talking, playing, or at task. They will also be reading to my aide or to me.

PRINCIPAL: I'll make a note of the reading aide, and I'll see you tomorrow.

Behavior	9:20	9:22	9:24	9:26	9:28	9:30	9:32	9:34	Total	%
A. At task, independent reading	4	1	2	2	2	4	2	0	17	18%
B. At task, reading with teacher or aide	0	0	1	1	2	1	1	2	8	8%
C. Out of seat	1	1	1	2	0	0	0	1	6	6%
D. Talking	5	8	2	0	0	2	2	3	22	23%
E. Out of room	0	1	5	5	5	5	5	5	31	32%
F. Playing	2	1	1	2	3	0	2	1	12	13%

Figure 11.2 Summary of at-task data from Figure 11.1.

The principal created several categories for recording data on a seating chart: at-task behavior while reading independently in a workbook at one's seat (A) or with the teacher or aide (B); out of seat (C); talking (D); out of room (E); and playing (F). The categories are shown in Figure 11.2, together with the completed at-task seating chart.

Analyzing At-Task Data

Figure 11.2 provides a convenient summary of the observations recorded on the seating chart (Figure 11.1). The teacher can see at a glance how many children were engaged in each category of behavior—either at a particular point in time or summed across all the time samples. The last column indicates the average percentage of students who were engaged in each category of behavior during the class period. For example, 6 percent of the children were out of their seat on average during the lesson. The numerator used to derive this percentage is the total of six children (see total column) who were out of their seat across the eight observations that were made of the lesson. The denominator (96) is the eight observations multiplied by the twelve children in the class. Dividing the numerator (6) by the denominator (96) gives the mean percent (6 percent).

Analysis of at-task data is illustrated by the feedback conference that occurred between the principal and the first-grade teacher. Part of it is reproduced below:

TEACHER: Let's see. Randall was at task once. Ronald was, too. Here is a shocker! Liz, Laura, and Sharon do a lot of visiting. I can see where I need to do some changes in the seating.

PRINCIPAL: That may solve some of your talking and visiting problems.

TEACHER: Boy, from 9:20 to 9:36, five of my students are out to music. This only leaves seven to work with. Gee, I only worked with two children, and the aide worked with one.

PRINCIPAL: It seems as though quite a few of your students are gone at one time.

TEACHER: Yes, I should try to work with these students before they go to music.

PRINCIPAL: That's a good idea! In that way you can usually have them read to you every day.

TEACHER: Maybe I could ask the aide to have Kathy only read a few pages and then listen to someone else.

PRINCIPAL: That sounds great!

TEACHER: This doesn't solve my problem with Randall and Ronald. Since Brian and Rick go to music, maybe I could put Ronald at Rick's desk. This way I can get a direct view of him. This also would separate the two boys.

PRINCIPAL: This sounds like a good step. Maybe you'll want to keep the boys apart permanently in the classroom.

TEACHER: I sure hope this works. If not, I'll find something else.

PRINCIPAL: I'm sure you will. You seem to have some good ideas already.

TEACHER: I could even have the aide work with Ronald and Randall in reading and have her play some phonics games with them. This would help expand their attention span, too.

PRINCIPAL: You're really getting some good ideas. It will be interesting to see how they work out. Maybe I could come back and do an at-task again.

TEACHER: Yes, I'd like to see if some of my ideas will help the children settle down, especially Ronald and Randall.

This interaction between the principal and teacher illustrates the importance of at-task data. They form the basis for the teacher and supervisor to identify and solve certain problems of practice that occur in classroom instruction.

OBSERVATION TECHNIQUE 7: RECORDING VERBAL FLOW PATTERNS

Verbal flow is similar to selective verbatim transcription (see Chapter 10) in that both deal with classroom verbal behavior. The difference is that selective verbatim transcription is concerned primarily with the actual content of classroom talk, whereas verbal flow focuses more on who the initiators and recipients of the classroom talk are. The collection of verbal flow data is particularly appropriate when the lesson involves discussion, question-and-answer recitation, or other methods that require many verbal interchanges between teacher and students.

In Chapter 4 we reviewed a study by Gregg Jackson and Cecilia Cosca, who found that teachers in the Southwest directed significantly more verbal behavior toward Anglo students than toward Chicano students. Research has identified other forms of bias in teachers' verbal behavior as well. Michael Dunkin and Bruce Biddle reached the following conclusions about one such bias in their review of research:

> The majority of both emitters and targets [of verbal behavior]—whether they be teachers or pupils—are located front and center in the classroom. Thus, pupils who are located around the periphery of the classroom are more likely to be spectators than actors in the classroom drama. It could be, then, that if the teacher wants to encourage participation on the part of a quiet pupil or silence on the part of someone who is noisy, she need merely move the pupil to another location in the room![5]

Although teachers tend to talk more to students seated closest to them, other location biases can occur. For example, one teacher found that he had a tendency to acknowledge more questions from students seated to his right than from students seated to his left. After learning of this tendency, the teacher realized that, in talking to a class, he usually looked to the right side of the classroom. Thus, students seated to this side were in the teacher's central line of vision, whereas students to the left were in his peripheral vision.

Sandra Bosacki studied why some adolescent students choose to remain silent during classroom instruction.[6] She found that silence can be helpful or harmful for adolescents. Being silent can help a student listen carefully to what classmates and the teacher are saying, reflect on instructional content, and think creatively. Silence is harmful, though, if it causes a student to feel isolated, alienated, and excluded from social interactions designed to promote self-development. Silence also can be an indicator of negative self-talk, in which a student tells himself that his ideas are not worthwhile or will be met with disapproval by the teacher or other students.

Teachers need to know which of their students are silent during classroom interaction and interpret whether this silence is helpful or harmful to them. Bosacki suggests several strategies for dealing with harmful silence, such as helping students develop communication skills and an understanding of their unique voice, others' voice, and the various meanings of silence. Another approach is for teachers to create varied forms of group instruction—whole-class question-and-answer activities, small cooperative learning groups, role-playing exercises—in the hope that students who feel uncomfortable speaking in one group setting will feel comfortable speaking in a different group setting.

Procedure for Recording Verbal Flow Data

As with other SCORE methods, the first step in recording verbal flow is to make a classroom seating chart. Each student is represented by a box on the chart. You will need to label salient characteristics of the student (e.g., male or female, talkative or quiet) if the teacher wishes to know whether his or her verbal behaviors are affected by these characteristics.

Arrows are used to indicate the flow of verbal interaction, as shown in Figure 11.3. The base of the arrow indicates the person who initiates a verbal interaction, and the head of the arrow indicates the person to whom the comment is directed. Box A indicates that the teacher (arrow pointed down) made four comments, and the student (arrow pointed up) made two comments.

Box A

Box B

Figure 11.3 Verbal-flow chart.

You can simplify the chart by marking notches in the arrow to indicate repeated interactions of the same kind. This notching method is illustrated in Box B of Figure 11.3. The arrow represents the first comment, and each succeeding comment is marked by a notch. You can see that Box B records the same data as in Box A, but in simpler form.

The standard verbal flow chart can be elaborated by using additional categories of observation, such as the following:

→ +   teacher praise or encouraging remark

→ −   teacher criticism or reprimand

→ F?   teacher fact question

→ T?   teacher thought question

Student verbal behaviors also can be differentiated, as in the follow examples:

→ C   student volunteered a relevant or correct response

→ I   student volunteered an irrelevant or incorrect response

→ ?   student question

→ }   student comment directed to the class as a whole

Some supervisors prefer to use an alphabetic notation system, in which letters of the alphabet indicate discrete categories of verbal interaction, for example:

Q   teacher question

P   teacher praise

C   teacher criticism

r   student volunteered a relevant or correct response

x   student volunteered an irrelevant or incorrect response

q   student question

In this notation system, teacher and student behaviors are easily distinguished by the use of uppercase and lowercase letters.

To illustrate these procedures, we refer to an assistant principal at a high school, one of whose responsibilities is teacher supervision. In a planning conference, a first-year English teacher asked her to determine which students were contributing to classroom and small-group discussions. The teacher's purpose to learn how she was influencing students' participation and how nonparticipating students could be encouraged to join the discussion. The teacher and assistant principal agreed that a verbal-flow chart was an appropriate technique for collecting the data. The assistant principal arranged to visit the teacher's class at a time when a discussion was scheduled.

The verbal-flow chart made by the assistant principal is shown in Figure 11.4. Horizontal lines are used to indicate empty desks. Students' gender is indicated by an M or F. The supervisor recorded verbal-flow data using four categories: teacher question, student response, teacher positive response, and teacher negative response. Because some students talked among themselves, the supervisor decided to record this behavior by drawing an arrow between the students engaged in such talk. The period of observation was 22 minutes.

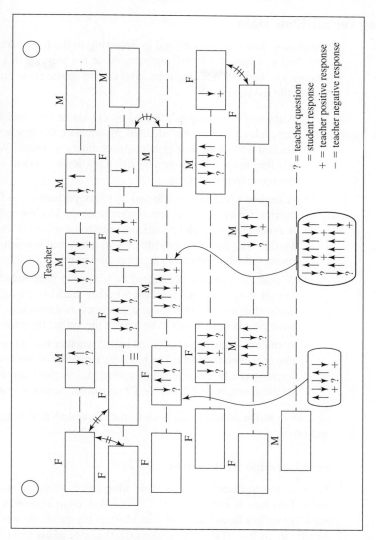

Figure 11.4. Supervisor's verbal-flow chart.

Note in Figure 11.4 that there are no arrows in the box indicating the teacher. The reason is that the teacher usually initiates most of the verbal interactions, so it would be awkward to have an arrow leading from his box to each student to whom he directs a comment. Arrows would be crisscrossing one another as they made their way from the teacher's box to boxes situated at diverse points on the seating chart. The problem is avoided by placing the arrow completely within the student's box. The base of the arrow should come from the general direction of the teacher to indicate that it was the teacher who initiated a comment or question.

Analyzing Verbal-Flow Data

Verbal-flow data can be analyzed by referring to the list of six learning principles that we described in Chapter 10 and summarized at the start of this chapter. The following are examples of how the learning principles can be applied (the numbers in parentheses below refer to the list numbers):

- A student's learning is affected by (1) his or her level of attention and (2) motivation, which in turn are affected by whether the teacher interacts directly with the student and gives him or her opportunities to speak. Verbal-flow data can indicate whether the teacher interacts with a particular student and whether that student has the opportunity to speak.

- A student's learning is affected by (3) opportunities to find personal meaning in the curriculum and (4) to practice what he or she has learned. Verbal interaction is one of the main ways in which students search for meaning and practice new information. Verbal-flow data can indicate how much verbal interaction is occurring in the classroom and which students are engaging in it.

- A student's learning is affected by (5) group processes among classroom members. Verbal-flow data can indicate whether students engage in relevant dialogue with each other and whether the group process is democratic in the sense that all students have equal opportunity to be part of the verbal interaction.

- A student's learning is affected by (6) whether the curriculum's focus is lower-cognitive or higher-cognitive. The teacher's emphasis on lower-cognitive or higher-cognitive learning can be determined by coding the teacher's questions in the verbal-flow chart by the symbols → **F?** and → **T?** or similar notation system.

We describe common analyses of data in verbal-flow seating charts in the next sections.

Seat-Location Preferences

Teachers might direct more of their attention to students seated in a certain part of the room. This bias is apparent in the verbal-flow chart shown in Figure 11.4. As the teacher put it, he suffers from tunnel vision. Most of his questions were directed to students seated directly in his line of sight. Students on either side of his line of sight were ignored, perhaps explaining why they were more likely to talk among themselves.

On seeing the verbal flow chart, the teacher commented that he might solve the problem of "tunnel vision" by seating students closer together, using the available empty seats. Another possibility is to place students in a circular seating arrangement so that everyone has eye contact with everyone else.

Student Preferences

Students are identified by gender in Figure 11.4 by the codes *M* and *F* next to each box. This coding system makes it easy to determine whether the teacher interacted equally with boys and girls, and whether he used each category of verbal behavior equally with them.

The verbal-flow chart indicates that 13 girls and 11 boys were present for the lesson. Of the 20 questions asked by the teacher, 12 (60 percent) were directed to boys, and 8 (40 percent) were directed to girls. Of the 12 positive responses by the teacher, 8 (66 percent) were directed to boys and 4 (33 percent) were directed to girls. The two negative responses by the teacher were both directed to girls. Nine of the 13 girls (70 percent) and 4 (36 percent) of the 11 boys did not participate in the lesson. These data suggest a gender bias favoring boys.

You might also note in Figure 11.4 that two students, a boy and a girl, dominated the participation. In fact, the assistant principal needed to create additional boxes to contain their data, as indicated by the oval-like boxes connected by long arrows to the two students. Thirty percent of the total number of questions asked by the teacher were directed to these two students. Moreover, these two students accounted for nearly half the student responses.

Jeffrey Wimer and his colleagues did a research study in which they used a seating chart form to examine the flow of teachers' higher-cognitive questions to boys and girls during mathematics lessons in third- and fourth-grade classrooms.[7] (They used the term "higher order" rather than "higher cognitive.") Examples of higher-order questions were "Why would you calculate a percentage in this case?" and "What if the number were 10 instead of 5?" Examples of lower-order questions were: "How many eggs are there in a dozen?" and "What is the '1' called?"

On the basis of previous research findings, the researchers predicted that teachers would direct more higher-order questions to boys than to girls. To test their prediction, they collected data on one lesson for each of 16 teachers using the seating chart form shown in Figure 11.5. You can see that the seating chart enabled them to record various types of information about each student, including the number of lower-order and higher-order questions directed to each student. Analyses of these data yielded several interesting findings. First, the teachers asked relatively few higher-order questions: Of the questions asked, only about one-third were higher order. Second, of the 249 students in the sample, only 15 percent had the opportunity to answer a higher-order question. Third, contrary to expectations, the teachers showed no bias in addressing higher-order questions to boys and girls. However, the researchers found that teachers were more likely to address a higher-order question to a boy who did not volunteer to answer it than to a girl who did not volunteer to answer it.

When teachers come across research findings such as these, it might arouse their interest in knowing their frequency of higher-cognitive questioning and whether it reflects gender bias or some other sort of bias. If this is the case, clinical supervisors can work with the teachers to collect question-asking data using a form such as the one shown in Figure 11.5.

Preferences for Certain Types of Verbal Behavior

Verbal-flow charts can be analyzed to determine how frequently teachers and students use various types of verbal behaviors and whether they emphasize certain types more than others. One comparison of interest in Figure 11.4 is the teacher's use of a positive verbal response, a negative verbal response, or no response to students' comments. Of the teacher's positive and negative responses, all but two were positive. The two negative responses were directed toward girls near the periphery of the classroom. We also find that of the 32 student responses or questions in the lesson, 11 (34 percent) were followed by a teacher positive response.

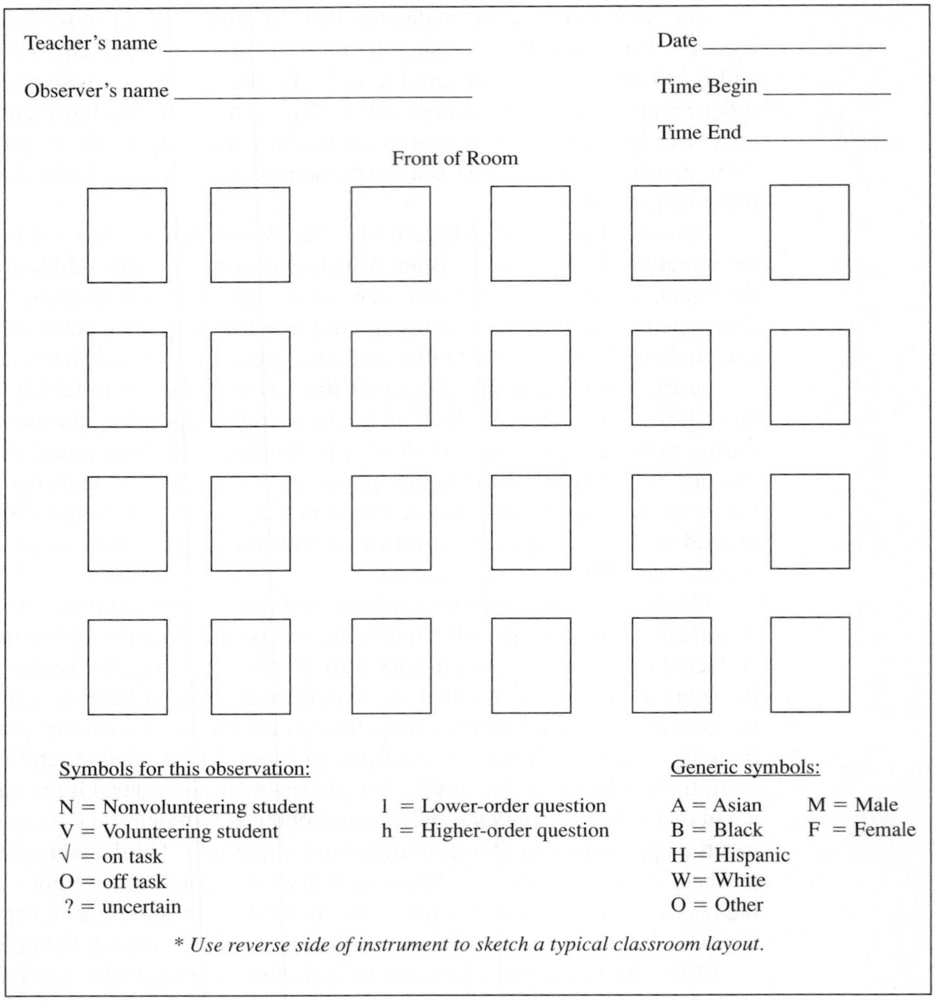

Teacher's name _____   Date _____

Observer's name _____   Time Begin _____

                                               Time End _____

Front of Room

☐ ☐ ☐ ☐ ☐ ☐

☐ ☐ ☐ ☐ ☐ ☐

☐ ☐ ☐ ☐ ☐ ☐

☐ ☐ ☐ ☐ ☐ ☐

Symbols for this observation: Generic symbols:

N = Nonvolunteering student   l = Lower-order question   A = Asian   M = Male
V = Volunteering student   h = Higher-order question   B = Black   F = Female
√ = on task   H = Hispanic
O = off task   W = White
? = uncertain   O = Other

Use reverse side of instrument to sketch a typical classroom layout.

Figure 11.5. Systematic Classroom Observation Instrument

Source: Wimer, J. W., Ridenour, C. S., Thomas, K., & Place, A.W. (2001). Higher order teacher questioning of boys and girls in elementary mathematics classrooms. *Journal of Educational Research, 95*(2), 84–92. (Chart appears on p. 88.) Reprinted by permission of Taylor & Francis Books.

OBSERVATION TECHNIQUE 8: RECORDING CLASSROOM MOVEMENT PATTERNS

Seating charts can be used to record how the teacher and students move around the classroom during a lesson. We call this SCORE technique "movement patterns." The supervisor's task is to record how the teacher and individual students walk from one section of the room to another during a given time interval. Many teaching situations, especially in primary and elementary school, require teachers to make decisions about where to position themselves in the classroom. For example, as students file into class after recess, the teacher needs to decide whether to stand by the door, at the desk, or elsewhere. When students are engaged in seatwork or group projects, the teacher must decide whether to stay at the desk or move around the room checking on students' work.

The nature of the teacher's movement patterns can affect students' attentiveness, motivation to perform learning tasks, and ability to practice and find meaning in new information. The teacher who "hides" behind a desk might experience more discipline problems and less student at-task behavior than the teacher who checks on students as they work at their desks. The teacher who always stands in one position while speaking to the class might not hold students' attention as effectively as the teacher who moves about for dramatic emphasis or to illustrate a concept on the blackboard or wall chart.

Teachers' movement patterns in the classroom might reveal a bias. Some prefer one part of the classroom over another, perhaps because certain students are seated there. Others tend to stand some distance away from students' seats while speaking to the class. This can create difficulties for students who do not see or hear well, and it might provide an excuse for some students to engage in off-task behavior ("the teacher can't see what I'm doing").

Students' movement patterns can reveal whether they are at task. Sometimes it is necessary for students to move about the classroom to complete an assigned activity. At other times, though, students move about to avoid an assigned task or because they have no assigned task. The latter situation often occurs when students finish their work early in the class period; they mill around to find another activity or a classmate to engage in conversation.

Movement patterns can be recorded during any lesson, but the technique is most useful when the teaching situation contains the potential for movement about the classroom. For example, seatwork and group projects provide situations where the teacher needs to move about—and where students move about even when they don't need to. On the other hand, there is not likely to be much movement behavior to record during the showing of a film.

PROCEDURE FOR RECORDING MOVEMENT PATTERNS

To record movement patterns, each student and the teacher should be represented by a separate box in the seating chart. Also, the seating chart should represent the physical layout of the classroom, including aisles and desks or tables where students might congregate.

Figure 11.6 shows a seating chart used to record movement pattern data. Teacher or student movement from one point in the room to another is indicated by a continuous line. The line for each person originates at the point where the teacher or student was located in the room when the supervisor began observing. The line ends where the teacher or student stopped, such as at a student's desk or a supply center. This stopping point can be indicated by an arrow point (>) or other symbol. If the person moves on to another location and stops there, the line on the seating chart can trace that path and the stopping point can be indicated by the stopping-point symbol. If the teacher or student returns to his starting point, this can be indicated by another symbol (e.g., a circle) placed at the start of the line.

For example, in Figure 11.6 the teacher went from her desk to Wes's desk and stopped there for a few minutes. This path is indicated by a line leading from her desk to Wes's

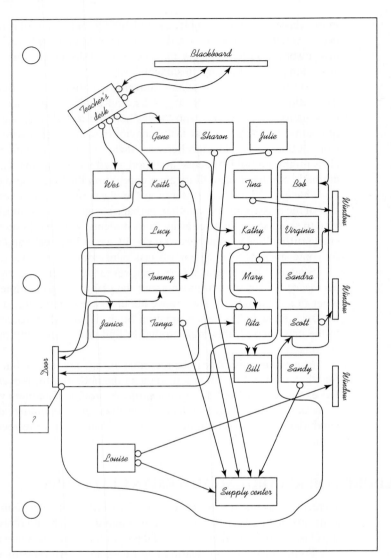

Figure 11.6 Movement pattern chart.

desk. The fact that she stopped there for a period of time is indicated by the arrow point. The fact that she then retraced her path back to her desk is indicated by the circle at the start of the line.

You might wish to indicate the pattern of movement at different points in the lesson. A supply of different-colored pencils is useful for this purpose. For example, you might record the first 10 minutes in yellow, the second 10 minutes in green, and so on. If the teacher plans to divide the lesson into different activities, this too can form the basis for color coding. Movement during each activity can be recorded with a different-colored pencil. This technique helps the teacher analyze the pattern of movement that occurred at different stages of the lesson.

So many students occasionally mill about in the classroom that you will not be able to record all their movements. When this occurs, you can suspend data recording for a few minutes. (Make a note that you did so somewhere on your movement pattern chart.) Another possibility is to limit your observation to only certain students in the classroom.

Analyzing Movement-Pattern Data

The movement pattern chart in Figure 11.6 was recorded in a high-school typing class. The teacher worried about whether he ran "too loose a ship." He didn't think that students should be "chained to their desks" during the entire class period, yet he wanted to instill in students a sense of discipline and self-control. He and the supervisor agreed that a movement pattern chart might be a good method for recording the level of orderliness in the classroom. The supervisor observed and recorded the class's movement behavior for approximately 30 minutes.

At first glance, a movement pattern chart such as the one shown in Figure 11.6 looks like a hopeless maze. However, if the teacher and supervisor isolate the behavior of one person or one section of the room, they usually can make helpful inferences from the chart.

The first thing that caught the teacher's eye was the door leading into the classroom. Five students entered or left the classroom after the lesson had begun. One student who was not enrolled in the class (indicated by a "?") apparently entered the classroom, talked to several friends, and then left. The teacher thought that the mystery student probably was wandering about during his free study period. One student (Keith) left the class while it was in session and then returned. The teacher did not realize this had happened.

After inspecting these data, the teacher decided he needed to monitor students' entry and exit behavior more closely. Also included in this resolution was the decision to give students some ground rules about leaving class while it is in session. The teacher then focused his attention on his own movement behavior. He recalled that he had gone to the blackboard at the start of the lesson to write key terms relating to typing business letters. Next the teacher decided to check on students' progress, so he visited a few students (Wes, Keith, and Gene), each time returning to his desk to catch up on some paperwork. Finally, he decided he should circulate a bit; this is reflected in a large loop starting and ending at his desk. (The loop is not shown in the figure.) Although he did not stop at every student's desk, he felt he got to each area of the classroom, so that if a student desired to speak with him, the student could get his attention easily. The teacher generally felt satisfied with his movement pattern in this lesson.

He and the supervisor next turned their attention to the supply center. Four students (Tanya, Sharon, Julie, and Sandy) went to the center for supplies during the observed part of the lesson. After seeing these data, the teacher wondered whether he should ask students to get any necessary materials at the start of the lesson. This procedure might create a more orderly class and might help students become more organized and systematic in their approach to typing. The supervisor suggested that the teacher experiment with this procedure and see for himself whether it produced the desired effects.

Finally, the teacher looked at other student behavior. He noted that several students had visited with each other. Four students (Tina, Mary, Scott, and Louise) had gone to the window to see what was happening outside. The supervisor told the teacher that most of this kind of classroom movement occurred near the end of the observation period. The teacher realized then that he had an activity planned for students who finished early, but had forgotten to relay it to them because he was preoccupied with some paperwork he wanted to complete during the lesson.

Summing up his inferences from the movement chart data, the teacher felt that he might make a few changes that would create a more orderly class without losing the relaxed atmosphere he valued.

ENDNOTES

1. MacGraw, F., Jr. (1966). The use of 35-mm time-lapse photography as a feedback and observation instrument in teacher education. *Dissertation Abstracts International, 26*(11), 6533. University Microfilms No. AAG66-02516.

2. These methods are described in: Chapman, E. (2003). Alternative approaches to assessing student engagement rates. *Practical Assessment, Research & Evaluation, 8*(13). Retrieved from http://PAREonline.net

3. Borg, W. R. (1980). Time and school learning. In C. Denham & A. Lieberman (Eds.), *Time to learn* (pp. 33–72). Washington, DC: U.S. Department of Education.

4. Rosenshine, B. V. (1980). How time is spent in elementary classrooms. In C. Denham & A. Lieberman (Eds.), *Time to learn* (pp. 107–126). Washington, DC: U.S. Department of Education.

5. Dunkin, M. J., & Biddle, B. J. (1974). *The study of teaching*. New York: Holt, Rinehart & Winston. Quote appears on p. 226.

6. Bosacki, S. L. (2005). *The culture of classroom silence*. New York: Peter Lang.

7. Wimer, J. W., Ridenour, C. S., Thomas, K., & Place, A. W. (2001). Higher order teacher questioning of boys and girls in elementary mathematics classrooms. *Journal of Educational Research, 95*(2), 84–92.

Chapter 12

Wide-Lens Techniques

It was a shock to listen to the audiotape of my lesson. I never knew before how I sounded when talking to students. The idea of audiotaping lessons is good. After all, students have to hear you talk, so you might as well know how you sound to them. Just listening for a few minutes to the audiotape helped me learn quite a few things about how I communicate. I'm ready now to have myself videotaped. I want to see what that's like!

—Comment of a preservice secondary teacher

INTRODUCTION

The observation techniques described in Chapters 10 and 11—selective verbatim and observation using seating charts—enable the teacher and supervisor to focus their attention on a few teaching behaviors. Their narrow lens screens out classroom "noise." But sometimes it is the "noise" (i.e., what you didn't plan to observe) that is most interesting. For example, an unanticipated teaching event might occur and strike you as noteworthy because of its effect on the class. Wide-lens techniques are well-suited for recording these situations. We use the term *wide lens* because these techniques have a wide focus for recording classroom events.

Wide-lens techniques make few prior assumptions about what is important or effective in teaching. For this reason, they provide a good starting point in supervising a teacher who is defensive or not ready to select particular teaching behaviors for improvement. After reviewing wide-lens data, the teacher might be more ready to reflect on his teaching, identify specific teaching or student behaviors for focused observations, and set self-improvement goals.

In this chapter we describe several wide-lens techniques that can be used to observe teaching techniques that researchers have found to be effective. In addition, you can refer to the appendix for a comprehensive list of effective teaching techniques and information about which ones are well-suited for observation by wide-lens methods.

OBSERVATION TECHNIQUE 9: CREATING ANECDOTAL RECORDS AND SCRIPT TAPES

Anecdotal records are an easy way to record classroom interaction using a wide lens. The basic technique is to make brief notes of events as they occur in the classroom. This is a favorite technique of anthropologists, who are highly trained in making descriptive ethnographic notes about what they are observing. In fact, anecdotal records in supervisory observations are similar to ethnographic notes in that both involve observation of a culture—in this case, the culture of a classroom.

We use the term *anecdotal record* to refer to this technique because it suggests informality and reminds the teacher and supervisor that the record is not complete. Madeline Hunter, the developer of the Instructional Theory into Practice teaching model (see Chapter 4), created a similar note-taking method called *script taping*, which is simply the process of taking notes about a lesson as it is happening.[1] Hunter claimed seven advantages for its use in the supervision process:

1. The only materials required are paper and pencil.
2. It can be used to record virtually anything that occurs in a classroom.
3. Events are recorded in a temporal order, making it easy to determine how teacher behavior affects student behavior and vice versa.
4. It is relatively unbiased, if used by a trained observer.
5. The script tape can be "played back" to the teacher in any location and at any time following the observation.
6. The script tape can be scanned quickly to find any part of the lesson.
7. Script tapes are easily stored.

Procedure for Making Anecdotal Records and Script Tapes

Anecdotal records have a wide focus, but you and the teacher will need to decide just how wide to open the lens. You can make anecdotal observations of the teacher, one particular student, one group of students, the whole class of students, or everyone in the classroom. As you widen the lens, you can observe more events. As you narrow it, you will observe a narrower range of behaviors, but you can make more intensive descriptions of them.

Anecdotal records usually consist of short descriptive sentences. Each sentence summarizes a discrete observation. It is helpful to start each sentence on a separate line and, every so often, record the time that an observation was made. These time markings help the teacher get a temporal sense of the flow of events that were observed.

The sentences should be as objective and nonevaluative as possible. Instead of writing, "Students are bored," you might write, "Several students yawn; Jane looks out window." Instead of writing, "Teacher does good job of giving directions," you might write, "Teacher gives directions for recording status of jar experiment. Asks if students understand. Most of class nod or say yes." If you make evaluative comments in your anecdotal record, the teacher is likely to react to the evaluation rather than to what occurred. If your comments are descriptive and neutral, teachers can more easily draw their own conclusions about the effectiveness of the lesson.

Carolyn Frank described an activity that supervisors and teachers can use to develop skill in distinguishing between objective description and interpretation.[2] The activity is called *notetaking/notemaking*. The first step is to observe a classroom lesson (or possibly a video of one). During and after the observation, they write their notes in two columns: a "notetaking" column for descriptive notes and a "notemaking" column for interpretive notes. The observers then compare their two columns of notes to determine whether each note is placed in the appropriate column and whether the interpretations in the notemaking column are grounded in the descriptions of the notetaking column. This activity can be recycled with new classroom events to improve proficiency. Figure 12.1 shows an example of notetaking/notemaking notes made by a student teacher who observed a bilingual fourth-grade classroom.

Teacher and student behaviors are not the only events to observe and describe in the anecdotal record. Observers also should be alert to the context of the teacher's lesson, for example:

"The room is warm. Wall thermometer reads 78 degrees."

"Teacher shows map to class. Map is faded. Names of countries are difficult to read."

"Lesson is interrupted by announcement over intercom."

"One of the fluorescent lights starts to hum loudly."

"Several students arrived late, with one coming in 10 minutes after class started."

"Some students had not done their homework."

Notetaking	Notemaking
A child is working at the computer. There are fourteen students working at their desks. Six students are working with another teacher (aide) in the back of the room. It is an English reading/writing group she is working with—speaking only in English. I see a mother working with one child only and she is helping the student with something in English. There is a baby in a carriage nearby the mother. I hear classical music playing very lightly. I can only hear the music every once in a while when the classroom is really quiet. I stand up and move around the room to see what the children at their desks are working on. They are writing scary stories. The baby makes a funny noise with her lips and everyone in the class laughs and stares for a few seconds, even the teacher. I look at the group working with the teacher and on the board I see: 5) Yo *quiero* a mi perrito 6) Yo voy a *querer* mucho ami perro 7) Vamos a *mioler* la tortilla	The class seems to be really self-directed. The children are really on task and each has their own thing that they are working on. I am not used to seeing students split up into different groups for Spanish and English readers because in my class they are Spanish readers, but it is really good for me to see this because it happens in a lot of upper grade settings, and I will be working in an upper grade bilingual setting next placement. I really like the idea of putting on music during work times. I know that when I hear classical music it really helps me to relax and calm [sic] as well as focus. I think that it has this same effect on the students in this class. I'm noticing more and more that I really cherish the laughter in a classroom when it comes from a sincere topic or source. It is also nice to see the students *and* the *teacher* laughing. It's good for students to see their teacher . . .

Figure 12.1 Example of the notetaking/notemaking method.

Source: Frank, C. (1999). *Ethnographic eyes: A teacher's guide to classroom observation.* (pp. 11–12) Portsmouth, NH: Heinemann.

An anecdotal record of these contextual phenomena can help the teacher interpret certain behaviors of students (or of the teacher) during the lesson. Figure 12.2 illustrates how much contextual detail can be found in classrooms. It is a sample of an ethnographic protocol made by a professionally trained ethnographer.

The anecdotal record can consist of handwritten notes made by the supervisor as he or she sits unobtrusively somewhere in the classroom. Unless you have good handwriting, the anecdotal record will be difficult for the teacher to read and analyze. Therefore, you

---

Protocol Number: 06
Name of Researcher: Gail
Date of Observation:
Subject of Observation:

2nd Grade Class, Open

1. Classroom. with two team teacher
2. and two other adults.
3. This is a joint observation with
4. Elizabeth. I will be observing two
5. reading groups today, simultan-
6. eously. including 9 children. Out of
7. the nine children. 2 are girls. 7 are
8. boys. 8:30 Noise level 2
10. At 8:30 the noise level is 2. The
11. children have just been let into the
12. classroom. taking their coats off
13. and wandering around the room.
14. Several boys are in the corner
15. fighting, and some girls are sitting
16. on the floor playing a puzzle. The
17. teacher is walking back and forth in
18. the back of the classroom not at-
19. tending the children. The noise
20. continues and the children are run-
21. ning around. There is much con-
22. fusion in the room. Two teachers
   8:35 23. stand at the desk talking
   to one
24. another. At 8:35. Mrs. Tyler
25. leaves the room. The team teach-
26. er stays seated behind the class-
27. room. At her desk. At 8:40 Hrs.
28. Tyler comes back into the room.
29. She walks to the desk at the far
30. left hand side of the classroom,

31. which is a round table, and sits
32. on the edge. She says "Blue
33. Group, get your folders and
   go up
34. in the front. Green Group. come
35. here." Noise levels drop to 1.
   and
36. the children begin to follow her
37. orders. She says, "Anybody
   lose
38. a quarter?" No one responds,
   and
39. she repeats the question again
40. with irritation in her
   voice. She
41. says I know someone found,
42. someone lost a quarter because
43. it was found in the coat room.
44. Look in your pockets and see."
45. No one says anything.
46. She now stands up and pulls a
47. pile of workbooks from across
48. the table over to her. They are
49. the reading workbooks,
50. She opens one of them on the
51. top and says, "Ah Daniel!" She
52. says this with a loud sharp
   voice.
53. She continues, "your work yes-
54. terday was not too bad but you
55. need some work. Evidently
   there
56. are still some words you don't
57. understand." She thumbs
   through
58. the rest of his lesson. Danny is

59. standing at the outside
   of the cir-
60. cle around her, not listening to
61. what she is saying. Mrs. Tyler
62. now stands and gives instructions
63. to the Green Group. She tells
64. them to go through 8 through 13.
65. reading the two stories between
66. those pages and to go over the
67. work in the workbooks that she is
68. about to give back, She tells them
69. that they may seat any place but
70. not together and she says. "And I
71. don't want any funny business."
72. She now opens the next work-
73. book which is Nicole's. She tells
74. Nicole that she is having the
75. same problem that Danny is hav-
76. ing without specifying further.
77. Nicole looks up at her
   with an ex-
78. pectant look on her face. She
79. then looks at a third book and
80. says "Michelle, you're having the
81. same problem." She says,
82. "Snatch means to grab. Beach,
83. what does it mean?" Michelle
84. doesn't answer. She has her fin-
85. ger in her mouth and looks anx-
86. ious. The teacher closes the
87. workbook and pushes it to
88. Michelle. Michelle takes it and
89. walks away, with Nicole. Teacher
90. then opens the next workbook
91. and says. "Mike. I don't appreci-
92. ate all these circles. She points

Figure 12.2 Example of an ethnographic protocol.

should have your notes typed, if possible, so that the teacher has a neatly typed transcript to reflect upon in the feedback conference. The best option is probably to type notes on a laptop computer and then make a printout of the anecdotal record.

If you write your notes by hand, it helps to use abbreviations so that you can keep up with the flow of events. Madeline Hunter provided the following example of a handwritten script tape with abbreviations:

Opn p. 43 I'm ask ver hd-use mark to find ans whn fnd sho me w/ sig who has lots of pets Every had mark on rt ans Who can't see Mr. Sleeper (wrong ans) that rt if askd who sees but can't see. Now just rt.[3]

In unabbreviated form, the script tape recorded the following teacher statement:

Open your book to page 43. I'm going to ask some very hard questions. Use your marker to find the answer. When you have found the answer, show me with the signal (thumbs up). Who has lots of pets? Everyone had the marker on the right answer. Who can't see Mr. Sleeper? (A girl gave the wrong answer.) That would be right if I asked who sees Mr. Sleeper, but I asked who can't see Mr. Sleeper? (Same child responds correctly.) Now you're just right![4]

In our experience, we have found it possible to record at least the main events of a lesson in neat handwriting and with only minor abbreviations.

Analyzing Anecdotal Records and Script Tapes

Jane Stallings, Margaret Needels, and Georgea Sparks provide an example of an anecdotal record based on observing a child who was proving to be a management problem for the teacher being supervised.[5] The supervisor made 60 pages (!) of handwritten notes about the child over a two-day period. The following is a partial summary of the information contained in the notes:

On the first day, Billy had wandered about the room 57 times. Since the school day was 5 hours long, this was about 10 times an hour. Billy had fallen off his chair 14 times, picked his nose 17 times, rubbed his eyes 23 times, received 13 smiles and 27 reprimands—mostly to stop falling off his chair and pay attention. Billy had initiated conversations with other children 44 times, but the interactions were only 1 or 2 sentences long. Billy spoke to everyone who passed his seat, tried to trip 3 people, succeeding twice. Billy was rejected 15 times by other children who were involved in some activity and was physically pushed away from a group of 3 who were working on a mural. During recess, he put a blanket over his desk, took his reading workbook and disappeared underneath. He stayed there for 5 minutes.[6]

The second day's observations were similar, and the picture that emerged was of a hyperactive, highly distractible child who needed help in screening out the myriad distractions in the classroom. This information was useful in working with the child's parents, the reading specialist, and the school psychologist to plan an educational program for the child.

Supervisors most likely would never collect this much anecdotal data about a teacher or her students. However, the example illustrates how data in an anecdotal record can be summarized and then used as part of a feedback conference, which can lead to instructional changes or another intervention.

OBSERVATION TECHNIQUE 10: MAKING VIDEO AND AUDIO RECORDINGS

Video and audio recordings are among the most objective observation techniques. They enable teachers to see themselves as students see them. Another advantage of recordings is their wide focus. They pick up a great deal of what teachers and students are doing and saying—and also the "feel" of classroom interaction, which includes emotional climate and nonverbal behavior.

Video recording is used in many professions and sports. Surgical operations are videotaped so that doctors can learn from them. Athletes and their coaches spend hours analyzing video recordings of games and individual player actions. Shouldn't we spend a fraction of our supervisory time with teachers reviewing video recordings of their classroom interaction?

The portable video recorder is often used in microteaching, a method of professional development that we describe in Chapter 3. In microteaching, the teacher practices a few specific teaching skills in a scaled-down teaching situation involving a 10- or 15-minute lesson with five or so students. [7] The microteaching lesson is videotaped and played back to the teacher so that his or her teaching performance, especially the use of the targeted skills, can be analyzed.

Teachers almost invariably find that a video recording, whether made in a microteaching situation or regular classroom, provides an important self-learning experience. However, there are several problems to avoid. First, supervisors must be careful to arrange the video recording equipment so that it does not interfere with the lesson. This is best done by setting up the equipment ahead of time, before students enter the classroom. Second, our experience indicates that, when first exposed to a videotape of themselves, teachers tend to focus on the "cosmetics" of their performance (e.g., physical appearance, clothes, and voice quality). In fact, a study by Gavriel Salomon and Fred McDonald revealed that in a videotape replay situation, 58 percent of teachers' self-observations were concerned with physical appearance, and only 18 percent were focused on teaching behavior.[8] This is a natural initial reaction.

Some teachers are initially anxious about the prospect of being videotaped. This problem can be alleviated by allowing teachers to experiment with the equipment before the classroom lesson is to be videotaped. Another helpful procedure is to allow teachers to keep their own videotape or show them how to erase it. This calms any fear that the video recording might get into the "wrong hands."

Although video recordings appear to be a more powerful observational tool than audio recordings, this may not be so. Teachers sometimes are captivated by the image on the TV screen and do not listen to what is being said. Audio recordings have fewer distracting cues, and so it is easier for teachers to concentrate on the verbal interaction. Research has shown that video feedback and audio feedback are equally effective in helping teachers improve their use of verbal teaching skills.[9]

Procedure for Making Video and Audio Recordings

Current models of video and audio recorders store the data on a hard drive, which can be linked to a TV or computer screen. Another option is to download the data to a computer and use software to cut out unwanted parts of the recording or to add subtitles. Editing of this type usually is unnecessary if the only individuals viewing the tape will be the teacher and supervisor.

However, editing might be desirable if the tape is to be viewed by a group, as might happen in a professional learning community (see Chapter 3). For example, Miriam Sherin describes how "video clubs" can be set up so that teachers can observe and learn from one another's practice.[10] In this use of a recorded lesson, it is necessary to follow legal requirements for obtaining prior written permission from the students and teacher and any other individual in the camera's view.

Audio recorders are much simpler than video recorders to set up and operate. Many models store the recording on a hard drive, which creates the option of downloading the recording to a computer's speaker system.

The recording process becomes more complicated as the size of the class increases. If you plan to record a regular classroom situation, it is a good idea to experiment beforehand with various camera and microphone placements in the classroom to get the best camera angle and sound. The microphone built into an audio or video recorder is likely to have a small pick-up range. As the focus of supervision is usually the teacher, we suggest that you place the microphone fairly close to the teacher. By doing so, you can record everything the teacher says and some of what students say. Another option is to use a wireless microphone that can be attached to the teacher's shirt pocket or other item of clothing. The supervisor can make the recording, and we have found that many students have the skills to do it.

Analyzing Video and Audio Recordings

An efficient procedure is to have teachers play back the entire recording for themselves. They can share insights about their teaching performance with you during the feedback conference. At this time you can select a short segment—or segments—of the recording (perhaps three to five minutes) for more intensive analysis. You will find that even a brief segment can yield important insights into the teacher's skill level and teaching style.

The wide focus of video or audio recordings is both a strength and weakness. The insightful teacher will be able to observe many different aspects of their behavior and their students' behavior. Some teachers will notice only a few aspects, however, and might focus on the "cosmetic" features mentioned earlier. The supervisor's role in the feedback conference is to encourage the teacher to draw inferences from comments that the two of them make about events in the recording, and also to draw the teacher's attention to significant classroom phenomena if he or she overlooked them.

Many teacher education programs have a required course on teaching strategies. One requirement of the course might be for the teacher to participate in microteaching sessions in which they practice several different teaching methods. They make an audio or video recording of their lesson for later analysis. They might also be required to make a transcript covering several minutes of the verbal behavior that was recorded. This procedure ensures that student teachers listen carefully to what was said in the lesson. For example, Figure 12.3 presents a partial transcript made by a preservice teacher who had presented a poetry lesson using the lecture method. This example shows that an audio recording and transcript made from it provided a rich source of feedback to the teacher on his teaching behavior.

Teachers might also be asked to write an analysis of their lesson based on the transcript and other feedback data. Figure 12.4 presents the first part of an analysis written by the preservice teacher who taught the poetry lesson. It illustrates that the process of teaching a lesson and recording it for later analysis is a powerful technique for helping the preservice teacher see areas for instructional improvement.

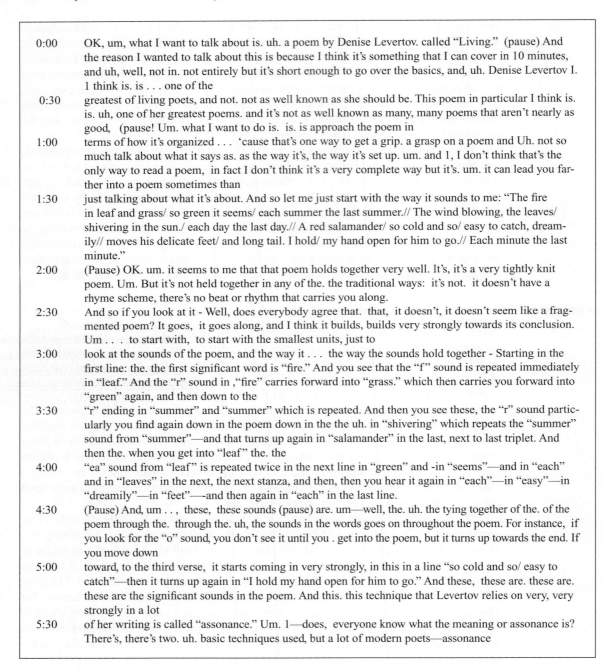

0:00	OK, um, what I want to talk about is. uh. a poem by Denise Levertov. called "Living." (pause) And the reason I wanted to talk about this is because I think it's something that I can cover in 10 minutes, and uh, well, not in. not entirely but it's short enough to go over the basics, and, uh. Denise Levertov I. 1 think is. is . . . one of the
0:30	greatest of living poets, and not. not as well known as she should be. This poem in particular I think is. is. uh, one of her greatest poems. and it's not as well known as many, many poems that aren't nearly as good, (pause! Um. what I want to do is. is. is approach the poem in
1:00	terms of how it's organized . . . 'cause that's one way to get a grip. a grasp on a poem and Uh. not so much talk about what it says as. as the way it's, the way it's set up. um. and 1, I don't think that's the only way to read a poem, in fact I don't think it's a very complete way but it's. um. it can lead you farther into a poem sometimes than
1:30	just talking about what it's about. And so let me just start with the way it sounds to me: "The fire in leaf and grass/ so green it seems/ each summer the last summer.// The wind blowing, the leaves/ shivering in the sun./ each day the last day.// A red salamander/ so cold and so/ easy to catch, dreamily// moves his delicate feet/ and long tail. I hold/ my hand open for him to go.// Each minute the last minute."
2:00	(Pause) OK. um. it seems to me that that poem holds together very well. It's, it's a very tightly knit poem. Um. But it's not held together in any of the. the traditional ways: it's not. it doesn't have a rhyme scheme, there's no beat or rhythm that carries you along.
2:30	And so if you look at it - Well, does everybody agree that. that, it doesn't, it doesn't seem like a fragmented poem? It goes, it goes along, and I think it builds, builds very strongly towards its conclusion. Um . . . to start with, to start with the smallest units, just to
3:00	look at the sounds of the poem, and the way it . . . the way the sounds hold together - Starting in the first line: the. the first significant word is "fire." And you see that the "f" sound is repeated immediately in "leaf." And the "r" sound in ,"fire" carries forward into "grass." which then carries you forward into "green" again, and then down to the
3:30	"r" ending in "summer" and "summer" which is repeated. And then you see these, the "r" sound particularly you find again down in the poem down in the the uh. in "shivering" which repeats the "summer" sound from "summer"—and that turns up again in "salamander" in the last, next to last triplet. And then the. when you get into "leaf" the. the
4:00	"ea" sound from "leaf" is repeated twice in the next line in "green" and -in "seems"—and in "each" and in "leaves" in the next, the next stanza, and then, then you hear it again in "each"—in "easy"—in "dreamily"—in "feet"—-and then again in "each" in the last line.
4:30	(Pause) And, um . . , these, these sounds (pause) are. um—well, the. uh. the tying together of the. of the poem through the. through the. uh, the sounds in the words goes on throughout the poem. For instance, if you look for the "o" sound, you don't see it until you . get into the poem, but it turns up towards the end. If you move down
5:00	toward, to the third verse, it starts coming in very strongly, in this in a line "so cold and so/ easy to catch"—then it turns up again in "I hold my hand open for him to go." And these, these are. these are. these are the significant sounds in the poem. And this. this technique that Levertov relies on very, very strongly in a lot
5:30	of her writing is called "assonance." Um. 1—does, everyone know what the meaning or assonance is? There's, there's two. uh. basic techniques used, but a lot of modern poets—assonance

Figure 12.3 Transcript of a lecture microlesson.

I would rate this lecture as a disaster, and this for two main reasons which are not unrelated; nervousness and poor organization. A sudden attack of stage fright was for some reason quite unexpected, and because I hadn't anticipated it I hadn't written out any more than a general outline of the points I wanted to cover. This, as it turned out. was not enough to see me through. Some of the faults in this lecture, such as the astonishing number of "um's." "uh's." and stuttering repetitions (e.g., "What I want to do is. is, is approach the poem . . .") are simply signs of nervous excitement: having heard tapes of myself in conversation. I know these mannerisms are not always present, at least not to this degree. These I can only expect to correct by calming down a bit, but this I think I will be able to do if 1 correct some of the more fundamental mistakes I made this time around. The most important thing missing from this lecture is an introduction. Immediately upon hearing the first questions after I finished, I was made aware that I had left out the necessary background for reading the poem, And even though biographical information about the author, for instance, was not what I was mainly concerned with, it would have given students some context, which is a necessary preliminary to any appreciation, A preliminary statement of what the poem is about, or perhaps simply some lead-in remarks about summer days and why some moments seem more alive than others, would have been very useful. And although before the lecture I had wanted not to seem too schematic, afterwards I realized that I needn't have worried: and I now regret not having outlined ahead of time the areas I was going to cover.

It now seems to me, also, that I went at the poem exactly backwards: for some reason I began with the smallest details; the sounds of the poem, and went on to its larger structure before talking about its over-all theme. This is absolutely perverse; it is almost as if I had been trying to keep the main point a secret until the last possible moment. Clearly, it would have been better to begin with the most general statements, and to proceed to the more particular ones only after these landmarks had been mapped out.

I feel that, even so, using a blackboard would have improved things immeasurably. Not only could I have communicated better by writing down a few terms like "assonance" and by marking the repetitions of sounds rather than simply listing them; but also I think it would have helped simply to get everyone's eyes and attention (not least of all my own) away from the handout sheet and out into a more central meeting place. I even think that just having something to do with my hands would have put me more at ease.

I only asked questions twice in the course of the lecture, and both questions were almost rhetorical, being put in such a way as to actually discourage a response: the first one beginning "does everyone agree . . ." and the second one beginning "does everyone know . . ." There were several other places in the lecture where a question would have been in order: and all of the questions should have been less leading, more open to genuine answers. This constricted questioning is, again, at least partly a function of nervousness; as is the fact that I forgot to ask for questions at the end

Figure 12.4 Analysis of a lecture microlesson.

OBSERVATION TECHNIQUE 11: KEEPING A TEACHING JOURNAL

In Chapter 1, we stated that an important goal of clinical supervision is to help teachers become reflective about their instruction. Reflection, among other things, involves being aware of the dilemmas inherent in teaching, one's belief systems and feelings and how they affect teaching, the consideration of choices among instructional strategies, and evaluation of the effect of those choices.[11] Journal writing is an effective self-observation technique for developing this type of reflectivity.

The technique simply involves having teachers keep a journal in which they regularly record their teaching experiences and raise questions about their teaching. Just as video or audio recordings mirror the external reality of teaching, so journals can mirror the internal reality of teaching. Although teachers can be asked to limit their journal entries to certain kinds of perceptions, they generally are left free to record whatever they wish. For this reason we classify journal writing as a wide-lens technique.

Journal writing has been used primarily in preservice clinical supervision. In that context, researchers have found that this technique helps prospective teachers become more reflective and less custodial in their attitudes toward students.[12] It seems likely that journal writing would have similarly positive effects on inservice clinical supervision.

Procedure for Keeping a Teaching Journal

Willis Copeland suggested that the effectiveness of journal writing depends on two factors.[13] First, teachers need to be taught explicitly how to keep a reflective journal. Simply telling them to keep a journal is not sufficient. Second, teachers need to receive thoughtful feedback about the content of their journal entries from their supervisor.

With respect to the first element, teachers need guidance about the kinds of content to include in their journal entries. One approach is to tell teachers to record problems and dilemmas that occur in their day-to-day teaching. Teachers also can be asked to report attempts to solve the problem or dilemma and the effectiveness of their solutions. Another approach is for teachers to focus on a particular teaching strategy or curriculum. For example, teachers can record their experiences in implementing a teaching method (e.g., project-based learning) or a new curriculum adopted by the school district.

Whatever the content focus of the journal, teachers should be allowed to describe relevant contextual factors. This means that teachers are not limited to what happens in their classroom. They can reflect on what is happening in the school, community, or the students' families that affects instruction.

All the other observation techniques in this book stress objectivity on the part of the observer. Journal writing is an exception. Teachers should be encouraged to record not only what happened in the classroom, but also their beliefs, feelings, insights, and evolving philosophy of education. This inner reality is important to understanding a teacher's behavior in the classroom.

The confidentiality of the journal will certainly influence what teachers are willing to record in it. Therefore, the supervisor should make explicit whether the journal is the property of the teacher and whether its contents will be shared with persons other than the supervisor.

The scope of the journal should be negotiated. For how long a period of time is the teacher to make journal entries? Are entries to be made daily, weekly, or whenever the teacher wishes? Should entries be made for each class period during the school day, or just for selected periods? Journal writing requires effort, so the teacher and supervisor should decide on a scope that does not exceed the goals of clinical supervision for the particular teacher.

Analyzing a Teacher's Journal

It is common practice in preservice education for the supervisor to write comments on the margins of teachers' journal entries. It seems unlikely that supervisors of inservice teachers would follow this procedure, though, because it puts teachers in too much of a student role. Instead, the supervisor can read the journal and mark entries, or make notes about entries that he or she wishes to discuss with the teacher. Another option is for only the teacher to read the journal, and for the teacher to decide which parts of the journal he or she wishes to talk about during the conference.

We can imagine a supervision process that is built entirely around the teacher's journal writing. The teacher and supervisor discuss what the content of the journal entries should be; the teacher makes journal entries; and the teacher and supervisor meet periodically to discuss problems, insights, beliefs, and feelings recorded in the entries.

This approach undoubtedly has value, but it also has the limitation that it might not correspond to what is actually happening in the teacher's classroom. Therefore, we recommend a process in which journal writing and direct classroom observation complement each other. For example, a journal entry can reveal a concern (see Conference Technique 1 in Chapter 8) that leads to direct classroom observation by the supervisor. Discussion of the observational data in a feedback conference can stimulate the teacher to engage in reflection, which he records in his journal. In this way, the supervisory process is informed both by the objectivity of observational data and the personal meaningfulness of recorded reflections.

Frances Bolin published examples of journal writing by a student teacher in the preservice program in Childhood Education at Teachers College, Columbia University.[14] The teacher, assigned the pseudonym Lou, kept a daily journal in which he reflected on his student teaching experiences and also a weekly journal in which he recorded reflections about his student teaching, his supervision, and the total preservice program. Lou's supervisor read the journal entries, wrote responses to them, and referred to them in supervisory conferences.

One of Lou's journal entries concerned classroom management:

> Sometimes I am not sure how "strict" I should be with the kids as a student teacher. Max [Lou's cooperating teacher] said he wants me not to be so timid. My timidness comes from not knowing the disciplinary boundaries at [the school]. Since I didn't know, I didn't really react. I am by no means timid, as the kids [I have worked with every summer] will attest. Now that I know what the system of discipline is I can implement it.[15]

The supervisor might help Lou with his management concerns by collecting data on students' at-task behavior (see Observation Technique 6) while Lou is teaching them. The data might indicate that his management style is fine as it is. If modification is needed, Lou can try different (possibly "stricter") management techniques, and the supervisor can collect more at-task data, which will provide Lou with feedback on the techniques' effectiveness.

Another of Lou's journal entries concerns creativity in teaching at the open-space school where he is student teaching and creativity in a traditional school, which he prefers:

> Maybe I am just old fashioned [sic]. I guess it depends on the kids and the school. Who said that a teacher in a typical, traditional school can't be creative and try new things. I hope that no matter what type school I work in I will be creative and not fall into a mold.[16]

In this journal entry and others, Lou expresses how important creative teaching is to him. The supervisor can respond to these entries by helping Lou clarify what he means by creative teaching (see Conference Technique 2). The supervisor then can collect observational data on Lou's use of creative teaching behaviors in the setting of the open-space school. In the feedback conference, Lou and the supervisor can review the data and consider whether the same creative teaching patterns would be possible in a traditional school.

OBSERVATION TECHNIQUE 12: CREATING PORTFOLIOS AND WORK SAMPLES

Portfolios serve a useful purpose in that they provide data on the totality of a teacher's work and professional competence, not just on a particular lesson that was observed by a supervisor. Dorothy Campbell and her associates describe this purpose well: "A portfolio is an organized, goal-driven documentation of your professional growth and achieved competence in the complex act called teaching."[17] Portfolios can include various kinds of evidence attesting to a teacher's instructional skill, subject-matter knowledge, or philosophy of education.

Portfolios are becoming increasingly popular in preservice and inservice teacher education. For example, they are a key feature of the National Board for Professional Teaching Standards (see Chapter 2). A key step in the process is for the teacher to assemble a portfolio containing various entries, four of which are classroom based: two ask candidates to videotape classroom interactions, and two ask candidates to collect student work of particular kinds. Candidates are required to write a detailed analysis for each portfolio entry.

Once teachers learn how to create a portfolio of their own work, they are in a good position to teach the process to others. In fact, a recent development in classroom teaching is to have students create portfolios to document their learning processes and accomplishments.[18] Students need instruction in portfolio construction for it to be effective. Teachers who have already created their own portfolio are well positioned to provide this instruction.

Work samples are another type of teacher portfolio.[19] Their special feature is that they focus on a specific domain of competence—namely, a teacher's ability to foster student learning under actual classroom conditions. This approach to observing teacher performance is becoming increasingly important as American education moves toward standards-based schooling and legislative mandates that hold schools accountable for student-learning gains.

Andrew McConney, Mark Schalock, and Del Schalock have standardized work samples and measures of student learning gains so that they can be used across different grade levels and school subjects.[20] The work sample comprises a portfolio that documents 10 steps of the design and teaching process in which a teacher engaged while teaching a unit of instruction, typically three to five weeks in duration. The 10 steps are shown in Figure 12.5. Six of the 10 steps (3, 4, 6, 8, 9, and 10) make explicit reference to teachers' assessment and interpretations of student learning gains. The findings of a research study by Stephen Koziol and colleagues suggest that this emphasis is different from what is typically found in teacher education programs.[21] They analyzed evaluation instruments used in teacher education programs at 11 research universities on the assumption that these instruments reflect what the programs consider most important in teaching. The researchers concluded that the teacher education programs overemphasize "management and the appearance of a smooth-running classroom over an attention to substantive teaching."[22] Substantive teaching includes the ability to facilitate students' learning of the curriculum.

It is too early to know whether work samples will become a prominent component of teacher portfolios, or perhaps a substitute for them. However, we believe that this is a likely scenario, given the current political and public support for standards-based schooling.

If work samples do achieve a position of prominence, supervisors will be called on to help teachers develop the skills needed to bring about student learning gains that can be demonstrated on externally developed or teacher-developed tests. This is no easy task. Among other things, teachers will need to learn how to align externally mandated standards with their curriculum, instruction, and assessment. Research by Gerald Tindal and Victor Nolet has found that this type of alignment is problematic for teachers.[23] Depending on

1. Define the sample of teaching and learning to be described.
2. Identify the learning outcomes to be accomplished within the work to be sampled.
3. Prior to instruction, assess students' status with respect to the postinstruction outcomes to be accomplished.
4. Develop instruction and assessment plans that align with proposed learning outcomes and the current status of students with respect to the proposed outcomes.
5. Describe the context in which teaching and learning are to occur.
6. Adapt the desired outcomes and the related plans for instruction and assessment to accommodate all students and the demands of the teaching-learning context.
7. Implement a developmentally and contextually appropriate instructional plan.
8. Assess the postinstructional accomplishments of learners, and calculate each student's growth in learning.
9. Summarize and interpret the growth in learning achieved (or lack thereof) for the class as a whole and for selected groups within the class.
10. Examine and reflect on student growth in learning in light of the preinstructional developmental levels of students, targeted learning outcomes, the context in which teaching and learning occurred, and personal professional effectiveness and development.

Figure 12.5 Steps in creating a work sample.

Source: McConney, A. A., Schalock, M. D., & Schalock, H. D. (1998). Focusing improvement and quality assurance: Work samples as authentic performance measures of prospective teachers' effectiveness. *Journal of Personnel Evaluation in Education, 11*, 343–363. (Quote appears on pp. 346–347). Copyright © Springer Publishing. Reprinted by permission of Sage Publications.

the teacher, concepts that are included in the curriculum might or might not be included in instruction or on tests. Most troubling is the situation in which key concepts are tested, but are not taught well—or not taught at all. Supervisors and teachers can review a work sample together to check for these alignment problems and design new instructional units that have better curriculum-instruction-assessment alignment.

Procedure for Creating Portfolios and Work Samples

As a supervisor, you can leave the planning of the portfolio entirely to the discretion of the teacher or plan it jointly. Another option is for groups of teachers to work with each other in planning their portfolio. If the portfolio is to be used as part of a supervisory process, you most likely will want to specify the products that you wish to see in the portfolio, how the products are to be organized, and criteria for judging their quality.

You should discuss with the teacher whether the portfolio is to have a one-time use or whether it will have multiple uses over time.[24] For example, preservice teachers might assemble a portfolio that can be used to assess their readiness for student teaching. The same portfolio might be used to introduce a preservice teacher to potential cooperating teachers for a practicum or student-teaching placement. As preservice teachers gain experience, they can revise the portfolio to include better examples of their capabilities and accomplishments. The revised portfolio might be submitted when applying for an initial teaching position. The portfolio might be revised further as the teacher's career advances; he or she might use it when applying for promotion and tenure or a new position.

The products to be included in the portfolio can be of various types, as shown in Figure 12.6. However, it is important not to include every possible product in the portfolio. The key is to include only those items that are relevant to the teaching principles, goals, or standards that are used to organize the portfolio. The completed portfolio can be in hard-copy form, such as a three-ring binder, with the products separated by from each other by binder dividers. Another option is to create an electronic portfolio.[25] Advantages of this

---

Action research projects, e.g., a report describing an action-research project that one has conducted and its impact on one's professional development.

Assessment results, e.g., test information illustrating skill in designing, administering, scoring, and interpreting tests that assess particular types of student learning.

Certificates, e.g., licenses, endorsements, diplomas, transcripts, or workshop documents recognizing completion of a course of study or set of professional requirements.

Curriculum materials, e.g., documents, handouts, exercises, videotapes, resource guides, or computer software created for use in instruction.

Evaluations, e.g., reports of student teaching performance; letters of recommendation from supervisors, cooperating teachers, and university instructors; and feedback from students.

Honors, e.g., letters, awards, and scholarships acknowledging personal merit or contributions to education.

Journals, e.g., a student-teaching journal demonstrating the ability to reflect on one's own teaching.

Lessons or other units of instruction, e.g., a detailed analysis of a lesson or longer instructional unit, including plans, instructional delivery, classroom management, and student learning.

Literature reviews, e.g., a synthesis of the literature to demonstrate expertise about a particular topic.

Media competencies, e.g., a list of the types of media equipment that one can operate or computer software that one can use for instruction or personal productivity.

Observational records, e.g., an organized set of notes or case study illustrating skill in observing and reflecting on the behavior of a particular type of student or classroom event.

Parent interactions, e.g., correspondence or records of in-person or phone interactions with parents demonstrating the ability to involve parents in the schooling of their children.

Philosophy, e.g., a course paper or other written statement explaining one's general philosophy of education or position on an educational issue or practice.

Photographs, e.g., photos of one's classroom layout, bulletin boards, and decor.

Professional organizations and committees, e.g., a list of organized groups of which one is a member and their role in one's professional life.

Student contracts, e.g., individualized educational plans (IEPs) in which one has participated, and statements describing modifications of instruction to accommodate particular student needs.

Videotapes, e.g., a video and accompanying analysis of a lesson that one has taught.

Work experience, e.g., a chronological list of all places of employment and relevant volunteer experiences.

Figure 12.6 List of possible products for inclusion in teacher portfolios.

type of portfolio are that it is easily stored and easily transmitted to other people, such as potential employers.

Analyzing a Portfolio or Work Sample

Dorothy Campbell and her associates presented examples of portfolio products created by preservice teachers.[26] Each product illustrates one of the teaching standards developed by the Interstate New Teachers Assessment and Support Consortium (INTASC—see Chapter 2). For example, a preservice teacher, Nicole, decided that clarity is particularly important when communicating with kindergarten children. Her initial practicum experiences demonstrated to her that vague, indefinite statements have an undesirable impact on children at this grade level. Therefore, she worked on developing her skill in making clear statements, and she chose to document her growth by the following portfolio entry:

> **ITASC Standard Six: Communication skills**
>
> I have included a lesson plan and a video of the same lesson in my portfolio to document how I achieved lesson clarity by utilizing effective verbal communication techniques. I have highlighted aspects of my lesson plan that indicate the techniques I used to achieve clarity and foster productive, active learning and collaboration. In this lesson, I planned for lesson clarity in a variety of ways. In the beginning, I demonstrated and discussed the entire process of terrarium construction. Later, when the students were in their carefully planned, heterogeneous learning groups, I reviewed the steps again using a picture and word chart to which they could refer. We also discussed the various jobs that could be shared among the group members and the value of allowing everyone to help. However, rather than assigning jobs, I allowed the groups to negotiate the assignment of these jobs. As my video shows, the children were successful in following directions and did an excellent job of sharing responsibilities.[27]

The supervisor can study this analysis and accompanying products, and then hold a feedback conference with Nicole to discuss them. The supervisor might note that there is a research literature on teacher clarity (see Chapter 4), including studies of how teachers use different techniques to achieve clear communication with students. Nicole could compare her techniques with those cited in the literature and consider goals for further development of her communication skills.

A supervisor and teacher can use this type of feedback conference for analyzing any portfolio product. Another option is to create a scoring guide that gives a teacher feedback about the quality of his or her portfolio. An example of a scoring guide for a work-sample type of portfolio is shown in Figure 12.7. One of the authors (M. Gall) created it to score work samples that preservice students created to satisfy a requirement for Oregon teacher licensure. The scoring guide includes each element of the work sample (e.g., Unit Goal), the Oregon professional standard (or standards) to which it relates, and a 6-point rating scale.

One of the required work samples was done as a course assignment in a large course for preservice secondary teachers, so the instructor needed to use a scoring guide as an efficient way to provide feedback. In addition to providing a numerical score for each work-sample product, the instructor and his aides also wrote brief feedback statements about selected products.

Scoring Guide for a Work Sample

The formal work sample provides evidence of many of Oregon's 39 Professional Standards. A score of 4 or 5 in a section can be used as evidence of meeting specific Professional Standard(s) within the domains indicated. The following descriptors are used to determine the score for each section:

0 = absent
1 = misses the criteria completely; needs to be corrected
2 = some criteria are missing, inaccurate, unclear or incomplete; needs development
3 = no serious weaknesses; approaches the criteria; needs minor revisions
4 = meets the criteria
5 = exceeds the criteria

_____ 1. **Background Information.**
      Professional Standard: (1) Instructional Planning
      - Described clearly and completely

_____ 2. **Unit Goal**
      Professional Standard: (1) Instructional Planning
      - Clearly stated as a performance
      - Appropriate for the particular group of students
      - Appropriate for the curriculum to be taught
      - Relates to the specified Oregon content standard(s) or benchmark(s)

_____ 3. **Unit Objectives**
      Professional Standard: (1) Instructional Planning
      - Vary in kind (i.e., factual, higher-cognitive, attitudinal)
      - Reflect meaningful learning outcomes (i.e., results relate to authentic, real-world contexts)
      - Are stated clearly
      - Are appropriate for the particular group of students
      - Are appropriate for the curriculum to be taught
      - Relate meaningfully to the overall goal of the unit
      - Relate to the Oregon content standard(s) or benchmark(s) specified

_____ 4. **Sequence of Unit Topics**
      Professional Standard: (1) Instructional Planning
      - Relate meaningfully to the unit goal and objectives
      - Show a clear rationale for the sequence as presented

_____ 5. **Primary Teaching & Motivational Strategies**
      Professional Standard: (1) Instructional Planning,
      (3) Implementation of Instruction
      - Are appropriate for the unit goal and objectives
      - Are varied
      - Include appropriate technology and media

_____ 6. **Lesson Plans for Minimum of Two Weeks**
      Professional Standards: (1) Instructional Planning,
      (2) Classroom Management, (3) Implementation of Instruction
      - Are original and creative
      - Are well-organized and clearly written
      - Incorporate effective technology

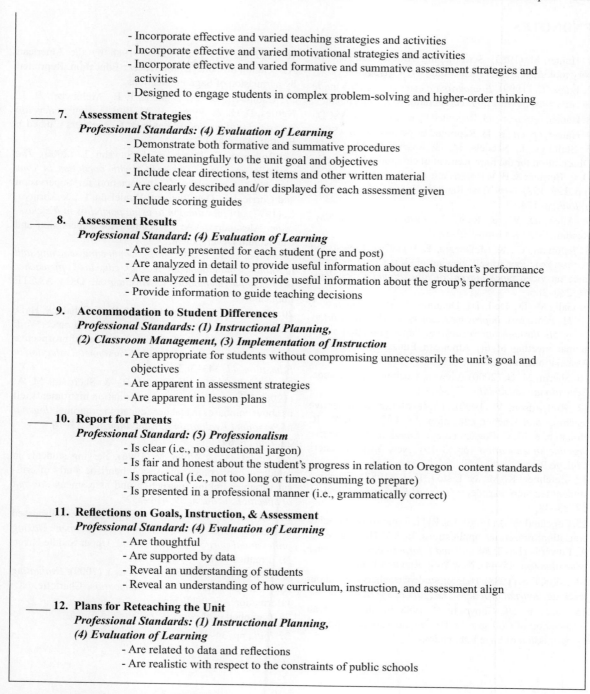

           - Incorporate effective and varied teaching strategies and activities
           - Incorporate effective and varied motivational strategies and activities
           - Incorporate effective and varied formative and summative assessment strategies and activities
           - Designed to engage students in complex problem-solving and higher-order thinking

_____ 7. **Assessment Strategies**
Professional Standards: (4) Evaluation of Learning
           - Demonstrate both formative and summative procedures
           - Relate meaningfully to the unit goal and objectives
           - Include clear directions, test items and other written material
           - Are clearly described and/or displayed for each assessment given
           - Include scoring guides

_____ 8. **Assessment Results**
Professional Standard: (4) Evaluation of Learning
           - Are clearly presented for each student (pre and post)
           - Are analyzed in detail to provide useful information about each student's performance
           - Are analyzed in detail to provide useful information about the group's performance
           - Provide information to guide teaching decisions

_____ 9. **Accommodation to Student Differences**
Professional Standards: (1) Instructional Planning,
(2) Classroom Management, (3) Implementation of Instruction
           - Are appropriate for students without compromising unnecessarily the unit's goal and objectives
           - Are apparent in assessment strategies
           - Are apparent in lesson plans

_____ 10. **Report for Parents**
Professional Standard: (5) Professionalism
           - Is clear (i.e., no educational jargon)
           - Is fair and honest about the student's progress in relation to Oregon content standards
           - Is practical (i.e., not too long or time-consuming to prepare)
           - Is presented in a professional manner (i.e., grammatically correct)

_____ 11. **Reflections on Goals, Instruction, & Assessment**
Professional Standard: (4) Evaluation of Learning
           - Are thoughtful
           - Are supported by data
           - Reveal an understanding of students
           - Reveal an understanding of how curriculum, instruction, and assessment align

_____ 12. **Plans for Reteaching the Unit**
Professional Standards: (1) Instructional Planning,
(4) Evaluation of Learning
           - Are related to data and reflections
           - Are realistic with respect to the constraints of public schools

Figure 12.7 Scoring Guide for a Work Sample.

ENDNOTES

1. Hunter, M. (1983). Script-taping: An essential supervisory tool. *Educational Leadership, 41*, 43.

2. Frank, C. (1999). *Ethnographic eyes: A teacher's guide to classroom observation*. Portsmouth, NH: Heinemann.

3. Hunter, *op. cit.*, p. 43. Reprinted by permission of ASCD.

4. Hunter, *op. cit.*, p. 43. Reprinted by permission of ASCD.

5. Stallings, J., Needels, M., & Sparks, G. M. (1987). Observation for the improvement of classroom learning. In D. C. Berliner & B. V. Rosenshine (Eds.), *Talks to teachers* (pp. 129–158). New York: Random House.

6. *Ibid.*, p. 144.

7. Allen, D. W., & Ryan, K. (1969). *Microteaching*. Reading, MA: Addison-Wesley.

8. Salomon, G., & McDonald, F. J. (1970). Pretest and posttest reactions to self-viewing one's teaching performance on video tape. *Journal of Educational Psychology, 61*, 280–286.

9. Gall, M. D., Dell, H., Dunning, B. B., & Galassi, J. (1971, February). *Improving teachers' mathematics tutoring skills through microteaching*. Paper presented at the annual meeting of the American Educational Research Association, New York.

10. Sherin, M. G. (2000). Viewing teaching on videotape. *Educational Leadership, 57*, 36–38.

11. Richardson, V. (1990). The evolution of reflective teaching and teacher education. In R. T. Clift, W. R. Houston, & M. C. Pugach (Eds.), *Encouraging reflective practice in education* (pp. 3–19). New York: Teachers College Press.

12. Zeichner, K. M., & Liston, D. P. (1987). Teaching student teachers to reflect. *Harvard Educational Review, 57*, 23–48.

13. Copeland, W. D. (1986). The RITE framework for teacher education: preservice applications. In J. V. Hoffman & S. A. Edwards (Eds.), *Reality and reform in clinical teacher education* (pp. 25–44). New York: Random House.

14. Bolin, F. S. (1988). Helping student teachers think about teaching. *Journal of Teacher Education, 39(2)*, 48–54.

15. *Ibid.*, p. 50. Copyright © 1988 by the American Association of Colleges for Teacher Education. Reprinted by permission of Sage Publications.

16. *Ibid.*, p. 51. Copyright © 1988 by the American Association of Colleges for Teacher Education. Reprinted by permission of Sage Publications.

17. Campbell, D. M., Cignetti, P. B., Melenyzer, B. J., Nettles, D. H., & Wyman, R. M. (2001). *How to develop a professional portfolio: A manual for teachers* (2nd ed.). Boston: Allyn and Bacon.

18. Rolheiser, C., Bower, B., & Stevahn, L. (2000). *The portfolio organizer: Succeeding with portfolios in your classroom*. Alexandria, VA: Association for Supervision and Curriculum Development; Danielson, C., & Abrutyn, L. (1997). *An introduction to using portfolios in the classroom*. Alexandria, VA: Association for Supervision and Curriculum Development.

19. Girod, G. R. (Ed.). (2002). *Connecting teaching and learning: A handbook for teacher educators on teacher work sample methodology*. Washington, D.C.: AACTE Publications.

20. McConney, A. A., Schalock, M. D., & Schalock, H. D. (1998). Focusing improvement and quality assurance: Work samples as authentic performance measures of prospective teachers' effectiveness. *Journal of Personnel Evaluation in Education, 11*, 343–363.

21. Koziol, S. M., Minnick, J. B., & Sherman, M. A. (1996). What student teaching evaluation instruments tell us about emphases in teacher education programs. *Journal of Personnel Evaluation in Education, 10*, 53–74.

22. *Ibid.*, p. 69.

23. Tindal, G., & Nolet, V. (1996). Serving students in middle school content classes: A heuristic study of critical variables linking instruction and assessment. *Journal of Special Education, 29*, 414–432.

24. Various uses for a professional portfolio are discussed in Martin, D. B. (1999). *The portfolio planner: Making professional portfolios work for you*. Upper Saddle River, NJ: Prentice-Hall.

25. Adamy, P., & Milman, N. B. (Eds.). (2009). *Evaluating electronic portfolios in teacher education*. Charlotte, NC: Information Age Publishing.

26. Campbell et al., *op. cit.*

27. *Ibid.*, pp. 34–35.

Chapter 13

Achievement Tests, Checklists, Rating Scales, and Timeline Coding

In almost any natural situation, particularly in one as phenomenally complex as a classroom, one perceives selectively. . . . The problem is not that perceivable phenomena vary in their duration and size and volume and other sensible characteristics but is, rather, to see things as they are objectively in their natural relationships, in their natural proportionalities, not as they are reflected by our mental fun mirrors.
—Robert Goldhammer[1]

INTRODUCTION

The observational methods described in the previous chapters do not predetermine what is to be observed. For example, in using selective verbatim, SCORE techniques, or video recordings, the teacher and supervisor jointly decide the categories of behavior to be observed. However, in certain situations, you might prefer a structured observation instrument that focuses on predetermined elements of teaching and learning. The use of such forms in educational practice and research has a long history, dating back at least to 1914.[2] Unless prohibited by the instrument's author or publisher, you have the option of modifying and adding categories to any of these instruments to suit your purposes.

This chapter presents a sample of structured observation instruments.[3] Also, we recommend that you examine the appendix, which lists research-validated teaching techniques that can be measured by these instruments. In reading about these instruments in this chapter, consider whether they generate data that reflect principles of learning you consider important. As we mentioned in Chapter 10, our review of research and theory suggests that students' learning is most affected by (1) their level of attention and motivation, (2) whether they can find personal meaning in the information being presented, (3) opportunities to practice using new information, (4) group processes in the classroom, and (5) whether the teacher focuses on lower-cognitive or higher-cognitive processes.

OBSERVATION TECHNIQUE 13: USING NCLB REPORT CARDS OF STUDENT ACHIEVEMENT

As we explained in Chapter 2, the No Child Left Behind (NCLB) Act of 2001 has been the most important policy initiative in the United States over the past decade. Among other provisions, NCLB requires that all states and school districts prepare "report cards" on their students' academic performance. These report cards are an important source of data for teachers and their clinical supervisors, especially if the report cards show that a district, school, or teacher is not making adequate progress in improving student performance to meet NCLB standards. Although one might criticize these report cards because they focus only on certain aspects of student learning, it is a fact that they are driving important governmental policies and funding decisions.

The format of NCLB report cards is left to the discretion of each state, but at the present time they must include the following statistical data:

- test results for reading/language arts and mathematics.
- the percentage of students who score at the advanced proficiency level, proficient level, basic level, and below basic level. Other terms for these levels can be used—for example, exceeds standards, meets standards, partially meets standards, and unsatisfactory. The levels are determined by establishing cutoff scores. For example, on a 100-item math test, scores over 90 might be considered to reflect advanced proficiency, scores between 70 and 89 might considered to reflect proficiency, and so forth.
- the percentage of students at each level of proficiency for students as a whole, male and female students separately, students in each major racial and ethnic group, students with disabilities, and students with limited English proficiency.
- the percentage of enrolled students who took each test.
- the graduation rates for secondary-school students and other student performance indicators, such as school attendance, that the state chooses.
- student performance goals for each assessment and other indicators, so that a comparison between annual goals and actual performance of each student group can be made.
- at least two years of data for each test and other performance indicators, so that "adequate yearly progress" toward stated performance goals can be determined. If schools are not making adequate annual yearly progress (AYP), they are formally identified as needing improvement.

The report card also must include data on the professional qualifications of teachers in the state.

States and school districts must present their report cards in easy-to-read format and distribute them so that they are easily accessible by parents, educators, and the general public. For example, the Washington, DC state superintendent's office presents several report cards for each school on the Internet.[4] Figure 13.1 shows a report card for one of its middle schools. It presents reading assessment results for all students tested (the bottom row labeled "School Total") and separately for various subgroups. Two years of data (2008 and 2009) are presented in order to determine whether the school met its AYP goal that 57.69 percent of students in each group achieve at the proficient or advanced proficient level in 2009. The only group that did not achieve this criterion level of performance was students identified as disabled. (32.35 percent of these students were proficient.)

We recommend that you search for information about the status of report cards and related data systems in your state. A survey conducted by the Data Quality Campaign, an

AYP REPORT						Met AYP?		
A Washington, D.C. Middle School						Acad. Target	Safe Harbor	
						YES	YES	

Year : 2009
Group : DCPS
Subject : READING (Click for Math)
Category : SECONDARY

GROUP	2008 % PROFICIENT	Number in Group	Number Tested	% Tested	% Proficient	Met % Tested (95%)	Met Prof. Target (1) (57.69%)	Safe Harbor (2)
					READING, 2009			
ETHNICITY								
Asian/Pacific Islanders*	-	1	-	-	-	-	-	-
Black/Non-hispanic	61.21%	332	330	99.40%	71.82%	Yes	Yes	-
Hispanic*	-	8	-	-	-	-	-	-
White/Non-hispanic	100.00%	51	51	100.00%	100.00%	Yes	Yes	-
GENDER (3)								
Female	69.12%	207	206	99.52%	80.58%	-	-	-
Male	63.33%	185	184	99.46%	68.48%	-	-	-
SPECIAL EDUCATION								
Disabled	16.67%	36	34	-	32.35%	-	No	-
ENGLISH PROFICIENCY								
Lep/Nep*	-	4	-	-	-	-	-	-
ECONOMIC STATUS								
Econ. Disadvantaged	55.12%	151	150	99.34%	60.00%	Yes	Yes	-
TOTAL	66.41%	392	390	99.49%	74.87%	Yes	Yes	-

* No data are displayed for groups with less than 25 students.
(1) AYP reading target 5 57.69%, AYP math target 5 55.41%
(2) Safe Harbor is achieved if a group that does not meet the proficiency target in the current year has at least 95% tested and reduces the percent not proficient from the previous year by 10%. In 2006 the reduction in percent not proficient has been adjusted because of the difference in proficiency standards on the DC-CAS and the SAT9.
(3) Females, males, and migrants are not subject to AYP targets.

Figure 13.1 NCLB report card for a Washington, D.C. middle school.

Source: http://www.nclb.osse.dc.gov/dccas_reportcards.asp

215

organization that promotes and studies the use of data in education, suggests that states vary in the quality of their data systems.[5] For example, at the beginning of 2010, only 17 states were creating reports with longitudinal statistics to guide systemwide improvement efforts; only four states were promoting strategies to raise awareness of available data; and no states were promoting educators' professional development in the use of data systems. At the national level, the What Works Clearinghouse has published an online manual on how to use student achievement data to support instruction.[6]

Initiatives currently exist to create report cards that show student learning outcomes, such as those shown in Figure 13.1, at the level of the individual teacher. Furthermore, there are initiatives to use these report cards for teacher evaluation, despite opposition by many teachers and teacher unions. If policy makers are successful in creating and disseminating report cards at the individual teacher level, this movement undoubtedly will create a great demand for clinical supervision of teachers whose AYP (adequate yearly progress) is inadequate.

NCLB report cards can be viewed either as an unwelcome burden or as an opportunity to improve classroom teaching. If it is viewed from the latter perspective, clinical supervision will have much to offer. Clinical supervisors can have a planning conference with teachers to interpret the report card results and explore what might be done to improve AYP. The effective teaching methods presented in Chapter 4 will be helpful in guiding this exploration. Observational data on the teacher's use of these and other methods then can be collected and reviewed in a feedback conference, most likely leading to new clinical supervision cycles.

NCLB report cards can provide summary results for each year, but they do not provide data about what teachers are, or are not, doing to produce those results. If some teachers are highly effective, as demonstrated by their report cards, a clinical supervisor might collect observational data in their classes to determine why they are effective. These data then can be used to guide the professional development of other teachers. Also, clinical supervisors can draw on their research-based knowledge about effective teaching (see Chapter 4) to suggest to school district educators what they might do to upgrade the teaching skills of the teacher workforce as a whole.

OBSERVATION TECHNIQUE 14: DETERMINING DEGREES OF CURRICULUM ALIGNMENT

The NCLB requirement that schools demonstrate adequate yearly progress (AYP) is causing educators to take a new look at their school curriculum. Students have a much better chance of doing well on NCLB-mandated achievement tests if their teachers' curriculum is *aligned* with the curriculum measured by the test items. For this reason, federal and state education agencies have ongoing initiatives to strengthen curriculum alignment, and these initiatives are very likely to affect individual teachers. Therefore, we present here several methods that clinical supervisors can draw upon if they are asked to help teachers with curriculum alignment.

Curriculum alignment involves several forms of alignment, which together form an interrelated system. This system of alignments is illustrated in Figure 13.2. Each double-arrowed line represents a particular type of alignment, and there are nine of them in the

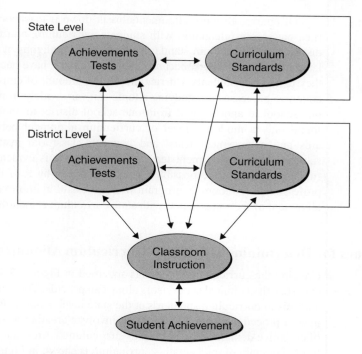

Figure 13.2 A system of curriculum alignments.

Source: Figure is based on Figure 2 in: Porter, A. C. (2002). Measuring the content of instruction: Uses in research and practice. *Educational Researcher, 31*(7), 3–14.

figure. The state-level curriculum standards are the starting point for the alignment process. Educators and other stakeholders develop these standards based on their content expertise and values, and possibly also on national curriculum standards developed by professional associations and federal agencies. Standardized achievement tests then are developed to measure students' achievement of these standards. The alignment between these tests and the curriculum standards is a *horizontal alignment,* because it is done within a particular organizational system.

Achievement tests and curriculum standards also need to be aligned horizontally within a school district. This too is a horizontal alignment. The NCLB Act determines adequate yearly progress based on students' performance on state-level achievement tests, so it is important that the district's curriculum standards are aligned with state-level curriculum standards and its achievement tests are aligned with state-level achievement tests. These are *vertical alignments,* which are represented by the double-arrowed vertical lines between the two boxes in Figure 13.2. One way that school districts can ensure these vertical alignments is by relying heavily or exclusively on state-level curriculum standards and achievement tests.

Of course, all these alignments break down if teachers do not align their instruction (i.e., classroom interaction with students, curriculum, and tests) with the state-level and district-level curriculum standards and tests. The alignment process will be a major challenge for many teachers, because they traditionally have had considerable latitude in what they teach their students. Curriculum topics, amount of emphasis on a topic, and required cognitive processes for studying a topic can vary widely from one teacher to another, from one school to another, and from one school district to another. In fact, researchers have found only a moderate level of curriculum alignment between state curriculum standards and achievement tests[7] and between classroom instruction and state curriculum standards and achievement tests.[8] However, there is evidence that improvements in curriculum alignment are possible. A research study by Rolf Blank and others found that a professional development program was successful in improving math and science teachers' alignment of their instruction with state curriculum standards.[9]

Techniques for Determining Degrees of Curriculum Alignment

Creating the curriculum alignments specified in Figure 13.2 requires many more types of expertise than clinical supervisors alone can provide. The critical first step is to do a careful analysis of curriculum standards at the state level. Andrew Porter and his associates developed a procedure for this purpose; it involves creating a matrix of topics and categories of cognitive demand for a particular curriculum.[10] An example of this type of matrix for a limited domain of mathematics curriculum is shown in Figure 13.3.

Once a matrix of this type is created, educators can use it to analyze curriculum standards, achievement tests, and classroom instruction. For example, a teacher might indicate on a four-point scale the extent to which he or she covered each of the six topics in Figure 13.3

	Category of cognitive demand				
Topic	**Memorize**	**Perform procedures**	**Communicate understanding**	**Solve nonroutine problems**	**Conjecture/ generalize/prove**
Multiple-step equations					
Inequalities					
Linear equations					
Lines/slope and intercept					
Operations on polynomials					
Quadratic equations					

Figure 13.3 Mathematics content matrix for use in curriculum alignment.

Source: Table 1 on p. 4 of: Porter, A. C. (2002). Measuring the content of instruction: Uses in research and practice. *Educational Researcher, 31*(7), 3–14. Copyright © 2002 by the American Educational Research Association. Reprinted by permission of Sage Publications.

during the school year. Suppose the teacher gave a rating of 4 to *multiple-step equations,* a rating of 1 to *inequalities,* a rating of 4 to *linear equations,* and a rating of 0 to the other three topics. These ratings then are converted to proportions by summing all the ratings $(4+2+4+0+0+0=10)$ and then dividing each rating by the sum. The resulting proportions are .40 for multiple-step equations, .20 for inequalities, .40 for linear equations, and .00 for the other three topics. We could have another teacher make these ratings for his classroom instruction, convert them to proportions, and then compare the two teachers to determine whether they place a similar emphasis on topics within the math curriculum.

Extending the procedure further, we could average teachers' ratings within each school district in a state to determine how similar or different they are in providing math instruction. On an even larger scale, we could compare math teachers across states. Note that these comparisons are possible because we have a predetermined list of topics and rating scale. Also, note that we could use the same procedures to determine teachers' emphasis on each category of cognitive demand in Figure 13.3 for all of a teacher's math instruction or within a particular topic, such as multiple-step equations.

Now suppose we wish to determine how well a teacher's math instruction is aligned with a school district's curriculum standards for his or her grade level. Experts could analyze those standards and rate the extent to which they emphasize each of the topics and categories of cognitive demand in Figure 13.3. These ratings could be converted to proportions, as described above, and compared to the proportions calculated for the teacher's instruction. The more similar these proportions, the more aligned is the teacher's instruction with the district's curriculum standards.[11]

The Council of Chief State School Officers has developed a systematic methodology for this approach to determining degrees of curriculum alignment. Working together with the Wisconsin Center for Education, the Council has developed and made available questionnaires for soliciting data from teachers about classroom curriculum and instructional practices. At the present time, four such questionnaires, called *Surveys of Enacted Curriculum,* are available. They cover the curriculum domains of K–12 mathematics, science, English language arts and reading, and social studies.[12] Teachers can complete the questionnaire in paper form or online, with scoring done by the Wisconsin Center for Education. Specialists affiliated with the Council of Chief State School Officers can create displays that indicate the extent to which a teacher's curriculum is aligned with state standards and assessment items. This analysis is possible because specialists previously coded the state's standards and assessment items using the same matrix of topics and cognitive demands as the matrix created for the Survey of Enacted Curriculum. Educators can examine the displays and determine whether a teacher or group of teachers have placed the same amount of emphasis on a particular topic or cognitive demand as the amount of emphasis in the state's curriculum standards and tests measuring those standards.

If the approach just described is not feasible, other approaches are possible. For example, teachers can be asked to create portfolios of their work that include such items as their instructional objectives for a curriculum unit of one or two weeks, lesson plans, tests, and samples of student work (see Observation Technique 12). Clinical supervisors can ask the teachers to analyze their portfolio to determine how the various elements in the portfolio relate to state or district curriculum standards, or perhaps the standards of an educators association such as the National Council of Teachers of Mathematics.[13] If a teacher can demonstrate meaningful relationships between the portfolio elements and the standards, this is feedback to the teacher and the supervisor that the teacher is aware of the curriculum standards and can align his or her instruction to it, more or less. If the teacher is unaware of these standards or has not thought about the alignment of his or her instruction with the standards, this can be a starting point for a clinical supervision cycle.

OBSERVATION TECHNIQUE 15: USING STUDENT RATING SCALES AND OPEN-RESPONSE FORMS

While students are in class, they are constantly observing their teacher's behavior. Having students record their observations is useful in clinical supervision, because teachers often are concerned about how their students perceive them—even more than they are concerned about how supervisors perceive them! The following sections describe instruments on which students can record their perceptions of the teacher and of themselves as learners.

Pupil Observation Survey Report

This student-administered checklist was developed in the 1960s, but is still useful in clinical supervision.[14] It measures the extent to which the teacher

1. is friendly, cheerful, admired.
2. is knowledgeable, poised.
3. is interesting and preferred to other teachers.
4. uses strict control.
5. uses democratic procedures.

These five dimensions are measured by 38 items that should be comprehensible to students in fifth grade and higher.

A shorter version of this instrument, called *Student Evaluation of Teaching,* is available. It is shown in Figure 13.4. The first five items measure, in order, the five dimensions listed above. The second five items also measure, in order, the same dimensions. For example, the first item ("is always friendly toward students") and sixth item ("is usually cheerful and optimistic") measure the first dimension listed above ("is friendly, cheerful, admired").

One way to summarize the data yielded by this checklist is to count the number of students in the class who circled each response option (F f t T) in each item. Another way is to score each item (e.g., F = 0, f = 1, t = 2, T = 3) and then compute the mean score for each pair of items that measure the same dimension.

Patterns of Adaptive Learning Scales

The measure of student at-task behavior (Observation Technique 6) described in Chapter 11 is useful in determining whether students are complying with instructional tasks. However, the measure does not directly determine whether students are cognitively and emotionally engaged in the learning process. Carol Midgley and her colleagues at the University of

STUDENT EVALUATION OF TEACHING

D. J. VELDMAN and R. F. PECK

TEACHER'S LAST NAME: _____

SUBJECT: _____

SCHOOL: _____

CIRCLE THE RIGHT CHOICES BELOW

Teacher's Sex: M   F

My Sex: M   F

My Grade Level:

3   4   5   6   7   8   9   10   11   12

DO NOT USE

CIRCLE ONE OF THE FOUR CHOICES IN FRONT OF EACH STATEMENT.
THE FOUR CHOICES MEAN:

F = Very Much False
f = More False Than True
t = More True Than False
T = Very Much True

This Teacher:

F f t T	is always friendly toward students.
F f t T	knows a lot about the subject.
F f t T	is never dull or boring.
F f t T	expects a lot from students.
F f t T	asks for students opinions before making decisions.
F f t T	is usually cheerful and optimistic.
F f t T	is not confused by unexpected questions.
F f t T	makes learning more like fun than work.
F f t T	doesn't let students get away with anything.
F f t T	often gives students a choice in assignments.

Figure 13.4 Pupil observation survey.

Michigan developed a set of student rating scales, called the Pattern of Adaptive Learning Scales (PALS), for this purpose.[15] A description of each student scale and sample items are shown in Table 13.1. Each item is accompanied by a five-point rating scale (not shown in Table 13.1) with three of them having a verbal descriptor: 1 = "Not at all true," 3 = "Somewhat true," and 5 = "Very true."

In addition to these scales, the PALS manual contains scales in which teachers can describe their personal teaching efficacy and how they go about engaging students in classroom instruction. The teacher or clinical supervisor can administer PALS to the teacher's students, perhaps telling them that the student's ratings will be confidential and used for the purpose of helping the teacher do a better job of helping them learn.

Direct observational data can help the teacher and clinical supervisor understand what is actually happening during classroom instruction. However, this type of data cannot tell them what is happening inside a student. PALS and other measures of its type are necessary for this purpose. Ideally, a teacher would have access to both types of data in order to develop a complete picture of the complexity and richness of teaching and learning. This does not mean, though, that a clinical supervisor should always collect both types of data. Some teachers might be only able to process and reflect on data from one source. As teachers move toward master teacher status, they will be more receptive to multiple data sources

Table 13.1 Pattern of Adaptive Learning Scales (PALS): Sample Items

Scales for Rating Personal Achievement Goal Orientations

Mastery Goal Orientation Scale. Measures whether a student perceive learning as inherently interesting and wish to achieve competence. 5 items.

- It's important to me that I thoroughly understand my class work.

Personal—Approach Goal Orientation Scale. Measures whether a student's goal is to demonstrate their competence as a learner. 5 items.

- One of my goals is to show others that I'm good at my class work.

Performance—Avoid Goal Orientation Scale. Measures whether a student's goal is to avoid the demonstration of incompetence. 4 items.

- It's important to me that I don't look stupid in class.

Scales for Rating Perceptions of Teacher's Goals

Teacher Mastery Goal Scale. Measures whether a student perceives that the teacher's goal is to have students engage in academic work in order to achieve competence. 5 items.

- My teacher gives us time to really explore and understand new ideas.

Teacher Performance—Approach Goal Scale. Measures a student's perception that the teacher wants students to engage in academic work in order to demonstrate competence. 3 items.

- My teacher points out those students who get good grades as an example to all of us.

Teacher Performance—Avoid Goal Scale. Measures a student's perception that the teacher wants students to engage in academic work in order to avoid the demonstration of incompetence. 4 items.

- My teacher tells us that it's important to join in discussions and answer questions so it doesn't look like we can't do the work.

Scales for Rating Perceptions of Classroom Goal Structures

Classroom Mastery Goal Structure Scale. Measures a student's perception of whether the purpose of engaging in academic work is to develop competence. 6 items.

• In our class, trying hard is very important.

Classroom Performance—Approach Goal Structure Scale. Measures a student's perception of whether the purpose of engaging in academic work is to demonstrate competence. 3 items.

• In our class, it's important to get high scores on tests.

Classroom Performance—Avoid Goal Structure Scale. Measures a student's perception of whether the purpose of engaging in academic work is to avoid demonstrating incompetence. 5 items.

• In our class, it's important that you don't make mistakes in front of everyone.

Scales for Rating Academic-Related Perceptions, Beliefs, and Strategies

Academic Efficacy Scale. Measures a student's perception of their competence to do class work. 5 items.

• I'm certain I can master the skills taught in class this year.

Academic Press Scale. Measures a student's perception of whether the teacher presses them for understanding. 7 items.

• My teacher asks me to explain how I get my answers.

Academic Self-Handicapping Strategies Scale. Measures a student's strategies for attributing low performance to circumstances rather than lack of ability. 6 items.

• Some students fool around the night before a test. Then if they don't do well, they can say that is the reason. How true is this of you?

Avoiding Novelty Scale. Measures a student's preference for avoiding unfamiliar or new work. 5 items.

• I would prefer to do class work that is familiar to me, rather than work I would have to learn how to do.

Cheating Behavior Scale. Measures a student's use of cheating in class. 3 items.

• I sometimes copy answers from other students during tests.

Disruptive Behavior Scale. Measures a student's engagement in behaviors that disturb the classroom. 5 items.

• I sometimes behave in a way during class that annoys my teacher.

Self-Presentation of Low Achievement Scale. 7 items.

• If other students found out I did well on a test, I would tell them that it was just luck even if that wasn't the case.

Skepticism about the Relevance of School for Future Success Scale. Measures a student's belief that doing well in school will not help them achieve future success. 6 items.

• Even if I am successful in school, it won't help me fulfill my dreams.

Source: Midgley, C., et al. (2000). *Manual for the Patterns of Adaptive Learning Scales*. Ann Arbor, MI: University of Michigan, School of Education. All the items for each scale and additional student scales for rating perceptions of parents, home life, and neighborhood are available in the manual, which can be viewed online at <http://www.umich.edu/~pals/PALS%202000_V13Word97.pdf>. The manual is copyrighted. The website contains information for contacting the scale developers. Reprinted by permission of Michael Middleton, Ph.D.

about their instruction. They will use the data to develop nuanced understandings of how to create a good learning climate in their classroom and meet the needs of students who require special attention.

Other Student Rating Scales

Figure 13.5 presents a series of survey items that students can use to provide feedback to their teacher. The items cover many important elements of classroom instruction. You are welcome to use or adapt them as you wish. You also can use a rating scale you prefer. One possibility is the rating scale format used on the *Student Evaluation of Teaching form* (described above). Another option is a scale with these five points: *never seldom sometimes often always.*

Open-Response Forms

If students have sufficient writing skills, the teacher and clinical supervisor can prepare simple open-response items to get feedback from students about the teacher's instruction. For example, the items might ask students to write comments about what they like or dislike

My teacher:
Clarity and task orientation
- explains things clearly.
- gives clear directions.
- makes it clear what we're supposed to learn.
- does not digress from the content we're supposed to learn.

Classroom management
- treats students fairly.
- knows how to manage students so they don't disrupt the class.
- is good about praising us when we deserve it.
- unfairly criticizes or punishes us.
- has reasonable classroom rules.

Learning and assessment tasks
- gives tests that evaluate us on what we've actually studied.
- gives tests that are too difficult.
- gives reasonable homework assignments.
- helps us review what we studied so we're prepared for the test.
- get us to think, not just learn facts.
- gives us worksheets and other class activities that are useful.

Motivating students to learn
- varies activities in order to hold our attention.
- gives us choices for projects, homework, and other assignments.
- is enthusiastic during class.
- teaches only from the textbook.
- does things to arouse our curiosity.
- makes the things we're studying interesting.
- makes it fun to learn.

Orientation to students
- talks too much.
- asks us good questions.
- lets us talk about our own ideas.
- listens carefully to what we have to say.
- answers our questions when we raise our hand.
- gives special help to students who need it.
- understands us.
- makes it comfortable for us to be in his/her classroom.
- does not have class "favorites."
- makes it possible for us to get to know each other.

Figure 13.5 List of items on which students can rate their teacher's behavior.

about the teacher's class, or how the class could be improved. For example, Edward Hootstein conducted a research study involving 60 middle-school students sampled from the classes of 18 U.S. history teachers in seven middle schools.[16] One of his goals was to learn what methods they would use to motivate their classmates if they were the classroom teacher. The open-response question they were given was this: "If you were the teacher in this class, what methods would you use to motivate students to learn?"

Hootstein's analysis of the students' responses is shown in Table 13.2. A teacher might administer the open-response question in her own classroom or use the list shown in the table. In a planning conference, the teacher and clinical supervisor could review the students' ideas and select one or several of them to incorporate in a lesson for which observational data were collected. In a feedback conference, the teacher and clinical supervisor could review the motivational effects of the ideas. A major advantage of this approach is that the ideas for instructional improvement are likely to have considerable credibility for teachers, as they come directly from students.

As with any student-generated data, you are likely to obtain more valid and useful data if students are told that their comments will be anonymous and used only to help the teacher learn how to provide better classroom instruction. If students are concerned that their handwriting will reveal their identity, you can consider telling students that an individual, such as the clinical supervisor or teacher colleague, will analyze the data and report them to the teacher only as a summary of all the students' comments.

OBSERVATION TECHNIQUE 16: USING OBSERVER-ADMINISTERED CHECKLISTS

Published checklists are available for observers to use to record data on teachers' use of various teaching methods. For example, Bruce Joyce and colleagues present rating checklists for observing teaching strategies organized into three models: information processing, social interaction, and personal.[17]

Clinical supervisors sometimes construct their own checklist for recording observations of classroom behavior. For example, the following are descriptions of several checklists that we constructed for our own use in supervision. You are invited to use them as shown here or adapt them for your particular purpose.

Table 13.2 Students' Ideas for Improving U.S. History Instruction

1. Act in dramatic presentations.
2. Watch videos and films of historical figures and events.
3. Role-play characters in simulations of historical or hypothetical events.
4. Play games with other students to review an understanding of facts and concepts.
5. Make learning fun.
6. Take the parts of characters in plays.
7. Role-play in interpersonal situations.
8. Use a variety of instructional methods, curriculum materials, and learning activities.
9. Assign students to read historical novels that provide details of everyday life.
10. Display objects that were used in the past and explain how and why they were used.

Source: Hootstein, E. W. (1993). *Motivational strategies and beliefs of social studies teachers in a U.S. history course for middle school students*. Unpublished doctoral dissertation, University of Oregon. Table appears on p. 75.

Questioning Behaviors

In Chapters 9 and 10, we show how selective verbatim and seating-chart observation records can be used to collect data about teachers' question-asking behavior in the classroom. A checklist also can be used for this purpose. Advantages of the checklist format are that it is relatively easy to use and a substantial number of teacher behaviors can be recorded on it. In contrast, the advantage of selective-verbatim and seating-chart procedures is that, although fewer questioning behaviors are observed, they are recorded more completely.

The checklist shown in Figure 13.6 is organized around three types of teachers' questioning behavior. The first set of behaviors is important because they usually produce increased student participation in the lesson. For example, the first behavior in the checklist is calling on nonvolunteers to respond. Teachers are likely to call on students who raise their hands and who customarily give good answers to their questions. Yet nonvolunteers often make good contributions if the teacher takes the initiative to call on them.

Student participation also can be increased by redirecting the same question to several students. The teacher might invite additional responses to a question by a nod acknowledging a particular student or by a statement such as "Does anyone have a different idea?" or "Would someone like to add to what Susie said?" Praising answers is a technique that helps students feel that their answers are worthwhile; as a result, they are encouraged to speak up when other questions are asked. Another good technique is to ask students whether they have any questions of their own about the lesson content. The teacher might choose to answer these student-initiated questions directly or call on other students to answer them.

The second category in Figure 13.6 refers to the cognitive level of the teacher's lesson. Educators generally agree that students should not just recite back the facts they have learned. (This is done by asking simple fact questions of the Who, What, Where, When variety.) Students also should be encouraged to think about the curriculum content. This goal is accomplished by asking higher-cognitive questions that elicit intellectual operations such as comparing and contrasting, speculating about motives or causes for observed phenomena, drawing conclusions, providing evidence, making predictions, solving problems, making judgments, and offering opinions.

To increase the likelihood of good student responses to higher-cognitive questions, one helpful technique listed in Figure 13.6 is to pause several seconds before calling on a student to respond. This gives students time to think. Another technique is to ask follow-up questions after the student has given an initial answer to a question. For example, the teacher might ask, "Did you agree with the jury's verdict?" and the student might respond, "No, I didn't." The teacher can follow up by asking the student to support his or her position (e.g., "Why didn't you agree?"). Follow-up questions also can be used to encourage a student to clarify a vague answer (e.g., "I'm not sure I understood what you said. Can you restate your answer?"), to generate additional ideas (e.g., "Can you think of other ways of solving the energy crisis?"), or to challenge the student (e.g., "That's a good idea, but have you considered possible adverse consequences that might occur if your idea were put into practice?"). Follow-up questions can be used, too, to prompt a student who is unable to respond to the initial question.

The third category in Figure 13.6 refers to the "don'ts" of question-asking. Teachers should avoid reacting negatively to student responses by making critical remarks (e.g., "That doesn't make any sense at all") or by showing annoyance. Critical behavior only

Behaviors That Increase Student Participation
1. Calls on nonvolunteers
2. Redirects question
3. Praises student responses
4. Invites student-initiated questions

Behaviors That Elicit Thoughtful Responses
1. Asks higher cognitive questions
2. Pauses 3-5 seconds after asking a question
3. Asks follow-up questions to an initial response

Negative Behaviors
1. Reacts negatively to student response
2. Repeats own question
3. Asks multiple questions
4. Answers own questions
5. Repeats student's answer
Strong Points of Lesson
Suggestions for Improvement

Figure 13.6 Checklist of questioning behaviors.

increases the likelihood that the student will volunteer no response in the future. The second negative behavior, repeating one's question, is to be avoided because it wastes class time and encourages students not to listen carefully the first time the teacher asks a question. The third "don't"—asking multiple questions—refers to the practice of asking several questions in a row before settling on a question to which a response is invited. Multiple questions waste class time, and they are likely to confuse students. The final "don't" is repeating student answers verbatim. A better practice is to praise the answer, extend the answer by adding new information, or invite another student to build on the answer.

The supervisor can use the right column of Figure 13.6 to make a rating of the teacher's use of each questioning technique (e.g., 0=unsatisfactory; 1=satisfactory; 2=exemplary) or to write comments. The bottom two headings of the checklist provide an open-ended opportunity for the observer to comment on the teacher's use of questions in the total context of the lesson.

Expository Behaviors

Researchers have found that teachers on average do two-thirds of the talking in elementary and secondary classrooms.[18] The percentage is probably higher in some settings (e.g., college teaching) and lower in others. Much of this talk time is spent in presenting new concepts and information to students, or in explaining difficult parts of the curriculum. The checklist and rating form shown in Figure 13.7 are designed for analyzing various techniques that might be present in teacher talk, which we label here as *expository behavior*. (Another label might be *delivery style*.) Research evidence supporting the effectiveness of these techniques is presented in Chapter 4.

BEHAVIORS TO BE TALLIED

Meaningful Content
1. Relates lecture content to content already familiar to students
2. Gives example to illustrate concept
3. Gives explanation for generalization or opinion

Student Involvement
1. Asks students if they have questions
2. Directs question to students
3. Has students engage in activity

BEHAVIORS TO BE RATED

Organization	good			needs improvement	
1. Lecture has clear organization and sequence	5	4	3	2	1
2. Uses blackboard, handout, etc., to show organization of lecture	5	4	3	2	1
3. Tells students what (s)he expects students to remember from lecture	5	4	3	2	1
4. Repeats key points and summarizes them at end	5	4	3	2	1
5. Avoids digressions	5	4	3	2	1

Delivery	good			needs improvement	
1. Speaks slowly and clearly	5	4	3	2	1
2. Conveys enthusiasm	5	4	3	2	1
3. Avoids reading from lecture notes	5	4	3	2	1
4. Avoids filler phrases such as "you know"	5	4	3	2	1
5. Avoids nervous gestures	5	4	3	2	1
6. Maintains eye contact with students	5	4	3	2	1
7. Uses humor	5	4	3	2	1

Figure 13.7 Checklist and rating form for expository behaviors.

You will note that the form is in two parts. The first part includes behaviors that can be tallied each time they occur. The second part of the form is a list of teacher behaviors that are assigned a quality rating by the observer. As in Figure 13.6, this checklist can be augmented by including space for comments about the strong points of the lesson and suggestions for improvement.

Constructivist Teaching Methods

We discussed constructivist theories of teaching and learning in Chapters 4 and 10. In brief, constructivist theorists believe that learners develop (or, in their term, *construct*) their own understandings of the world. These theorists also believe that students in conventional classrooms often acquire new knowledge and skills, but without understanding what they are learning.

Educators who subscribe to constructivism have developed various teaching methods to promote student understanding. Jacqueline and Martin Brooks organized these methods into a list and contrasted them with conventional teaching methods.[19] We organized their list into a checklist form shown in Figure 13.8. The observer can place a check in one of the two checkmark columns to indicate the presence or absence of a particular method of instructional planning or classroom instruction.

Methods for Accommodating Student Diversity

Carol Ann Tomlinson compiled a list of methods that experts recommend for differentiating instruction so that the needs and interests of all students in a classroom are met.[20] Tomlinson contrasted these methods with a list of methods found in classrooms where students are treated as if they were homogeneous. We reorganized the lists into checklist form in Figure 13.9 (note that it parallels Figure 13.8 in format.)

The terminology used in Figure 13.9 is in common use, except perhaps for *learning profile options.* According to Tomlinson, a learning profile has to do with how a student learns. For example, students with a certain learning profile need to talk about new concepts in order to learn them, whereas students with a different learning profile can learn new concepts better if left alone. Some students learn analytically (details first and then the big picture), whereas others learn holistically (big picture first and then the details). To be effective, teachers need to include instructional options that accommodate these different learning profiles.

A quick inspection of the checks in the two columns will reveal the extent to which the teacher is using differentiated teaching methods to accommodate student diversity. The form can be adapted, if you wish, by adding or subtracting items or by changing the check columns to rating scales—for example, 1 = used rarely or to a minor degree; 2 = used sometimes or to a moderate degree; 3 = used regularly or to a significant degree.

Of the methods presented in Figure 13.9, perhaps the most critical is "Time is used flexibly in accordance with student need." In Chapter 4, we reviewed research evidence demonstrating that the teacher's allocation of time affects students' learning. Because students learn at different rates, allocating more time for slower learners increases their opportunity for academic success.

OBSERVATION TECHNIQUE 17: USING THE FLANDERS INTERACTION ANALYSIS SYSTEM

The Interaction Analysis System (FIAS) developed by Ned Flanders is one of the best-known techniques of classroom observation.[21] It was widely used in teacher training and in research during the 1960s and 1970s. Less use of it is made now as other conceptualizations of effective teaching have come into prominence. Nonetheless, the Interaction Analysis System records aspects of teaching that continue to be important in American education.

FIAS has two principal features: (1) verbal-interaction categories and (2) timeline-coding procedures for using the categories to make classroom observations.

CONSTRUCTIVIST CLASSROOMS	√	√	TRADITIONAL CLASSROOMS
• Curriculum is presented whole to part, with emphasis on big concepts.			• Curriculum is presented part to whole, with emphasis on basic skills.
• Pursuit of student questions is highly valued.			• Strict adherence to fixed curriculum is highly valued.
• Curricular activities rely heavily on primary sources of data and manipulative materials.			• Curricular activities rely heavily on textbooks and workbooks.
• Students are viewed as thinkers with emerging theories about the world.			• Students are viewed as "blank slates" onto which information is etched by the teacher.
• Teachers generally behave in an interactive manner, mediating the environment for students.			• Teachers generally behave in a didactic manner, disseminating information to students.
• Teachers seek the students' points of view in order to understand students' present conceptions for use in subsequent lessons.			• Teachers seek the correct answer to validate student learning.
• Assessment of student learning is interwoven with teaching and occurs through teacher observations of students at work and through student exhibitions and portfolios.			• Assessment of student teaming is viewed as separate from teaching and occurs almost entirely through testing.
• Students primarily work in groups.			• Students primarily work alone.

Figure 13.8 Checklist for constructivist teaching methods.

Source: Brooks, J.G., & Brooks, M.G. (1999). *The case for constructivist classrooms*. Alexandria, VA: Association for Supervision and Curriculum. Development, p. 17.

Categories of Verbal Interaction

The interaction categories in FIAS are shown in Figure 13.10. With the exception of category 10 (silence or confusion), all categories pertain to a specific type of verbal behavior. Any verbal statement by a teacher or student is classifiable by one of the 10 categories. This is true irrespective of grade level, subject area, or teacher and student characteristics. Indeed, one of the major appeals of interaction analysis is its universality. For example, a first-grade reading group and a graduate-level seminar could be compared for similarities and differences using the system.

Three kinds of interaction categories are shown in Figure 13.10. Some verbal behaviors are responses, either made by a teacher to a student (categories 1, 2, and 3) or by a student to a teacher (category 8). Other verbal behaviors are intended to initiate communication.

DIFFERENTIATED CLASSROOMS	√	√	TRADITIONAL CLASSROOMS
Planning • Teacher analyzes how students in the class differ and plans accordingly. • Student readiness, interest, and learning profile shape instruction. • Excellence is defined in large measure by individual growth from a starting point. • Focus on multiple forms of intelligences is evident.			**Planning** • Student differences are ignored in planning phase of instruction. • Coverage of texts and curriculum guides drive instruction. • A single definition of excellence exists. • A relatively narrow sense of intelligence prevails.
Curriculum • Key concepts and principles are the focus of learning, • Multiple materials are provided.			**Curriculum** • Facts and skills out-of-context are the focus of learning. • A single text prevails.
Instruction • The teacher facilitates students' skills at becoming self-reliant learners. • Students are frequently guided in making interest-based learning choices. • Many learning profile options are provided for. • Many instructional arrangements are used. • Multi-option assignments are frequently used. • Time is used flexibly in accordance with student need. • Multiple perspectives on ideas and events are routinely sought. • Students help other students and the teacher solve problems.			Instruction • The teacher directs student behavior. • Student interest is infrequently tapped. • Relatively few learning profile options are taken into account. • Whole-class instruction dominates. • Single-option assignments are the norm. • Time is relatively inflexible. • Single interpretations of ideas and events are sought. • The teacher solves problems.
Assessment • Students are assessed in multiple ways. • Assessment is ongoing and diagnostic to understand how to make instruction more responsive to learner need. • The teacher works with students to establish both whole-class and individual standards for grading.			**Assessment** • A single form of assessment is used. • Assessment is most common at the end of learning to see "who got it." • The teacher provides whole-class standards for grading.

Figure 13.9 Checklist for methods of accommodating student diversity.

Source: Adapted from page 16 of: Tomlinson, C. A. (1999). *The differentiated classroom: Responding to the needs of all learners*. Alexandria, VA: Association for Supervision and Curriculum Development.

Teacher Talk	Response	1. *Accepts feeling.* Accepts and clarifies an attitude or the feeling tone of a student in a nonthreatening manner. Feelings may be positive or negative. Predicting and recalling feelings are included. 2. *Praises or encourages.* Praises or encourages students; says "um hum" or "go on"; makes jokes that release tension, but not at the expense of a student. 3. *Accepts or uses ideas of students.* Acknowledges student talk. Clarifies, builds on, or asks questions based on student ideas.
		4. *Asks questions.* Asks questions about content or procedure, based on teacher ideas, with the intent that a student will answer.
	Initiation	5. *Lectures.* Offers facts or opinions about content or procedures; expresses his own ideas, gives *his own* explanation, or cites an authority other than a student. 6. *Gives directions.* Gives directions, commands, or orders with which a student is expected to comply. 7. *Criticizes student or justifies authority.* Makes statements intended to change student behavior from nonacceptable to acceptable patterns; arbitrarily corrects student answers; bawls someone out. Or states why the teacher is doing what he is doing; uses extreme self-reference.
Student Talk	Response	8. *Student talk—response.* Student talk in response to a teacher contact that structures or limits the situation. Freedom to express his own ideas is limited.
	Initiation	9. *Student talk—initiation.* Student initiates or expresses his own ideas, either spontaneously or in response to the teacher's solicitation. Freedom to develop opinions and a line of thought; going beyond existing structure.
Silence		10. *Silence or confusion.* Pauses, short periods of silence, and periods of confusion in which communication cannot be understood by the observer.

Figure 13.10 Flanders interaction analysis categories.

No scale is implied by these numbers. Each number is classificatory; it designates a particular kind of communication event. To write these numbers down during observation is to enumerate, not to judge, a position on a scale.

Source: Based on: Flanders, N.A. (1970). *Analyzing Teaching Behavior.* Reading, MA: Addison-Wesley, p, 34.

Either a student (category 9) or the teacher (categories 5, 6, and 7) can play the role of initiator. Categories 4 and 10 are considered neutral with respect to the response-initiation distinction.

The most critical distinction in FIAS is between response and initiation. When teachers make a responsive comment (categories 1, 2, or 3), they are said to be using an "indirect" style of teaching. You will note that these indirect behaviors are also associated with positive affect—accepting feelings, praising, and acknowledging students' ideas. When teachers initiate a verbal interchange (categories 5, 6, or 7), they are said to be using a "direct" style of teaching. According to Flanders, a teacher question can be either direct, as in a narrow or specific question, or indirect, as in a broad or open question. Flanders and other researchers have found consistently that a teacher's use of an indirect style of teaching (categories 1, 2, and 3) encourages students to offer their own ideas and opinions (category 9). In contrast, a teacher's use of a directive style (categories 5, 6, and 7) has been found consistently to channel students' ideas and behavior to meet teacher expectations (category 8).

Which is better—an indirect or a direct teaching style? As we stated in Chapter 4, research on teaching effectiveness using FIAS as the observation instrument suggests that use of an indirect teaching style is associated with more positive student attitudes and higher student achievement. But this does not mean that a direct style is necessarily poor teaching. Flanders suggests that there are occasions when the teacher needs to be direct, as in presenting new content to students and giving directions. When using direct teaching, though, opportunities to use some indirect verbal behaviors are also present. For example, the teacher might be giving an extended series of directions for conducting an experiment (category 6). While doing this, the teacher might consider pausing to praise or encourage the students for their efforts and success in following directions (category 2).

A similar situation can occur in indirect teaching. For example, the teacher might be moderating a discussion in which students are encouraged to state their own opinions on an issue (category 9). The teacher might acknowledge students' ideas (category 3), encourage silent students to talk (category 2), and verbalize awareness of the feelings that underlie students' opinions (category 1). All these are indirect verbal behaviors. At some point in the discussion, though, the teacher might discover that students are misinformed about a particular issue and therefore decides to interrupt the discussion temporarily to provide information (category 5) and direct students to do homework reading (category 6). Thus, the teacher has interspersed direct teaching into a predominantly indirect, student-centered lesson.

Timeline Coding Procedures

Supervisors use a timeline to record FIAC data while observing a teacher's classroom instruction. Figure 13.11 shows two examples of these timelines. The first thing to notice about each timeline is its columns. Each column represents a three-second interval. The three-second interval is long enough that the observer need not become preoccupied with recording data. In most lessons there usually are several periods of time lasting a minute or more when only one interaction category is being used (usually categories 4, 5, or 6.) The observer can relax during these time intervals until the pace of interaction increases again.[22]

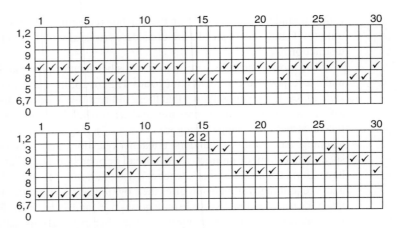

Figure 13.11 Timelines used for recording data in Flanders' Interaction Analysis System.

The other salient feature of a FIAC timeline is the rows. Each row represents one or two categories. The middle row is for teacher questions (category 4), which often are a stimulus for a series of interactions between teacher and students. Categories reflecting an indirect teaching style (1, 2, and 3) are above the middle row, as is the category reflecting open, student-initiated responses (category 9). Categories that indicate a direct teaching style (5, 6, and 7) are below the line, as is the category for structured, restricted student responses (category 8).

Category 10 (silence or confusion) is not represented by a discrete row. Tallies for this category are made below the timeline. Several categories (1 and 2, 6 and 7) share the same row in order to conserve space. Observers can use different tallies in the cells to differentiate 1 from 2 or 6 from 7, or they can simply change the timeline form by adding two rows so each category has its own row.

The organization of the FIAC categories on the timeline helps the supervisor and teacher detect verbal patterns that occurred during an observed lesson. For example, a majority of tallies above the middle row indicates that the lesson was indirect in style. A majority of tallies below the middle row indicates that the lesson was direct in style. These patterns can be detected much more quickly than by playing back a video or audio recording of a lesson. Also, software is available so that a supervisor can record FIAC data efficiently on a Palm Pilot or similar device.[23]

The first timeline in Figure 13.11 is characterized by alternating 4s and 8s. This pattern suggests that the teacher was engaged in a rapid question-and-answer interchange with students, with the level of discourse probably focused on fact recall. The second timeline in Figure 13.11 suggests a richer, more indirect dialogue. The teacher starts by giving some information on a curriculum topic. Then students are invited to offer their own ideas on the topic. After each student response, the teacher takes care to acknowledge the student's idea and, in some instances, to praise it.

When teachers first become exposed to interaction analysis, they might find that they use a few simple patterns in interacting with their students. As they see these patterns recorded on a timeline, they likely will wish to explore how they can become more flexible in their use of verbal behavior. Sometimes, but not always, this involves a shift from a more direct to a more indirect style of teaching.

Other Timeline Coding Procedures

Our discussion of timelines has focused on its application to the Flanders Interaction Analysis System. Timelines are a generic recording device, however. For example, you can create categories for other classroom phenomena and use them instead of, or in addition to, the FIAC categories.[24] Also, the three-second interval represented by the columns of the timeline can be varied.

Supervisors might want to consider an alternative observation system that generates timeline data, but with categories that record other kinds of classroom events that are relevant for particular teachers. For example, a method developed by Jane Stallings has been used in research,[25] inservice education,[26] and preservice education.[27] It can be used at any grade level and with any subject area, and it can be adapted for observing special situations.

The Stallings Observation System is similar to the Flanders Interaction Analysis System in its coding procedure and emphasis on observable classroom behaviors. However, whereas the Flanders system measures 10 types of teacher and student behavior, the Stallings system measures 64 types. Another difference is that the Flanders system is based on group process theory and research, whereas the Stallings system is based on research on effective teaching of academic knowledge and skills (see Chapter 4 for a review of this research).

The Stallings Observation System has two components: (1) the classroom snapshot and (2) the five-minute interaction (FMI). The snapshot data show how the teacher and students spend their time during a lesson and the types of activities in which they engage. The FMI data show how the teacher and student verbally interact with each other during a lesson. Together the snapshot and the FMI provide a comprehensive picture of what happened during the lesson.

OBSERVATION TECHNIQUE 18: USING EVALUATION RATING SCALES

The purpose of observation in the clinical supervision cycle is to collect *objective data* about the teacher's classroom behavior. In teacher evaluation, however, the supervisor collects *evaluative data.* The purpose of these data is to judge the teacher's competence. Observation instruments used for this purpose generally consist of evaluative rating scales. The observer makes a check or circles a point on the scale that corresponds to his or her rating of the teacher's performance. States and school districts have developed formal scales of this type to evaluate whether a teacher has sufficient skills to be certified or to be offered continued employment.

A typical teacher evaluation instrument contains 10 to 15 items. Most of them typically concern the teacher's classroom behavior, for example:

1. teaches accurate content.
2. makes learning outcomes explicit to students.

3. includes both lower-cognitive and higher-cognitive objectives in instruction.

4. uses curriculum materials and technology that are appropriate to the lesson objectives.

5. motivates students to achieve the lesson objectives.

6. uses a variety of teaching strategies.

7. demonstrates effective classroom management.

8. gives students adequate feedback on their performance, and reteaches if necessary.

9. maintains a positive, cooperative classroom climate.

10. adjusts instruction appropriately for unexpected events and time constraints.

11. assesses student progress and achievement regularly and in a manner consistent with curriculum objectives.

The evaluator should have a rationale for each item included in the instrument. Making the rationale explicit to the teacher being evaluated is also important. This can be done by showing the teacher the instrument and explaining it as part of the clinical supervision process.

Other items in teacher evaluation instruments typically involve qualities of professionalism such as the following:

1. demonstrates ethical, professional behavior.

2. contributes to colleagues' development and to the school as an organization.

3. communicates effectively with parents and other members of the community.

4. demonstrates continued professional development.

The evaluator obviously would need to make observations outside the classroom context in order to make valid ratings on these items.

Some teacher evaluation instruments include "indicators" that clarify what is meant by each item. It is helpful both to the teacher and the evaluator if these indicators are stated as observable behaviors. For example, consider the item stated above, "Motivates students to achieve the lesson objectives." Indicators of what is meant by this item might include the following:

- exhibits enthusiasm (varied voice inflection, lively facial expressions, energetic body movements).

- praises and acknowledges students when they demonstrate interest or give a correct response.

- relates the curriculum content to phenomena within the range of students' experience and interest.

These indicators increase the credibility and comprehensibility of evaluation items. They also help teachers identify what they can do to improve their ratings on the items.

An important element of an evaluative rating instrument is the scale itself. The following are two examples:

Low Competence	Average Competence	Exceptional Competence	NA
1 2	3 4 5	6 7	

Unsatisfactory	Satisfactory	Excellent	NA
1 2	3 4	5	

The evaluator circles the appropriate point on the scale for each item. Each scale includes an "NA" (not applicable) option, because a particular item might not be appropriate for a teacher's job description.

ENDNOTES

1. Goldhammer, R. (1969). *Clinical supervision: Special methods for the supervision of teachers.* New York: Holt, Rinehart & Winston. Quote appears on pp. 288–289.

2. A history of structured classroom observation instruments is presented in Meehnan, M. L., Cowley, K. S., Finch, N. L., Chadwick, K. L., Ermolov, L. D., & Riffle, M. J. S. (2004). *Special strategies observation system-Revised: A useful tool for educational research and evaluation.* Charleston, WV: Appalachia Educational Laboratory.

3. Many other checklists are described and presented in Borich, G. D. (2008). *Observation skills for effective teaching* (5th ed.). Upper Saddle River, NJ: Merill; see also Borich, G. D., & Madden, S. K. (1977). *Evaluating classroom instruction: A sourcebook of instruments.* Reading, MA: Addison-Wesley.

4. The web address for this office is http://www.nclb. osse.dc.gov

5. Aarons, D. I. (2010, January 29). States said to lag in using data systems well. *Education Week.* Retrieved from http://www.edweek.org/ew/articles/2010/01/29

6. What Works Clearinghouse (2009). *Using student achievement data to support instructional decision making.* Washington, DC: U.S. Department of Education, Institute of Education Sciences. Retrieved from ERIC database. (ED506645)

7. Porter, A. C. (2002). Measuring the content of instruction: Uses in research and practice. *Educational Researcher, 31*(7), 3–14.

8. Blank, R. K., Smithson, J., Porter, A., Nunnaley, D., & Osthoff, E. (2006). Improving instruction through school-wide professional development: Effects of the data-on-enacted-curriculum model. *ERS Spectrum, 24*(2), 9–23.

9. *Ibid.*

10. Porter, *op cit.*

11. Porter, *ibid.*, has developed a mathematical index for extent of alignment. Its values range from .00 to 1.00.

12. The questionnaires can be viewed at http://www.ccsso. org/projects/Surveys_of_Enacted_Curriculum/7805.cfm

13. The NCTM standards can be viewed at http://standards. nctm.org

14. A copy of the full instrument appears in: Veldman, D. J., & Peck, R. F. (1963). Student teacher characteristics from the pupils' viewpoint. *Journal of Educational Psychology, 54,* 346–355.

15. Midgley, C., Maehr, M. L., Hruda, L. Z., Anderman, E., Anderman, L., Freeman, K. E., Gheen, M., Kaplan, A., Kumar, R., Middleton, M. J., Nelson, J., Roeser, R., & Urdan, T. (2000). *Manual for the patterns of adaptive learning scales (PALS).* Ann Arbor, MI: University of Michigan. The scales and a manual for them are available at http://www.umich.edu/~pals/PALS%202000_V13Word97.pdf

16. Hootstein, E. W. (1993). Motivational strategies and beliefs of social studies teachers in a U.S. history course for middle school students. *Dissertation Abstracts International: Section A. Humanities and Social Sciences, 54*(04), 1216.

17. These checklists are called Teaching Analysis Guides by Bruce Joyce and colleagues. They are included in a set of three books: Weil, M., & and Joyce, B. (1978). *Information processing models of teaching.* Englewood Cliffs, NJ: Prentice-Hall; Joyce, B., & Weil, M. (1978). *Social models of teaching.* Englewood Cliffs, NJ: Prentice-Hall; and Joyce, B., Weil, M., & Kluwin, B. (1978). *Personal models of teaching.* Englewood Cliffs, NJ: Prentice-Hall.. See also: Borich *ibid;* Borich & Madden, *ibid.*

18. This research is reviewed in Flanders, N. A. (1970). *Analyzing teaching behavior*. Reading, MA: Addison-Wesley.

19. Brooks, J. G., & Brooks, M. G. (1999). *The case for constructivist classrooms*. Alexandria, VA: Association for Supervision and Curriculum Development.

20. Tomlinson, C. A. (1999). *The differentiated classroom: Responding to the needs of all learners*. Alexandria, VA: Association for Supervision and Curriculum Development.

21. Flanders, N. A., op cit. See also Acheson, K. (1989). *Another set of eyes: Techniques for classroom observation* (video and trainer's manual). Alexandria, VA: Association for Supervision and Curriculum Development.

22. When a simple interaction category occurs for any length of time, the observer can abbreviate the record-keeping process. For example, if the teacher launches into an extended explanation of a concept, the observer may place a few tallies in the row designated by category 5, and then draw a short arrow with a note indicating approximately how many minutes or seconds this category of verbal behavior was used.

23. Crippen, K. J., & Brooks, D. W. (2000). Using personal digital assistants in clinical supervision of student teachers. *Journal of Science Education and Technology, 9*, 207–211.

24. For an example of how the Interaction Analysis System can be adapted, see Sakaguchi, H. (1993). A comparison of teaching methods in English-as-a-Second-Language conversation courses and reading courses in Japanese universities. *Dissertation Abstracts International: Section A. Humanities and Social Sciences, 54*(10A), 3692.

25. Sirotnik, K. A. (1983). What you see is what you get—Consistency, persistency, and mediocrity in classrooms. *Harvard Educational Review, 53*, 16–31.

26. Stallings, J. A. (1986). Using time effectively: A self-analytic approach. In K. K. Zumwalt (Ed.), *Improving teaching* (pp. 15–27). Alexandria, VA: Association for Supervision and Curriculum Development.

27. Freiberg, H. J., & Waxman, H. C. (1990). Reflection and the acquisition of technical teaching skills. In R. T. Clift, W. R. Houston, & M. C. Pugach (Eds.), *Encouraging reflective practice in education* (pp. 119–138). New York: Teachers College Press.

Appendix

Effective Teaching Practices and Methods for Observing Them

In Chapter 3 we reviewed teaching practices that research has found to be effective. These practices are listed in the left column of the following list. The right column lists methods for collecting observational data on how frequently or how well the teacher uses each practice. These methods are described in more detail in Chapter 10 (selective verbatim); Chapter 11 (seating charts); Chapter 12 (wide lens); and Chapter 13 (checklists and time coding).

Most of the effective teaching practices can be observed using methods other than those listed here. In fact, virtually any observation method can be adapted to observe virtually any teaching practice. This list only includes the method that we believe is most convenient and appropriate for each practice.

1.	Clarity	Wide lens (audio recording)
2.	Variety	Wide lens (audio recording)
3.	Enthusiasm	Wide lens (video recording)
4.	Task-oriented approach	Wide lens (video recording)
5.	Avoidance of harsh criticism	Selective verbatim (teacher feedback)
6.	Indirect teaching style	Timeline coding (interaction analysis)
7.	Teaching content covered on criterion test	Wide lens (anecdotal record)
8.	Structuring statements	Selective verbatim (teacher directions and structuring statements)
9.	Questions at multiple cognitive levels	Selective verbatim (teacher questions)
10.	Praise and encouragement	Selective verbatim (teacher feedback)
11.	Explicit teaching model	Wide lens (anecdotal record)
12.	Discussion method	Checklist
13.	Allocated time	Timeline coding (anecdotal record)
14.	Student at-task behavior	Seating chart (at task)
15.	Homework	Wide lens (anecdotal record)

16.	Cooperative learning method	Seating chart (at task; movement patterns)
17.	Use of value statements and success to motivate students	Wide lens (anecdotal records, reflective journal)
18.	Equitable treatment of students varying in achievement, ethnicity, and gender	Seating chart (verbal flow)
19.	Classroom management	Selective verbatim (classroom management statements)
20.	Changing strategy based on decisions while teaching	Wide lens (video recording)
21.	Curriculum implementation	Wide lens (reflective journal)

Name Index

Subject Index

Curriculum (*continued*)
  change, 94–96
  implementation, 240
  in constructivist instruction, 230
  standards, 45–46, 218–219

D

Data Quality Campaign, 214, 216
Data–based teaching, 81
Decision making in instruction 93–94, 240
Department heads, 16
Direct
  supervision style, 127–129
  teaching style, 72, 233–234
Discussion method, 75, 80, 86, 89, 233, 239

E

Education Resources Information Center, 57
Ego development of teachers, 36–37
Electronic portfolios, 208–209
Emotional engagement of students, 220, 222
Engaged time in teaching, 77
Enthusiasm in teaching, 71, 122–123, 144, 239
Equity in teaching, 240
ERIC, 57
Espoused theories, 23–26, 154
Ethnic diversity of students, 89–90
Ethnographic observation, 195–198
Evaluation of teachers. *See* Teacher evaluation
Expertise in teaching, 14–15
  Leithwood's model of, 33–35, 45–46
  Berliner's model of, 37–39
Explicit teaching method, 72–74, 80, 239
Expository teaching method, 227–228, 233

F

Feedback conferences
  as phase of clinical supervision, 8
  in teacher evaluation, 109–112
  purpose of, 149–150
  techniques in, 150–156
Feedback to students, 169–173
Flanders Interaction Analysis System, 89, 151, 229–235
Formative assessment, 34

G

Gates Foundation, 156
Graphic organizers, 76
Gender of students, 90–91, 188–189, 214

H

Hamilton Project, 115
Higher–cognitive curriculum objectives, 74
Higher–cognitive questions
  in teaching, 75–76, 80
  observation of, 164–167, 189, 226
High–stakes testing, 46
Homework, 77–78, 239
Horizontal curriculum alignment, 217
Hypotheses in teaching, 76

I

Indirect
  supervision style, 127–129
  teaching style, 71–72, 79, 233–234, 239
Inservice teacher education, 5, 14–15, 26, 111–112. *See also* Teacher development
Inspection as supervisory style, 5–6
Instructional
  coaching, 59
  leadership, 34, 63–64
  rounds, 60–62
Instructional Theory into Practice, 73, 174
INTASC, 40, 105–106, 209
Interaction analysis, 89, 151, 229–235
Interactive decisions, 94
Intercultural communication, 135–136
International Society for Technology in Education, 40
Interstate New Teacher Assessment and Support Consortium, 40, 105–106, 209
Iowa teaching standards, 102–104
ISTE, 40
ITIP, 73, 174

L

Learning communities, 41, 64–65, 201
Learning organizations, 64
Learning, principles of, 159, 188
Learning profile options, 229
Lecture method, 86, 227–228
Lesson study, 65–66
Listening in supervision, 129
Lower–cognitive objectives, 74
Lower–cognitive questions, 164–165

M

Mentoring, 14, 34–35, 53, 136–137
Microteaching, 54–56, 200
Minicourses, 17, 54–55
Modeling of teaching methods, 155